Understanding American History through Children's Literature: Instructional Units and Activities for Grades K-8

by Maria A. Perez-Stable and
Mary Hurlbut Cordier

Oryx Press
1994

The rare Arabian Oryx is believed to have inspired the myth of the unicorn. This desert antelope became virtually extinct in the early 1960s. At that time several groups of international conservationists arranged to have 9 animals sent to the Phoenix Zoo to be the nucleus of a captive breeding herd. Today the Oryx population is nearly 800, and over 400 have been returned to reserves in the Middle East.

Copyright © 1994 by The Oryx Press
4041 North Central at Indian School Road
Phoenix, Arizona 85012-3397

Published simultaneously in Canada

Printed and Bound in the United States of America

∞ The paper used in this publication meets the minimum requirements of American National Standard for Information Science—Permanence of Paper for Printed Library Materials, ANSI Z39.48, 1984.

Library of Congress Cataloging-in-Publication Data

Pérez-Stable, María A.
  Understanding American history through children's literature: instructional units and activities for grades K–8 / by María A. Pérez-Stable and Mary H. Cordier.
    p. cm.
  Includes bibliographical references and indexes.
  ISBN 0–89774–795–X
  1. United States—History—Study and teaching (Elementary).
2. Children's literature—Study and teaching (Elementary)—United States. 3. United States—History—Juvenile literature—Bibliography.
I. Cordier, Mary Hurlbut, 1930– II. Title.
LB1582.U6P47   1994   94–2636
372.89'0973—dc20   CIP

*This book is dedicated to the future of the children in our lives:
Jennifer, Matthew, Sarah, Rachael, Hannah, Sara Ellyn, Christianna,
Nora, and their contemporaries; and to the memory of Dr. Ralph W.
Cordier, Academic Dean Emeriti, Indiana University of Pennsylvania;
leader in developing social studies curricula, K-12; past president of the
National Council for the Social Studies; and father-in-law, grandfather,
great-grandfather, and friend.*

CONTENTS

* * * * * * * *

ACKNOWLEDGMENTS

❖ ❖ ❖ ❖ ❖ ❖ ❖ ❖

We would like to extend our special appreciation to the following people who helped to make this book possible:

For the fine graphics found throughout the text, we thank Dr. J. William Armstrong of Vision Tree Associates, Portage, Michigan.

The Staff of the Resource Sharing Center, Waldo Library, Western Michigan University, deserves our sincere gratitude. This efficient group of professionals— Judy Garrison, Kristen Badra, Kirk Evans, Toyka King, and Marsha Santow—was able to locate and borrow every book that we requested. In addition, during the two and one-half years that we researched this book, they were always pleasant and supportive in our efforts.

Appreciation is also extended to Dr. Howard R. Poole, Director of the Division of Media Services, Western Michigan University, for his assistance in the dreaded Macintosh to IBM file transfer.

Finally, we would like to thank our families, colleagues, and friends for their steadfast support and encouragement during the writing of this book.

INTRODUCTION

* * * * * * * * *

INTEGRATING AMERICAN HISTORY AND CHILDREN'S LITERATURE

American history for many children is a fragmented, hit-or-miss portion of the curriculum often lacking in roots, continuity, personal relevance, and comprehension of the multiple causes and effects of historical events. Traditionally, the study of history in elementary and middle schools has emphasized wars, treaties, and political leaders. American children need not be ignorant of any aspect of their nation's history, nor do teachers need to reinvent the wheel in order to teach the major concepts and events of history within a context of chronology and location. Children will, however, more easily comprehend historical events that are set within the context of time-and-place and cause-and-effect relationships that embody the disciplines of history, political science, geography, sociology, and the humanities.

For children, it is vital that American history be the chronological story of the diverse races, religions, and ethnic origins of the American people: the leaders and followers, the innovators and traditionalists, the activists and reactionaries, the everyday folks and authority figures. How better to tell children the story of the American people than through historical literature written specifically for children? The integration of children's literature with American history is a vehicle for bringing the time and place of historical events within the understanding of young children and children of limited experience. The stories of the diverse peoples of the United States are told through biography, fiction, nonfiction, folk tales, and legends, all easily available through school and public libraries. Our nation's history comes alive when, through literature, history is infused with the lives of people, great and small, who lived at another time and another place. Through the vicarious experiences of people of the past as conveyed through literature, children can be aided in understanding the significance of historical events. This combination of history and literature provides both the "roots and the wings" for children: the roots of their national heritage and their personal identities through history, and the wings of self-respect and national identity through literature.

In order to adequately describe America's story, the historical concepts of change, leadership, conflict, cooperation, nationalism, exploration, historical bias, power, and justice must be explored. To comprehend our nation's history, these concepts must be combined with multicultural diversity and understanding, and with the geographic concepts of location, place, region, immigration, and interaction with the environment. A conceptual approach to history will be enhanced through the integration of selected children's literature, both fiction and nonfiction.

The continuous process of history with its multiple causes and effects is fundamental in understanding the past. For example, change is inevitable, but the results of change have variable consequences. In *Small Wolf*, a book for early elementary children, a young Native American boy watches the Dutch settlers on the island of Manhattan.[1] His family and the other members of the tribe are concerned that their land is being occupied by the strangers, so they move on "again and again and again." The displacement of the Native Americans by white settlers illustrates the concepts of change, conflict, historical bias, multicultural diversity, movement of people, and the relationship of people and the environment. In the case of *Small Wolf*, we see the colonization of North America from the viewpoint of the Native American.

In *New Providence: A Changing Cityscape*, a book for later elementary children, the change within a community over time is visually illustrated, showing how technology, community economy, and architectural tastes change along with the population of the community.[2] *Sarah Bishop*, for later elementary and middle school students, offers a very different view of change.[3] An adolescent named Sarah heads into the wilderness to escape the conflicts of the Revolutionary War after both her Loyalist father and her rebel brother are killed. In this book, the concepts of change, conflict, and movement of people are illustrated by the Revolutionary War, the emerging nation's government, the settlement of the land by white people, and, of course, Sarah herself as she learns once again to trust people.

In each of these books, the concepts are evident, but the continuity of history is remote. In each example, children can identify the cause-and-effect relationships specific to the events of the story line, but the larger picture encompassing the relationships of local, state, and national history is lost without the continuity of a chronological approach to the nation's history. The story of *Small Wolf* needs the context of European exploration and colonization of North America. For primary children, this context will be superficial to be sure, but through maps, globes, and the stories of people, both real and fictional, the foundations of American history are laid.

New Providence will become something more than a series of colorful illustrations when compared with the history of the students' own community. *Sarah Bishop* and her life and times become even more interesting when the events leading to the Revolutionary War are examined in a chronological context. To see the advent and effects of the American Revolution through the experiences of a girl caught between the Loyalists and the Patriots brings special meaning to this momentous event, but reading *Sarah Bishop* does not replace a study of time and place.

The case for emphasizing the concepts of history, geography, and multicultural understanding is evident, for without understanding the concepts, history is no more than a list of dates and names. The concepts without the context of chronology and location make the causes, effects, and relevance of events merely a hodge-podge of unrelated adventures. Therefore, we propose that American history at each grade level from kindergarten through middle school have a context of geographic concepts combined within a chronological framework. Organized around such a framework, we have developed learning objectives and activities based on historical content set in locations appropriate to the events and illustrated through selected children's literature applicable to the topic and the grade level.

ORGANIZATION OF THE PARTS AND UNITS

This volume has been organized into two sections: Part 1 covers the primary grades, kindergarten through grade 3; and Part 2 covers the intermediate grades 4–6 and the middle school grades 6–8. Parts 1 and 2 are divided into units of instruction that explore the history of the United States, pre-Columbus to the present. Each unit includes "Objectives," "Learning Activities," and the annotated "Book List."

In the units in both parts 1 and 2, teachers and librarians will choose from among the learning activities and the extensive book lists by determining which are appropriate for the learning levels of their students and will fulfill the skills and content goals of the curriculum. Helping elementary and middle school students select books for independent reading will necessarily be based on the teacher's and librarian's knowledge of the individual student's skills and interests; therefore, the grade level designations in the book lists are to be used as guidelines for selection, not precise measurements of reading levels. For example, 32-page books are generally appropriate in content for young children; however, not all "picture books" are easy to read. In primary grades with beginning readers, teachers customarily read aloud books that are above the independent reading comprehension of their students. Thus, adults can share the rich stories of the American experience and heritage that are beyond the children's independent reading comprehension, and the independent readers can read the books on their own.

The learning activities, arranged in topical units, will need to be adapted to the local curriculum and the learning levels of the students. For example, if a learning activity is designed to trace the route of the Pilgrims to the New World, the teacher will trace the route of the Pilgrims to North America for young children on the globe or wall map; for children in second and third grade, this may be a teacher-directed activity using one large map for the class; fourth and fifth graders may individually record the routes on teacher-constructed maps; and middle school youngsters may draw their own maps, research the routes from a variety of sources, and compare the routes taken by other colonists. If the learning activity calls for writing about the book characters, teachers will adapt the lesson so that young children will draw a picture or tell about the characters, while those students who can write will be expected to write to the best of their ability. The content of the writing, drawing, or verbal explanation should then reflect the level of maturity of the students.

A number of objectives indicate that the activity may be pursued "As a class, in groups, or independently. . . ." These and other learning activities may be teacher-directed with young or inexperienced learners or when the constraints of time and resources prevent implementing cooperative group work. When the skills of the students and resources are available, the activities can be accomplished through individual or small group work. The units are meant to provide a framework of concepts, skills, and activities that can help children learn about the history of their nation. The learning activities and book lists in Part 1 may be used with the units in Part 2. The book lists in Part 2 may provide read-aloud books for the primary grade units. Teachers and librarians will surely want to adapt these resources according to their own goals and the needs of their students.

THE BOOK LISTS

In developing the bibliography of children's literature for this book, we consulted numerous evaluative sources and inservice teachers and librarians. Vital to our search of the literature were the evaluative reviews found in *School Library Journal, Booklist, Horn Book,* and the yearly listing of outstanding trade books found in the April issues of *Social Education.* A bibliography of these and other sources will be found in the "Select Bibliography" at the end of the book.

In Part 2, as an aid to teachers and librarians in the selection of appropriate literature suited to the reading levels of their students, we have designated books as appropriate for grades 4-6 or for grades 6-8. Overlapping the grade levels of the book lists recognizes the differences in content, concepts, and skills from the later elementary grades to middle school. The middle school designation (6-8) indicates more complex ideas, skills, and content than later elementary (4-6). For students with reading problems in grades 4-8, the book lists in Part 1 may provide the best choices; for advanced readers in grades K-3, the book lists in Part 2 may be used. The extensive book lists give teachers and librarians many options in selecting books for their students.

As we read and examined the books to be included in the book lists, we applied the following criteria:

1. **Realism of Time, Place, Events, and Characters.** The learning activities and books cited in the Book Lists relate America's story from the discovery of the Americas by the Europeans prior to the year 1000, with America defined as the contiguous United States, Alaska, and Hawaii. While the illustrations and characters in the books selected represent the multicultural peoples of America, all books are written in English. A few of the selected books are bilingual. For inclusion, the settings, time periods, and events of a book had to be realistic representations.

In the units based on folk tales, the learning activities and books have been selected to represent a wide variety of American stories.

2. **Literary Qualities.** The story lines, characters, language, vocabulary, and actions of selected books are appropriate to the historical settings, while also stimulating interest through well-written stories. The themes of children's literature selected for inclusion in the book lists authentically represent historical events that are often seen through stories about family life and children's lives. Many of the books selected, including some of the nonfiction works, are suitable for reading aloud. Nonfiction books included are of high interest and supplement the content found in history and social studies textbooks.

3. **Availability of the Books.** The books cited are generally recent publications from the 1980s and 1990s and are in print or are widely available in school, public, or academic libraries.

Annotations

The annotation for each book includes the standard bibliographic data; an indication of whether the book is fiction, nonfiction, folk tale, biography, or poetry; and, for most books, a descriptive synopsis. The number of pages for each book is included; a number in brackets—for example, [32] p.—indicates the pages are not numbered. In Part 2, a general grade level of the content is also given. In the synopsis, we have cited the time and place of the events, plus the race, sex, age, and nationality of the central characters. Strengths of the book, such as the illustrations or use of primary sources, are noted. The annotations about each book will aid the teacher or librarian to select from among the books recommended for each unit.

In order to include a wide variety of selected, recommended books within the space constraints of this book, we have chosen to include only the bibliographic data and no synopsis for some books that are generally well known or have descriptive titles, such as biographies and other nonfiction works. *The omission of these synopses in no way implies that these books are of lesser value than the others*, but allows space for an additional 130 titles that are, perhaps, not as well known. All books included in the book lists have been carefully reviewed and are recommended.

Examples of books with descriptive titles for which synopses have been omitted are *Daniel Boone* by Laurie Lawlor; *Columbus and the World Around Him* by Milton Meltzer; *Bully for You, Teddy Roosevelt* by Jean Fritz; *Always to Remember: The Story of the Vietnam Veterans Memorial* by Brent Ashabranner; and *The Great American Gold Rush* by Rhoda Blumberg. Examples of well-known titles that have been included without reviews are *Sarah, Plain and Tall* by Patricia MacLachlan; *Across Five Aprils* by Irene Hunt; and *The Witch of Blackbird Pond* by Elizabeth George Speare.

THE LEARNING ACTIVITIES

Both the learning activities and the children's literature cited are selective and illustrative. For example, in developing understanding of the settlement of the West, Wilder's *Little House on the Prairie* may be cited in a learning activity that could also be used with *Wagon Wheels, Addie Across the Prairie*, or *First Farm in the Valley*. The learning activities are sufficiently open-ended so that the teacher may determine the depth of the learning experience and the literature appropriate to the concepts. The learning activities may be teacher-directed and simplified for the beginners, or expanded for students with more skills, independence, and experience. Throughout the units, many of the learning activities are sequential, one lesson building on the previous lesson, while other activities may be implemented out of the sequence.

The learning activities emphasize the continuum and connections of history and the involvement of multicultural peoples. Teachers and librarians working with children in grades 4 through 8 may wish to consult the learning activities in Part 1 for students with little experience with historical perspectives. The Select Bibliography at the end of the book cites sources for additional learning activities and book titles.

Through the reading and the learning experiences, concepts are developed that involve children with understanding their national heritage. We wish you and your students the wings of literature and roots of history!

NOTES

1 Nathaniel Benchley, *Small Wolf* (Harper & Row, 1972).

2 Renata Von Tscharner and Ronald Lee Fleming, *New Providence: A Changing Cityscape* (Harcourt Brace Jovanovich, 1987).

3 Scott O'Dell, *Sarah Bishop* (Houghton Mifflin Co., 1980).

Primary Grades: Kindergarten through Grade 3

THE PEOPLE OF AMERICA

❀ ❀ ❀ ❀ ❀ ❀ ❀ ❀

INTRODUCTION TO UNITS 1, 2, AND 3

The foundations of American history begin with young children learning who they are and where they live through development of the concepts of location, national identity, and historical perspective. In Unit 1, "Locating the United States and the Children's Community and State," children will locate the United States and their home state and community on a map, thus initiating an understanding of the relationship of people to the land and water masses of the earth. By learning the names and locations of their nation, state, and community, an aspect of national identity falls into place for the children. The children identify themselves and their families as Americans by consciously examining the diversity of the American people; children will come to understand that the population of the United States includes women and men of various races, ethnic groups, and ages. For children, developing a concept of national identity that encompasses our multicultural population is basic to understanding the history of our nation.

In Unit 2, "Comparing Families of the Past and Present," children begin to recognize life in the "olden days" by comparing their own lives with the lives of people from other times and places. The concepts of historical perspective are richly supported through children's literature. Reading about the children and families of another time and place helps today's children understand that people existed before they were born. Children's literature brings to life the events and adventures of the American people. Constructing a time line to be used throughout the school year adds a visual representation of the passage of time and the relationship of events. Using maps lays the foundations for understanding location and land forms.

Unit 3, "Folk Tales and Songs of America," will help children enjoy these rich and varied expressions of the American people. Folk tales and songs help children understand events and human concerns expressed through fantasy, humor, and commentary.

UNIT
one

Locating the United States and the Children's Community and State

OBJECTIVES

1. Children will locate and name their nation, state, and community on the map of North America.
2. Children will recognize the diversity among their classmates and within their community, state, and nation.
3. Children will draw and label simple maps showing land forms associated with a story or book.

LEARNING ACTIVITIES

1. United States Map-Collage, "We Are Americans"

Using the overhead projector or an opaque projector, make a large outline map of the United States. Have the children cut out magazine pictures of people—all races, ages, males and females—and paste the pictures on the outline map of the United States as a collage of Americans. Highlight the children's state and community with a brightly colored marking pen. Title the map: "We are Americans." Make a second outline map to use in subsequent units.

If there are immigrant or non-resident children in the class, the teacher or librarian may make a special effort to make the children welcome and part of the learning activities. The title of this map and the map in Activity #2 may be changed to "We Are Children Living in. . . ."

2. "We Are Americans Living in [community], [state], United States"

Make a large outline map of the children's state. Have the children cut out or draw and label pictures of families of all races, ages, and both sexes, working and playing together. Labels will indicate family members, such as mother, sister, brother, father; names of family members; and activities portrayed, such as having a picnic, working in the office, and going to school. As an alternative to family pictures, use photographs of the children. Display this map along with the "We Are Americans" map-collage. With brightly colored yarn, connect the home state map to the home state shown on the "We Are Americans" map-collage. Title the state map: "We Are Americans Living in [name of community], [state], United States of America."

3. Drawing Picture Maps

After reading books with well-defined locations and natural features, in small groups or individually, children can draw simple picture maps showing the land forms portrayed in the story. The Book List provides sources about mapping and about different regions of the United States. Depending on the stories and the previous mapping experience of the children, include land forms, such as mountains, rivers, lakes, islands, oceans, plateaus, and plains. Beginners can draw their own representations of the lands forms, while more experienced students can use more standard map symbols and include a map key.

BOOK LIST

Anno, Mitsumasa. *Anno's USA.* Putnam, 1983. [32]p. Fic.

In this wordless picture book, Anno presents, in double-page spreads, his conceptualization of the vastness of the United States. Anno begins his journey on America's west coast and moves eastward. Some of the people and scenes depicted are Tom Sawyer, the Alamo, Charlie Chaplin, the Pilgrims, Paul Bunyan, and the Pueblo Indians.

Baylor, Byrd. *The Desert Is Theirs.* Ill. by Peter Parnall. Macmillan, 1975. [32]p. Non-fic.

The beauty of the desert is portrayed with line drawings showing animals and the landscape. The Papago Indians' way of life, including their respect for the environment, is shown clearly through pictures and poetic text.

Cooney, Barbara. *Island Boy.* Viking, 1988. [32]p. Fic.

Set in nineteenth-century New England on an island, this book's text and pictures convey the changes in everyday life and the dependence on ships on the island and in the city. The story is told through the life of Matthias, who served as a cabin boy, later became master of his own ship, and eventually retired to his beloved island. This is a good read-aloud story with full-page illustrations.

Feeney, Stephanie. *A is for Aloha.* Photos. by Hella Hammid. University Press of Hawaii, 1980. [63]p. Non-fic.

This book uses the ABC format to present some of the faces, places, and experiences that constitute the everyday life of children in Hawaii. Canoe, beach, gecko, pineapple, hibiscus, muumuu, octopus, net, and ukelele are just some of the words shown in this easy-reading book. The large black-and-white photographs are delightful and portray the people of Hawaii well. An author's note at the end of the book explains more about Hawaii and some of the words included. Another book by Feeney that is recommended is *Hawaii Is a Rainbow* (University of Hawaii Press, 1985), which uses the colors of the rainbow to show the people, plants, places, and animals of Hawaii.

Hall, Donald. *The Ox-Cart Man.* Ill. by Barbara Cooney. Viking, 1979. [32]p. Fic.

In this Caldecott award-winning book, the author traces a year in the life of a nineteenth-century New England family. In October, Papa loads his wagon with the goods his family has produced over the year—a bag of wool, mittens, candles, maple sugar, brooms, and shingles—and he makes his rounds to sell and barter his products. Cooney's full-page drawings resemble the early American technique of painting on wood. This is an excellent book for identifying the sequence of events.

Hartman, Gail. *As the Crow Flies: A First Book of Maps.* Ill. by Harvey Stevenson. Bradbury, 1991. 32p. Non-fic.

Lambert, David. *Maps and Globes.* Bookwright Press, 1987. 32p. Non-fic.

Mango, Karin N. *Map Making.* Ill. by Judith Hoffman Corwin. Julian Messner, 1984. 106p. Non-fic.

This book begins with an explanation of how humans orient themselves, and then explains how maps are made and their many uses. This is followed by a discussion of how the world came to be mapped over the centuries and discussions on the mapping of outer space and imaginary places. Illustrations, including reproductions of ancient maps, liberally sprinkle the pages of this well-researched book. This work will best be used as a resource book by the teacher. Includes an index and bibliography.

Radin, Ruth Yaffe. *High in the Mountains.* Ill. by Ed Young. Macmillan, 1989. [32]p. Fic.

Lyrical language and striking watercolor illustrations take the reader through a day in the mountains near Grandpa's house. The child in this story travels from dewy morning, through the sunny meadow filled with flowers at midday, into the nearby stream as afternoon falls, and finally to a cricket concert as the tent is pitched in anticipation of the morning sun.

Rylant, Cynthia. *The Relatives Came.* Ill. by Stephen Gammell. Bradbury, 1985. [32]p. Fic.

In this picture book, the relatives from Virginia drive north over the mountains to visit their family. Delightful illustrations convey the humor, love, and fun connected with this family reunion, which takes place in a present-day, rural setting.

Siebert, Diane. *Heartland.* Ill. by Wendell Minor. Crowell, 1989. [32]p. Poet.

This poem, written in the first person by the land, celebrates the American Midwest—the great heartland of the United States that grows so much of the world's grain. The stunning paintings depict modern farm life, the local community, and the weathered farmer wearing his favorite hat from the feed-and-seed store. This beautiful book is suitable for reading aloud. Other recommended books by Siebert are *Mohave* (Crowell, 1988) and *Sierra* (HarperCollins, 1991).

UNIT

two

Comparing Families of the Past and Present

OBJECTIVES

1. After reading or listening to books about American family life of the past and present, the children will construct Then and Now Charts to identify the similarities and differences among the book families and their own families.
2. Through constructing a Then and Now Chart showing seasonal changes, children will identify their own jobs, responsibilities, and worth in their families, as well as those of children in the past.
3. Children will examine the lives of children in several books, consult with their own parents and guardians, and recognize the traditions passed from one generation to the next.
4. By examining the changes that occur from one generation to the next, children will identify environmental changes over time, such as from forest to farm land to community.
5. By constructing a time line, children will compare the past and the present through the visual representation of time.

LEARNING ACTIVITIES

1. American Family Life, Then and Now Chart

After reading or listening to books about American family life in the past, the children will construct a Then and Now Chart comparing the lives of the book characters with their own lives. To expand the students' concepts of the American people, take time to read books that represent the ethnic and cultural backgrounds of children in your classroom, as well as of other American children.

Using large chart paper, list the categories to be compared down the left side of the chart. Under the heading "Then," list a book title and the date of its setting. Under the "Now" heading, children should describe their own lives. The teacher should help the children fill in the information for each category. Keep the chart displayed so that additional books may be added to the chart throughout the school year.

Other suggested categories to compare include:

• How families meet human needs of food, clothing, shelter, and love.

• How technologies have brought about changes in homes, transportation, and communication.

• How children of the past and present learn at home and at school.

• The past and present work of adults and children at home, on farms, in factories, in mines, in businesses, and in communities.

	1870s *Little House on the Prairie*	1990s Our town today
toys	corncob doll, rag doll, homemade toys & games	bikes, video games, Nintendo, electronic & battery-operated games
clothing	petticoats, pantaloons, barefoot in summer, handmade dresses, shirts	store-bought jeans, overalls, running shoes, many choices
chores	churn butter, milking cow, watch younger children, work in garden, herd cows	taking out trash, watch younger children, load dishwasher, feed dog, make bed
homes	log cabin built by family	3-bedroom, ranch-style houses, apartments, mobile homes
contributions of family	built new towns, built schools, help neighbors, vote, follow laws	keep home & town clean, maintain schools, help neighbors, vote, follow laws

CHART 1   American Family Life, Then and Now

• The contributions to America by children of the past and the present.

The category of "contributions to America" may be difficult for children at first. They may need help in identifying children as responsible citizens who attend school, obey laws, and have the potential to help other people.

Individuals or small groups who have read the same book may cooperatively construct a Then and Now Chart comparing that book with their own lives. The individual or small group charts may be displayed together for comparisons.

2. Changes in Seasonal Activities

Young children can easily identify seasonal changes through the illustrations in books, such as *Yonder* and *Hannah's Farm*. Have children fold drawing paper into four sections. Label the sections "Fall," "Winter," "Spring," and "Summer." Ask children to draw four pictures of themselves pursuing a favorite activity for each season. Next, the children should draw their seasonal activity pictures as though they lived at the same time and in the same place as Hannah or some other book character with whom they are familiar. Ask children to label the pictures or tell how their seasonal activities help the family.

3. Generational Changes

Changes occurring from one generation to the next can be found in *Yonder*, *Island Boy*, and *The Keeping Quilt*. Reading and examining the illustrations in *Cornrows* and *The Quilt Story* will help children identify the traditions and customs within their own families that have been passed on from one generation to the next. Help the children write a letter to their parents or guardians, asking for their help in identifying such family traditions as favorite ways to celebrate a birthday, traditional family names, and favorite foods or family activities for particular holidays, such as the Fourth of July. After the children have gathered information from their families, have each child write a sentence or paragraph, depending on their skills, about one of their family traditions. Children may wish to draw pictures of their traditions. Put all the traditions and drawings into a class scrapbook titled "Our American Traditions." Share the scrapbook with parents and other classes.

4. Changes in How We Use Our Land

Read aloud several children's books that demonstrate changes in land use over time. In groups, as individuals, or with the entire class, list or draw the main events from one of the books in chronological order on mural paper.

Where appropriate, discuss or record the causes and effects of the events. For example, using Virginia Lee Burton's *Little House*, children can deduce from the illustrations that the little house in the country gradually became part of the city because more and more people moved to the city to build their homes and businesses. Thus the amounts of open space around the little house and the city disappeared. In the illustrations in books such as *Little House*, *Window*, and *The Land of Gray Wolf*, children can easily identify changes in the land, water, air, and lives of people to show on their murals.

5. Time Line

Construct a time line on a long, continuous roll of paper, starting with the year 1000, and marking segments of 10 or 25 years up to the present. Put the time line at the children's eye level so they can easily read it. As books are read, place the titles at the appropriate place on the time line. As information about American history is presented, place the data on the time line. Place the birth dates of the students, their parents, teachers, and famous Americans on the time line. Compare placement of the childhood years of today's children with the childhood years of book characters, past generations, and famous Americans. Display the time line throughout the year. Add significant events from the present, as well as from the past.

The sample time line given below, showing only the nineteenth century, lists a few major events of American history and some relevant book titles for primary grades. A time line constructed as one continuous horizontal chart showing the years 1000-2000 is most effective for creating a visual display of the passage of time and how events are related.

BOOK LIST

1. Changes in How We Use Our Land

Baker, Jeannie. *Window.* Greenwillow, 1991. [32]p. Fic.

This wordless story is told through collages portraying the view from a window over a long period of time. The mother and child in the first picture grow older as the scene changes from forest to town to overcrowded city. Each picture has context clues that will help develop the viewer's visual literacy. The implied cycle of events presented would be an excellent basis for discussion with children.

Burton, Virginia Lee. *The Little House.* Houghton Mifflin, 1942. [32]p. Fic.

Through pictures and text, this timeless story shows how the little house in the country becomes part of the city. The portrayal of change over time is

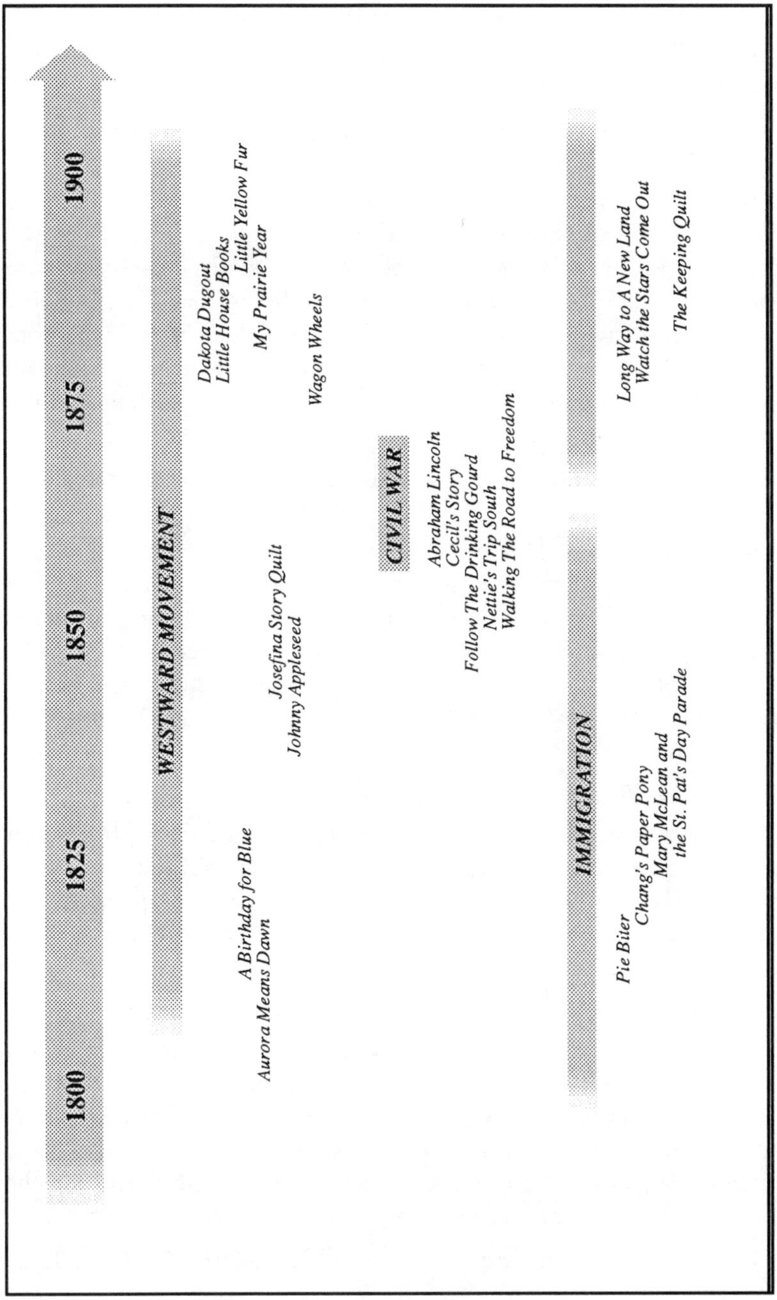

1800	1825	1850	1875	1900

WESTWARD MOVEMENT

Dakota Dugout
Little House Books
Little Yellow Fur
My Prairie Year

Wagon Wheels

Josefina Story Quilt
Johnny Appleseed

A Birthday for Blue
Aurora Means Dawn

CIVIL WAR

Abraham Lincoln
Cecil's Story
Follow The Drinking Gourd
Nettie's Trip South
Walking The Road to Freedom

IMMIGRATION

Long Way to A New Land
Watch the Stars Come Out

The Keeping Quilt

Pie Bier
Chang's Paper Pony
Mary McLean and
the St. Pat's Day Parade

CHART 2   Time Line—1800 to 1900

clearly shown, and when the little house becomes surrounded by the tall buildings of the city, the granddaughter of the original owners moves the house back to the country.

Cherry, Lynne. *A River Ran Wild: An Environmental History.* Harcourt Brace Jovanovich, 1992. [32]p. Non-fic.

This beautifully illustrated picture book traces the life of the Nashua River in New England from the time before humans, to the arrival first of the Native American peoples, and then of the white settlers. Each two-page spread shows the changes people brought to the river and surrounding environment, many of them detrimental after the Industrial Revolution. Eventually, the polluted river was cleaned up in the 1970s. This is an excellent book for showing young children the results of humankind's interaction with its natural habitat.

Dragonwagon, Crescent. *Home Place.* Ill. by Jerry Pinkney. Macmillan, 1990. [32]p. Fic.

As a present-day family is hiking in the woods, they discover the remains of the foundation of a house, a blue glass marble, a nail, a horseshoe, a piece of a plate, a china doll's arm, and a small bottle. The modern family imagines the people who might have lived there—an African-American family who loved each other, worked hard, and one summer night, experienced a thunderstorm. Pinkney's extraordinary watercolors fill each page with feeling and natural beauty.

Johnston, Tony. *Yonder.* Ill. by Lloyd Bloom. Dial, 1988. [32]p. Fic.

Vivid illustrations tell the story of a young man riding a horse "over yonder," who becomes a farmer, takes a wife, builds a cabin and barn, plants a tree for each child he has, and watches his children grow up, marry, and have children of their own. The beauty, harmony, and usefulness of the land plays a prominent role in this story.

Locker, Thomas. *The Land of Gray Wolf.* Dial, 1991. [32]p. Fic.

Set during early colonial times, this book shows events through the eyes of a young Indian boy, Running Deer, as the white settlers come to his tribal lands. After the Indians are displaced, the forests are cut down, towns are built, the land is used up, and the white people move on. The land eventually returns to its natural state, full of new growth, deer, and the sounds of wolves. Exceptional full-page paintings accompany the text.

Lyon, George Ella. *Dreamplace.* Ill. by Peter Catalanotto. Orchard, 1993. [32]p. Fic.

As a modern-day girl visits the courtyards and kivas built by the Pueblo Indians at Mesa Verde, Colorado, she imagines the life of the people who lived there 800 years earlier. The softly colored illustrations depict the Anasazi at home, work, prayer, and play. The time of drought and sickness is presented and how the people deserted their cities in search of a better life. The story has an other-world quality to it and could be used nicely to connect past with present.

Lyon, George Ella. *Who Came Down That Road?* Ill. by Peter Catalanotto. Orchard, 1992. [32]p. Fic.

As a young boy and his mother walk through the woods, they discover a buffalo trace and the mother tells her son that the road is very old. When he asks who came down the road, she tells how her great-grandparents came down it to homestead, before that came soldiers during the Civil War, before the soldiers came pioneers settling the Old Northwest, before them Wyandot and Chippewa Indians hunting deer, before them buffaloes, bears, and elk, before them mastodons and woolly mammoths, and so on. The soft illustrations help convey the sense of time and place over the aeons.

Pryor, Bonnie. *The House on Maple Street.* Ill. by Beth Peck. Morrow, 1987. [32]p. Fic.

Two little girls who live at 107 Maple Street in the present day find a tiny china cup and an arrowhead. As the story unfolds, readers will learn about the various people who lived on Maple Street, including a Native American tribe and a pioneer farm family whose little daughter owned a blue china tea set. This well-crafted book presents the history of a place over the course of 300 years of development and change.

Turner, Ann. *Heron Street.* Ill. by Lisa Desimini. Harper & Row, 1989. [32]p. Fic.

This simply written picture book demonstrates how land usage changes over time. What began as a marsh by the sea, becomes a town as the Pilgrims arrive and build homes. With the passage of time, the green grasses disappear as paved streets, automobiles, and suburbia take over. Poetic language, accompanied by vibrant drawings, demonstrate how difficult it is to maintain harmony between nature and human progress.

Yolen, Jane. *Letting Swift River Go.* Ill. by Barbara Cooney. Little, Brown, 1992. [32]p. Non-fic.

Based on a real event in the twentieth century, this picture book tells of the small towns along the Swift River in western Massachusetts that were purchased by the government and flooded in order to form the Quabbin Reserve. Young Sally Jane remembers growing up in one of these towns, walking to school and fishing in the Swift River with her friends. In mid-century, however, the cemeteries were moved, houses were torn down, trees were felled, and whole villages disappeared in order to create the reservoir. The soft, detailed illustrations depict the end of a way of life.

2. Changes in Seasonal Activities

Note: Starred (*) books are reviewed in a previous section or unit of this book.

*Johnston, Tony. Yonder. Dial, 1988. Fic. (Unit 2, Sect. 1)

MacLachlan, Patricia. Three Names. Ill. by Alexander Pertzoff. HarperCollins, 1991. 31p. Fic.

The author's great-grandfather recalls his childhood years in the late 1800s, growing up on the prairie with his dog, Three Names. He recalls walking to the one-room schoolhouse in the fall, Christmas parties, playing marbles, sudden spring storms, and summer commencement. Throughout the days, Great-Grandfather's dog accompanied him, even to school! This is a beautifully written and illustrated story of a bygone way of life.

McCurdy, Michael. Hannah's Farm: The Seasons on an Early American Homestead. Holiday, 1988. [32]p. Fic.

Rylant, Cynthia. When I Was Young in the Mountains. Ill. by Diane Goode. Dutton, 1982. [32]p. Fic.

A girl remembers her early years living with her grandparents in the Appalachian Mountains. She recalls swimming in the pond, eating beans and okra, Grandfather coming home covered in coal dust, and having to go to the "johnny-house" by candlelight at night. The soft watercolor drawings convey information about a bygone lifestyle and the love among the family members.

3. Generational Changes

Note: Starred (*) books are reviewed in a previous section or unit of this book.

*Cooney, Barbara. Island Boy. Viking, 1988. Fic. (Unit 1)

Crews, Donald. Bigmama's. Greenwillow, 1991. [32]p. Fic.

The author, who is African-American, reminisces about the trips he took with his family every summer to visit his grandparents, Bigmama and Bigpapa, on their Florida farm. The family traveled for three days by train and the children were delighted to find everything the same each year— the comfortable house, the cold well water, the chicken coop in the backyard, and the outhouse behind the shed. The soft drawings evoke images of a close-knit, loving family enjoying their summers together in a former era. The author continues his story in *Shortcut* (Greenwillow, 1992).

Friedman, Ina R. *How My Parents Learned to Eat.* Ill. by Allen Say. Houghton Mifflin, 1984. 30p. Fic.

A little girl tells the story of how her parents met in Yokohama, Japan, when her father was in the U.S. Navy and her mother was a young Japanese woman. They both go to great lengths to learn each other's cultures, and that is why their daughter sometimes eats with chopsticks and sometimes with a knife and fork. This is a good read-aloud choice for young children.

Howard, Elizabeth Fitzgerald. *Aunt Flossie's Hats (and Crab Cakes Later)* Ill. by James Ransome. Clarion, 1991. [32]p. Fic.

On Sunday afternoons, two African-American girls, Susan and Sarah, visit their Great-Aunt Flossie, trying on her wonderful collection of hats and eating crab cakes. With each hat, Aunt Flossie has a story to tell—the great fire in Baltimore, the parade of soldiers returning from World War I, or losing her best Sunday hat in the pond—and her nieces learn of life in the not-too-distant past. Based on the author's childhood reminiscences of her aunt, the rich oil paintings express personal history and family affection.

Johnston, Tony. *The Quilt Story.* Ill. by Tomie dePaola. Putnam, 1985. [32]p. Fic.

During the late nineteenth century, a mother completes a beautiful quilt for her daughter, Abigail, who not only uses it to keep warm, but also as a tablecloth for tea parties, to dress up, and to shield her from her siblings. Over the years the quilt is tucked in the attic until a modern-day girl discovers it and uses it much as Abigail did.

***Johnston, Tony.** *Yonder.* Dial, 1988. Fic. (Unit 2, Sect. 1)

Polacco, Patricia. *The Keeping Quilt.* Simon & Schuster, 1988. [32]p. Fic.

When Anna comes to the United States as a girl, the only things she has of "backhome Russia" are her brightly colored blue dress and red babushka. Long after Anna outgrows her clothes, the neighborhood ladies piece together a quilt, using scraps of fabrics that belonged to various members of the family. As the generations progress, Anna's quilt serves as a tablecloth for the Sabbath celebration, a wedding canopy, a baby blanket, and a play tent.

Precek, Katharine Wilson. *Penny in the Road.* Ill. by Patricia Cullen-Clark. Macmillan, 1989. [32]p. Fic.

A young Pennsylvania boy in 1913 finds a 1793 penny in the road as he is walking to school and he wonders who might have been its owner. He imagines a boy in a three-cornered hat and knee breeches who plowed the fields, studied his lessons, and played marbles with his friends. Softly colored illustrations depict both the contemporary boy and his counterpart from 200 years ago.

Yarbrough, Camille. *Cornrows.* Ill. by Carole Byard. Coward, McCann & Geoghegan, 1979. [32]p. Fic.

Grandmaw tells her grandchildren about the great spirit of the African people and how the people translated their spirit into symbols, such as braided hair. She explains how one could identify someone's clan or village by the style of her or his hair. When the proud African peoples were taken into slavery, their spirit did not die, but could still be seen in the old symbol of cornrowed hair.

4. American Family Life Then and Now

Note: Starred (*) books are reviewed in a previous section or unit of this book.

Anderson, Joan. *Spanish Pioneers of the Southwest.* Photos. by George Ancona. Dutton, 1989. [62]p. Fic.

This story of Spanish family life in the middle 1700s in New Mexico is one of the few books about early Hispanic heritage in the United States. Photographs show a reenactment of an eighteenth-century settlement of Spanish pioneers. The story tells of the daily activities of a Spanish family, including the responsibilities of the children.

Benchley, Nathaniel. *Small Wolf.* Harper & Row, 1972. 64p. Fic.

A young Native American boy, Small Wolf, learns about hunting and fishing from his father in their home village in what is now Manhattan, New York. One day as Small Wolf is hunting, he sees white settlers establishing their village. Fearing the intrusion by these people, Small Wolf's family and tribe move away, time and time again. This is a simply told story of displacement as Small Wolf's people try to maintain their way of life.

Brenner, Barbara. *Wagon Wheels.* Harper & Row, 1978. 64p. Fic.

Based on a true event, this story of bravery and cooperation tells of the African-American pioneer settlers in Kansas shortly after the Civil War. With the help of neighbors in the village of Nicodemus, and food from friendly Indians, three young brothers take care of themselves while their father searches for good farmland. When their father sends them a map, the boys walk 150 miles to meet him at their new homestead.

Bunting, Eve. *The Happy Funeral.* Ill. by Mai Vo-Dinh. Harper & Row, 1982. [40]p. Fic.

This timeless story tells of a young girl's coming to terms with the death of her grandfather. Laura's family is Chinese American and the funeral customs depicted reflect the family's heritage, including the burning of incense, giving little gifts to Grandfather, and burning offerings for his journey in the afterlife. Laura remembers happy times with Grandfather and readers will learn about a view of death rather different from the one typically held by other Americans.

Clark, Ann Nolan. *In My Mother's House.* Ill. by Velino Herrara. Viking, 1991. 56p. Non-fic.

While teaching Tewa Indian children in the 1930s and 1940s, the author records the children's views of the world. Through simple statements and descriptions, the daily life of the Pueblo people comes alive, and its important aspects are defined, including the Pueblo spiritual views of life.

de Paola, Tomie. *An Early American Christmas.* Holiday, 1987. [32]p. Fic.

Dorros, Arthur. *Abuela.* Ill. by Elisa Klevin. Dutton, 1991. [40]p. Fic.

As a young Hispanic-American girl and her *abuela* (grandmother) board a bus to go to the park, the girl imagines the two of them flying over the city. They pass by the Statue of Liberty, the airport, skyscrapers, her father's office, Central Park, and other New York landmarks. The forthright text is interwoven with Spanish words, some of which are translated, some of which children will understand in context. The brightly colored, detailed illustrations are a visual delight. This is a good choice for a read-aloud or for newly independent readers. Includes a glossary of Spanish words.

Faber, Doris. *The Amish.* Ill. by Michael E. Erkel. Doubleday, 1991. 45p. Non-fic.

*Friedman, Ina R. *How My Parents Learned to Eat.* Houghton Mifflin, 1984. Fic. (Unit 2, Sect. 3)

Hamilton, Virginia. *The Bells of Christmas.* Ill. by Lambert Davis. Harcourt Brace Jovanovich, 1989. 59p. Fic.

The year is 1890 and the Bells, an African-American family who have lived for generations on the same land near Springfield, Ohio, are preparing to celebrate Christmas. For 12-year-old Jason the two days before Christmas pass much too slowly—he is anxious for his cousins to arrive, and he wishes it would snow. Eventually the big day arrives and so do the Bell cousins. This is a warm-hearted reminiscence of how a loving and extended family celebrated Christmas a century ago. Softly colored paintings accompany a text based on the recollections of the author's mother.

Harvey, Brett. *Immigrant Girl, Becky of Eldridge Street.* Ill. by Deborah Kogan Ray. Holiday, 1987. 36p. Fic.

Becky Moscowitz, a 10-year-old Jewish girl, lives with her parents, siblings, aunt, and grandmother in a three-room tenement apartment on New York City's lower east side in 1910. Fleeing the *pogroms* in Russia, Becky's family finds life in America very different, much noisier, and full of surprises. The experiences of this family typify the experiences of thousands of immigrants who came to the United States at the turn of the century. Includes a glossary of Yiddish terms.

Haskins, Francine. *I Remember "121."* Children's Book Press, 1991. [32]p. Fic.

In this picture book, the author reminiscences about her childhood living with her extended African-American family in a three-story brick house in Washington, D.C., in the 1950s. She remembers the birth of her new brother, watching "Howdy Doody" on television, family dinners, shopping in Baltimore, making mischief, playing dress-ups, jumping double dutch with her friends, and, finally, moving to a new house in 1956. The stylized, colorful illustrations will help readers picture family life in the 1950s.

Hendershot, Judith. *In Coal Country.* Ill. by Thomas B. Allen. Knopf, 1987. [32]p. Fic.

Based on the author's experiences, this story of a coal-mining family in southern Ohio in the 1920s and 1930s is told through the eyes of a young girl. The girl recollects such things as Papa coming home from the night shift all covered in coal dust, swimming under Bernice Falls in the hot summers, eating Eskimo pies, playing hopscotch, and Mama's fresh flowers on the table. This book depicts a way of life that is still a reality for some people.

Howard, Elizabeth Fitzgerald. *Chita's Christmas Tree.* Ill. by Floyd Cooper. Bradbury, 1989. [32]p. Fic.

Set in Baltimore, Maryland, in the early 1890s, this is the story of the Christmas traditions of an African-American family. Young Chita and her doctor father leave early one morning for the country to select a Christmas tree, and Chita and Mama bake cookies. On Christmas Eve, the entire family gathers at Chita's house to celebrate and dance. The brilliant watercolor drawings present a wonderful visual depiction of this family's holiday customs.

Keegan, Marcia. *Pueblo Boy: Growing Up in Two Worlds.* Cobblehill Books, 1991. [48]p. Non-fic.

Concise text and stunning photographs show the home, school, and cultural life of a young Native American boy growing up in the San Ildefonso Pueblo in present-day New Mexico. Ten-year-old Timmy Roybal does the normal things for his age—he attends school, uses a computer, plays baseball and pocket pool, and rides his bike. As a Pueblo Indian, Timmy also learns the ancient ways of his people—respect for the land, the spiritual beliefs of the Pueblo, and the dancing that accompanies the Corn Dance celebration in the fall. A very similar book, focusing on a young Cochiti Pueblo girl named April, is Diane Hoyt-Goldsmith's *Pueblo Storyteller* (Holiday, 1991). Also of interest is Rina Swentzell's *Children of Clay: A Family of Pueblo Potters* (Lerner, 1992), which tells of a Tewa Indian family in the Santa Clara Pueblo in New Mexico that has created pottery for centuries.

Kroll, Virginia. *Masai and I.* Ill. by Nancy Carpenter. Four Winds, 1992. [32]p. Fic.

A young black girl named Linda, who lives in a crowded city, learns at school about the Masai people in East Africa and she imagines how life would be if she was part of the tribe. In Africa, she would know all of her neighbors, there would be no stairs to climb in her hut and no beds with ruffled bedspreads. She would see zebras and giraffes grazing, and she would run barefoot through the fields. Two things would be the same—love of family and joy in celebrations. The colorful paintings show Linda in her American home and her Masai counterpart in Africa.

Locker, Thomas. *Family Farm.* Dial, 1988. [32]p. Fic.

This timeless story tells about one family's struggle to save their farm from bankruptcy. The children plant flowers and pumpkins that they sell to help pay the bills. This is a tale of family pride and cooperation, and Locker's illustrations richly depict the countryside and farm life. Young children will learn much from the outstanding illustrations and from the story as a read-aloud.

Lomas Garza, Carmen. *Family Pictures/Cuadros de Familia.* Children's Book Press, 1990. 32p. Non-fic.

Based on recollections of her childhood in Kingsville, Texas, near the Mexican border, Lomas Garza presents vignettes in the life of her Hispanic-American family. With the aid of detailed drawings, the book recounts some of the events in her life, such as attending a fair in Mexico, making tamales, a birthday piñata, enacting *posadas* at Christmas, and picking cactus with her grandparents. This is a loving and brightly illustrated tribute to a close-knit family. Contains Spanish and English text.

O'Kelley, Mattie Lou. *Moving to Town.* Little, Brown, 1991. [32]p. Fic.

This story tells of a family's move from an old farm in the country to the city in the opening decades of the twentieth century. After packing three wagonloads, the family travels over hills and through valleys before spotting the first tall buildings of the city. The children in the family are thrilled to go to a movie, visit the zoo, shop downtown, and eat in a restaurant, but they miss their old home. The colorful illustrations present a myriad of details that celebrate life in the big city.

Polacco, Patricia. *Just Plain Fancy.* Bantam, 1990. [32]p. Fic.

Set in present-day Lancaster County, Pennsylvania, this story emphasizes the importance to Amish people of maintaining their simple lifestyle. With illustrations and story line, the Amish way of life is lovingly told through Naomi's finding of a peacock egg that is later hatched by the chickens. Naomi worries that the bird is too fancy for the Amish way, but she is reassured that the peacock is acceptable because it is one of God's most beautiful creatures. This is a charming read-aloud book to share with primary children as they learn about different American lifestyles.

Ringgold, Faith. *Tar Beach.* Crown, 1991. [32]p. Fic.

Black artist Faith Ringgold has transformed her art-form quilt into a story of the early 1930s, showing the simple pleasures and everyday life of a black family in Harlem. The folk-tale style is evident as Cassie and her little brother fly into the sky, an escape theme of tales from slavery. The rich illustrations are vivid in colors and characters, reflecting the strong family ties of the African-American family.

Rosen, Michael J., ed. *Home: A Collaboration of Thirty Distinguished Authors and Illustrators of Children's Books to Aid the Homeless.* HarperCollins, 1992. [32]p. Non-fic.

This is a collection of 15 works written and illustrated by 30 well-known children's authors and illustrators, such as Virginia Hamilton, Leo and Diane Dillon, Jerry Pinkney, Myra Cohn Livingston, Cynthia Rylant, Jane Yolen, Laurence Yep, James Marshall, and Sheila Hamanaka. Each collaboration tells of a special meaning of "home"—a comfortable old chair, the front stoop, Grandmother's tiny apartment, a back porch, the attic, or the kitchen table. The illustrations are as diverse as the contributors, and the proceeds of this book benefit the Share our Strength (SOS) organization to provide help for the homeless.

Rylant, Cynthia. *Appalachia: The Voices of Sleeping Birds.* Ill. by Barry Moser. Harcourt Brace Jovanovich, 1991. [32]p. Non-fic.

Rylant, a native of West Virginia, has teamed with Moser, a Tennesseean, to create this ageless tribute to the Appalachian people, their way of life, and how they perceive themselves. The author presents everyday life—cooking and canning, visiting the general store, going to church, making a living from coal mining, and the company of people and family dogs. This is a splendid blend of text and art, well-suited for reading aloud.

*Rylant, Cynthia. *When I Was Young in the Mountains.* Dutton, 1982. Fic. (Unit 2, Sect. 2)

Sanders, Scott Russell. *Aurora Means Dawn.* Bradbury Press, 1989. [32]p. Fic.

The year is 1800 and the Sheldon family has left Connecticut to travel by covered wagon to their new home in Aurora, Ohio. During their journey they encounter a terrific thunderstorm that fells trees and makes the road impassable. As Mr. Sheldon seeks help, he finds no town in Aurora, just a surveyor's post. He eventually finds help in Hudson and the Sheldons reach their destination. The natural beauty of the land is clearly evident in the soft watercolor drawings. The story of the Sheldon family continues in *Warm as Wool* (Bradbury, 1992) as they raise sheep during the first year on their new homestead.

Smalls-Hector, Irene. *Irene and the Big, Fine Nickel.* Ill. by Tyrone Geter. Little, Brown, 1991. [32]p. Fic.

For young Irene, this summer day in 1957 in her Harlem neighborhood holds many adventures. She visits her next-door neighbor hoping for some of her banana pudding, plays with her best friends in the street, and is excited when she finds a bright, shiny nickel. In her generous fashion, Irene buys a raisin biscuit and shares it with friends and foes alike. Text and art combine successfully to evoke a feeling of love and community in an African-American urban setting.

Smucker, Anna Egan. *No Star Nights.* Ill. by Steve Johnson. Knopf, 1989. [48]p. Fic.

A steel-mill town in West Virginia is the setting for the author's reminiscences of growing up in the middle decades of the 1900s. The steel furnaces turned the sky red at night and a fine coating of grit always covered everything. The children in this town played around the slag hills, watched Fourth of July parades, and attended Pirates baseball games in Pittsburgh. In this heart-warming account of growing up in an industrial town, shadowed illustrations in somber colors convey the frequent drabness of the environment.

Sneve, Virginia Driving Hawk, selector. *Dancing Teepees: Poems of American Indian Youth.* Ill. by Stephen Gammell. Holiday, 1989. 32p. Poet.

This collection of 19 poems celebrates the Native American tradition of respect for the family and the natural world. Some of the poems are in the oral tradition and others are written by contemporary tribal poets. Many nations are represented, including the Osage, Apache, Lakota Sioux, Ute, Navaho, Dakota Elk, Paiute, and Hopi. Gammell's soft illustrations complement the text.

Turner, Ann. *Dakota Dugout.* Ill. by Ronald Himler. Macmillan, 1985. [32]p. Fic.

A grandmother tells a story to her grandchild about what it was like to live in a sod dugout on the Dakota prairie in the late 1800s when she was a young bride. She tells of the loneliness and of the hardships of winter and summer. Eventually the couple move into a clapboard house and the young woman is surprised to discover that she misses the warm, safe feeling of the dugout. Although the imagery may be too advanced for young readers, this is an excellent story to read aloud and discuss with children.

Waters, Kate. *Sarah Morton's Day: A Day in the Life of a Pilgrim Girl.* Photographs by Russ Kendall. Scholastic, 1989. 32p. Non-fic.

This full-color photo essay recreates a day in the life of a real, nine-year-old girl whose life in Plimoth Plantation in 1627 has been verified in several journals and histories of the period. Sarah is shown getting dressed, doing chores and lessons, playing with friends, and interacting in the tiny settlement. The book was photographed on location in Plimoth Plantation in Plymouth, Massachusetts, and an author's note tells about Plimoth, the real Sarah Morton, and Pilgrim customs. A companion volume is *Samuel Eaton's Day: A Day in the Life of a Pilgrim Boy* (Scholastic, 1993), which takes the reader through a typical day in the life of a seventeenth-century Pilgrim boy.

UNIT
three

Folk Tales and Songs of America

OBJECTIVES

1. As children learn folk songs and other songs about America, they will identify the sources of the songs.
2. With the assistance of the teacher or librarian, children will identify the sources of the folk tales.
3. Through reading, illustrating, and dramatizing American folk tales, children will identify similarities among the folk tales, such as the role of the trickster, inclusions of humor, exaggerations, and the *pour quoi* tales.
4. Children will write, tell, or draw their own original folk tales.
5. After reading or listening to folk tales from various regions and peoples of America, children will differentiate between facts and folk tales.

LEARNING ACTIVITIES

1. Singing Songs of America

Teach children American songs from various regions and cultures. When introducing a song, locate the origin of the music on the map and tell children the background of the song. For example, "Swing Low, Sweet Chariot" is a song from the days of slavery; "This Land is Your Land" is a song composed by the American folk singer Woody Guthrie. Some collections of songs provide this information for each song. Be sure to check the music textbooks for sources of American music. The music teacher can aid in selecting and teaching the music. As a culminating activity, perform the American songs for parents and other classes.

2. Where Do Folk Tales Originate?

People and Regions. Select a folk tale, such as a Brer Rabbit story. After the children have identified the main characters and their attributes, both good and bad, help them identify the source of the tale. Many publications of folk tales include information about the sources of the tales. For example, tell the children how long ago African-American slaves told the Brer Rabbit stories as a way to poke fun at those in control. For centuries, Native Americans have told *pour quoi* stories, such as why the bluebonnets bloom in the hills as Texas, as told by Tomie de Paola in *The Legend of the Bluebonnet: An Old Tale of Texas*. The legendary hero Paul Bunyon was created by people who lived in areas where lumbering was an important source of income.

Record the titles of the stories on the Outline Map drawn in Unit 1 to show their origins.

Real Events that Become Folk Tales. Some folk tales are based on real events. Read Paul Goble's *Death of Iron Horse* or Reeve Lindbergh's *Johnny Appleseed*. Discuss how a real event can become the basis of a folk tale. What events have happened in your community that could become a folk tale? Was someone very brave? Did something funny happen during the Fourth of July parade?

Make a bulletin board display listing these events that could become folk tales.

3. What Do Folk Tales Tell About People?

Folk Tale Characters. In small groups, as individuals, or as a whole class activity, select a few of the children's favorite folk tale characters. For each character, list the ways that the character can be recognized. Include the physical characteristics, what the character does, how the character speaks, what the character wears, and how the character relates to other people or characters in the tale. Use the list as a way to build vocabulary, including the ethnic names and words from the tale, and as preparation for the next dramatic activities.

Readers' Theater. The teacher or librarian may need to edit or revise some stories in order to create a readers' theater script from a story with a dialogue among the characters, as in *The Talking Eggs*, or with a clearly defined storyteller's portion plus the dialogue. Children will be assigned parts to read out loud as readers' theater.

Creative Dramatics and Puppet Plays. After reading the story, identify the characters, their behaviors, and the sequence of events. Select children to play each part and dramatize the story, keeping to the sequence of events. Simple paperbag puppets can be used to tell the folk tales.

Illustrating Folk Tales. A small group of children, working cooperatively, can identify the sequence of events and the characters of the story. The children will make a series of drawings that illustrate the story, or construct a mural that tells the story.

4. Creating Folk Tales

Creating Exaggerated Characters. Read or tell a Paul Bunyon or Pecos Bill story. Help children identify the exaggerated characteristics of the lumberman or the cowboy. With the children, invent a similar character. Could this character be like Viola Swamp, the all-time worst substitute teacher?[1] Or the best crossing guard who ever single-handedly held back the traffic? Or the super soccer player who could win every game? Or the stupendous second grader who could learn all the spelling words there ever were in the whole wide world without really trying?

After making a list of descriptive words and phrases, ask the children to draw pictures of their character and write about the character's fantastic experiences.

Creating New Folk Tales. Children can write, tell, dramatize, or draw their own stories about a trickster, such as Iktomi; exaggerated characters, such as Paul Bunyon or Ann Thunder Ann Whirlwind, both found in *American Tall Tales*; a *pour quoi* folk tale that explains why events or things are the way they are; or a tale based on a real event or person, such as Johnny Appleseed or a local event identified in Activity 2. The students may wish to combine folk tale styles as in *Iktomi and the Boulder*, which is both a tale about the trickster, Iktomi, and a *pour quoi* tale that explains why bats have flat faces and why there are rocks scattered across the Great Plains.

Take Time to Share. In the folk tradition, stories and songs are shared with others. Arrange time to have the children share their stories, dramatizations, and drawings with each other, another class, or with parents. Display the children's stories and drawings during open house. In these ways, children will be part of the folk tradition of sharing stories with others.

5. How to Tell the Real Americans from the Folk-Tale Americans

Choose a folk-tale American and a real American, such as a member of the class or a realistic character from a book, such as Laura Ingalls. Construct a chart comparing the real American and and the folk-tale American. Reality

---

[1] Viola Swamp is the nasty substitute teacher in humorous books written by Harry Allard and James Marshall: *Miss Nelson Is Missing* (Houghton Mifflin, 1977); *Miss Nelson Is Back* (Houghton Mifflin, 1982); and *Miss Nelson Has a Field Day* (Houghton Mifflin, 1985).

	REAL AMERICANS	FOLK TALE AMERICANS
HOMES		
FOOD		
CLOTHING		
RECREATION		
SCHOOL		
JOBS		
CONTRIBUTIONS TO AMERICA		

CHART 3   Comparing Real Americans and Folk Tale Americans

and fantasy will be apparent to the children as they fill in the categories. This can be a total class activity, or pursued in small groups or by individuals.

BOOK LIST

1. Singing Songs of America

Axelrod, Alan. *Songs of the Wild West.* Music by Dan Fox; ill. with reproductions from the Metropolitan Museum of Art and the Buffalo Bill Historical Center. Simon & Schuster, 1991. [128]p. Non-fic.

Bryan, Ashley. *All Night, All Day: A Child's First Book of African-American Spirituals.* Musical arr. by David Manning Thomas. Atheneum, 1991. 48p. Non-fic.

Spirituals, written as an artistic response to slavery, are unique in the song literature of the world. From over 1,000 spirituals collected since the Civil War, Bryan has selected 20 of the best-loved, including "This Little Light of Mine," "O When the Saints Go Marching In," "There's No Hiding

Place," and "He's Got the Whole World in His Hands." Manning has written rhythmic and harmonic piano accompaniments and guitar chords for the songs. The brightly colored double-page spreads depict the stories in the songs.

Cohn, Amy, compiler. *From Sea to Shining Sea: A Treasury of American Folklore and Folk Songs.* Scholastic, 1993. 416p. Folk.

This is a splendid collection of over 140 folk tales, songs, poems, and essays by authors as diverse as Walt Whitman, Mark Twain, Virginia Hamilton, Emma Lazarus, Woody Guthrie, and Ralph Waldo Emerson. Each of the 15 sections is illustrated by award-winning artists, such as Donald Crews, Chris Van Allsburg, Barbara Cooney, Ed Young, Molly Bang, Jerry Pinkney, and Anita Lobel. Each section offers a blend of the voices and visions that shaped the nation, including Native American myths, tales told by immigrants, songs of the American Revolution, and the tragedy of slavery. The book contains explanatory notes, indexes, background annotations for each tale or song, and suggestions for further reading.

Durell, Ann, compiler. *The Diane Goode Book of American Folk Tales and Songs.* Ill. by Diane Goode. Dutton, 1989. 64p. Folk.

Glazer, Tom, compiler. *Tom Glazer's Treasury of Songs for Children.* Ill. by John O'Brien. Doubleday, 1988. 256p. Non-fic.

Johnson, James Weldon. *Lift Every Voice and Sing.* Ill. by Elizabeth Catlett. Walker, 1993. 36p. Non-fic.

The African-American National Anthem was written in 1900 by James Weldon Johnson, a school principal and civil rights leader, and his brother J. Rosamond Johnson, for the celebration of Abraham Lincoln's birthday. Words tell of the long struggle of black people for equality, their joy and hopes, and their enduring faith in God. The strong linocuts by Elizabeth Catlett, made in the 1940s, portray black women and men and are especially well suited for the song. The piano score and all verses are included in this attractive book.

Krull, Kathleen, compiler and arranger. *Gonna Sing my Head Off! American Folk Songs for Children.* Ill. by Allen Garns. Knopf, 1992. 145p. Non-fic.

This collection of over 60 contemporary and traditional folk songs includes such favorites as "Buffalo Gals," "Go Tell It on the Mountain," "If I Had a Hammer," "Red River Valley," "Sweet Betsy from Pike," and "Turkey in the Straw." The compiler successfully strikes a regional balance, and the motifs of the songs include a mix of themes, historical periods, emotions, and types. Each song includes a brief paragraph providing the regional location and origin of the song, which is helpful. The piano and guitar arrangements are simple and in keys that are easiest for average people to sing and play. Colorful illustrations accompany the alphabetically arranged songs.

Mattox, Cheryl Warren. *Shake It to the One That You Love the Best: Play Songs and Lullabies from Black Musical Traditions.* With ill. from the works of Varnette P. Honeywood and Brenda Joysmith. Warren-Mattox Productions, 1989. 56p. Non-fic.

The compiler has brought together 16 play songs and 10 lullabies, recalled from her youth, that embody an important part of the African-American musical heritage. Included are "Kumbaya," "Loop de Loo," and "Short'ning Bread." The play songs fall into three categories—ring games, line games, and clapping rhymes—and Mattox appends directions on how to play the games. Also included is a brief description of the origin of each song. The illustrations by renowned contemporary black artists will introduce young children to their works.

2. Folk Tales of America

Aardema, Verna. *Borreguita and the Coyote: A Tale from Ayutla, Mexico.* Ill. by Petra Mathers. Knopf, 1991. [32]p. Folk.

In this simple tale, the little lamb called Borreguita outwits Coyote when he plans to eat her for supper. She convinces Coyote that she is too skinny to eat, that the reflection of the moon on the pond is cheese, that he needs to hold up a mountain, and that he can swallow Borreguita whole. After the last incident, Coyote leaves with a horrible ache in his mouth, never to bother Borreguita again. Children will enjoy this classic tale of a smaller opponent besting a more powerful adversary. Brightly colored illustrations enhance the text.

Ata, Te. *Baby Rattlesnake.* Adapted by Lynn Moroney. Ill. by Veg Reisberg. Children's Book Press, 1992. [32]p. Folk.

The story of Baby Rattlesnake has been told for many decades by Te Ata, a 92-year-old Chickasaw Indian storyteller. Now written down for the first time, children will read this classic tale about a young rattlesnake who gets something he greatly desires before he is ready for it. Family love and forgiveness are prominent themes in this delightful story illustrated with brilliant drawings designed from cut paper and gouache paints.

Bierhorst, John. *The Woman Who Fell from the Sky: The Iroquois Story of Creation.* Ill. by Robert Andrew Parker. Morrow, 1993. [32]p. Folk.

In this retelling of the Iroquois creation myth, the woman who falls out of the sky lands on the water, forms mud, and then uses her powers of creation to make the earth, the stars, and the sun. The woman gives birth to two very opposite sons, Sapling and Flint; each of them participates in the creation process by creating streams, rivers, animals, birds, fish, and even monsters. When their work is done, the sons rise up from the Earth along the Milky Way, and the sky woman throws herself into the fire, rising up in smoke. Vivid watercolor paintings accompany the simple text.

Bruchac, Joseph, and Jonathan London. *Thirteen Moons on Turtle's Back: A Native American Year of Moons.* Ill. by Thomas Locker. Philomel, 1992. [32]p. Poet.

This beautiful collection of poems, based on Indian legends, explains the 13 moon cycles each year as interpreted by different Native peoples. The close bond of the People with their natural world is revealed in the Cherokees' "Moon of Falling Leaves," the Winnebagos' "Moon When Deer Drop Their Horns," and the Potawatomis' "Baby Bear Moon." Locker's stunning paintings accompany and enhance each splendid poem.

Caduto, Michael J., and Joseph Bruchac. *Keepers of the Earth: Native American Stories and Environmental Activities for Children.* Ill. by John Kahiones Fadden and Carol Wood. Fulcrum, 1988. 209p. Folk.

These folk tales, gathered from Native Americans from all parts of the United States, focus on aspects of the environment: creation, fire, wind, weather, water, sky, plants and animals, life, death and spirit, and the unity of the earth. Each story is accompanied by a discussion of the story, questions that check comprehension, and activities that focus on sensory awareness, and an understanding of, and caring for, the earth and its people. The stories are told in an easy-to-understand, story-telling style, well suited for reading aloud. The activities, which can be adapted for either younger or older students, can be integrated across the curriculum for grades K-8. A companion volume by the same authors is *Keepers of the Animals: Native American Stories and Wildlife Activities for Children* (Fulcrum, 1991).

Cohlene, Terri, adapter. *Little Firefly: An Algonquian Legend.* Ill. by Charles Reasoner. Rourke Corporation, Inc., 1990. 47p. Folk.

In this variation of the Cinderella story, Little Firefly is treated very badly by her two older sisters, who keep her constantly working and tending the fire. In a dream, Little Firefly is told to go to the wigwam of the Invisible One where she will find happiness. Dressing herself in the best clothes she can find, Little Firefly sets off across the water and is welcomed by the Invisible One's sister. Because of her kind heart, the Invisible Being chooses Little Firefly for his bride. A short chapter at the end of the story provides some information about the Algonquian Indians. A similar tale is

Rafe Martin's *The Rough-Face Girl*, illustrated by David Shannon (Putnam, 1992).

DeArmond, Dale. *The Seal Oil Lamp: Adapted from an Eskimo Folktale*. Sierra Club, 1988. 32p. Folk.

A seven-year-old Eskimo boy named Allugua is left to die alone by broken-hearted parents because his blindness will make him a burden to the people of his village. This is a sensitive and well-told adaptation of an Eskimo folk tale of despair and triumph over adversity. The black-and-white woodcuts depict the Eskimo people in harmony with their environment.

de Paola, Tomie. *The Legend of the Bluebonnet: An Old Tale of Texas*. Putnam, 1983. [32]p. Folk.

de Paola, Tomie. *The Legend of the Indian Paintbrush*. Putnam, 1988. 40p. Folk.

Little Gopher is small for his age and cannot hunt nor fight very well. He can draw, however, and as he grows older he has a dream vision that tells him his role is to record the history of his people on painted animal skins. His greatest dream is to capture the colors of the sunset, and, one night, his wish is granted. The legend recounts how Little Gopher's paintbrushes are transformed into the brightly colored flowers that dot Wyoming, Texas, and the high plains. Brilliant illustrations accompany the text.

Esbensen, Barbara Juster. *The Star Maiden: An Ojibway Tale*. Ill. by Helen K. Davie. Little, Brown, 1988. [32]p. Folk.

This legend, illustrated with wonderful full-page paintings, tells of the beautiful star maiden who, tired of wandering the skies, decides she wants to become part of the earthly world. The Ojibway people are delighted and prepare to welcome her. She cannot decide—should she be a rose, a prairie wildflower, or what? In the end, she and her star sisters settle over the water and in the morning, the people are astounded to see water lilies floating as far as they can see. Another recommended folk tale by Esbensen is *Ladder to the Sky: How the Gift of Healing Came to the Ojibway Nation* (Little, Brown, 1989).

Goble, Paul. *Crow Chief: A Plains Indian Story*. Orchard, 1992. [32]p. Folk.

This is a tale of the wise Savior, often known as Falling Star, who selflessly comes to help his people during times of stress. This story, which explains how crows became black in color, tells of how Crow Chief continually warned the buffalo about the dangers of approaching Indian hunters. Falling Star comes and tricks Crow Chief, eventually establishing peace between the animals and humans. Goble's brilliant trademark drawings accompany the text.

Goble, Paul. *Death of the Iron Horse.* Bradbury, 1987. [32]p. Folk.

Based on an historical event, this is the story of the bravery of the Cheyenne Indians in derailing a Union Pacific freight train as part of their struggle to maintain their integrity and way of life. The tale illustrates how a relatively insignificant event can become a folk tale of pride and courage.

Goble, Paul. *Iktomi and the Boulder: A Plains Indian Story.* Orchard, 1988. [32]p. Folk.

Iktomi is the hero of many funny stories—he is very clever, a liar, a mischief-maker, a trickster, up to no good, and always in trouble. In this story, as he is walking to a nearby village, he gives his blanket to a large boulder to shield it from the sun. He then decides to take it back, angering the boulder, who rolls on top of him. In the evening, bats come and chip away at the rock thus freeing Iktomi, which explains why bats have flat faces and why there are rocks scattered across the Great Plains. Other *Iktomi* stories include *Iktomi and the Berries* (Orchard, 1989), *Iktomi and the Ducks* (Orchard, 1990), and *Iktomi and the Buffalo Skull* (Orchard, 1991).

Goble, Paul. *The Lost Children: The Boys Who Were Neglected.* Bradbury, 1993. [32]p. Folk.

This book is based on the Blackfoot myth that tells the origins of the Pleiades stars, which the Blackfoot called the Bunched Stars or the Lost Children. When none of the People will help the six, ragged orphaned brothers who are caring for themselves, the boys decide they no longer want to be part of the world. They decide to become stars because stars remain forever and will always be beautiful. They are helped by Sun Man and Moon Woman and the Lost Children can still be seen today in the night sky. Goble's vivid illustrations fill the pages, and he includes a note at the end of the book regarding the tipi designs in the story.

Note: Although we have cited only a few of Paul Goble's books, all of his many works are highly recommended.

Harris, Joel Chandler. *Jump on Over! The Adventures of Brer Rabbit and His Family.* Adapted by Van Dyke Parks. Ill. by Barry Moser. Harcourt Brace Jovanovich, 1989. 40p. Folk.

Hooks, William H. *The Ballad of Belle Dorcas.* Ill. by Brian Pinkney. Knopf, 1990. 40p. Folk.

An example of a conjure tale from the Gullah people of the Carolina coast, this story tells of Belle Dorcas, a free black woman who falls in love with and marries a slave man named Joshua. When Joshua's new master plans to sell him, Belle goes to Granny Lizard for a spell to save her husband. The magic turns Joshua into a great cedar tree and allows him to become a man at night. This beautifully told and illustrated tale is haunting and deep, and demonstrates how magic was a method to "escape" slavery.

Hunter, C. W. *The Green Gourd: A North Carolina Folktale.* Ill. by Tony Griego. Putnam's, 1992. [32]p. Folk.

An old woman ignores the saying "Never pull a gourd afore it's ripe, or it'll witch ye sure." By picking a green gourd, she gets more than she bargained for. Her fractious, unripe gourd attacks her, and then when a panther and fox try to help, they, too, are overpowered by the gourd. It is up to a clever boy to outwit the gourd and restore order. Colorful illustrations accompany the text, and an author's note explains the origins of the tale.

Jaquith, Priscilla, reteller. *Bo Rabbit Smart for True: Folktales from the Gullah.* Ill. by Ed Young. Philomel, 1981. 55p. Folk.

This is a collection of four folk tales from the Gullah—a people brought as slaves to the Georgia and South Carolina coastal plantations in the 1700s. Wily characters feature prominently in these stories, especially little Bo Rabbit who manages to outsmart both a whale and an elephant. An author's foreword explains the history of the Gullah people, and the book includes background notes and a bibliography.

Kellogg, Steven. *Mike Fink: A Tall Tale.* Morrow, 1992. [40]p. Folk.

Born in the Allegheny Mountains, Mike Fink ran away at the age of two days, apparently destined for a life of action right from the start. Mike became the King of the Keelboatmen, those rough men who navigated cargo boats up and down the Mississippi, Missouri, and Ohio Rivers to New Orleans. Growing up on the frontier, Mike learned how to wrestle, eventually wrestling with grizzly bears in an effort to defeat the strongest of the keelboatmen. This American tall tale is full of humor, action, and colorful, detailed drawings. Three other tall tales by Steven Kellogg are recommended: *Johnny Appleseed: A Tall Tale* (Morrow, 1988); *Paul Bunyan: A Tall Tale* (Morrow, 1984); and *Pecos Bill: A Tall Tale* (Morrow, 1986).

Lacapa, Michael, reteller. *Antelope Woman: An Apache Folktale.* Northland Pub., 1992. 44p. Folk.

Illustrated with Lacapa's dazzling and stylized art, this folk tale explains why the Apache never hunt or kill antelope and remember to respect all things great and small. A young Apache woman admires the man who comes to her village to teach the People to respect all creatures. When she follows him through the four sacred hoops, she sees him turn into an antelope, and so does she. He instructs her so that she, too, can teach the People to honor all life. After a while, they return to her People, are married, but then are rejected when she bears twins. They then pass through the hoops once again and become antelopes, forever making them special to the Apache nation. Another recommended folk tale by Lacapa is *The Flute Player: An Apache Folktale* (Northland Pub., 1990).

Lester, Julius. *The Tales of Uncle Remus: The Adventures of Brer Rabbit.* Ill. by Jerry Pinkney. Dial, 1987. 153p. Folk.

Lester retells these African-American stories with relish, humor, and a few contemporary twists that will help children relate to the tales. Written in the storyteller's style, these tales, in part, represent an allegorical response to slavery by black people. The stories should be read aloud and some of them would be excellent choices for readers' theater. Additional "Uncle Remus" books by Lester include *More Tales of Uncle Remus: Further Adventures of Brer Rabbit, His Friends, Enemies, and Others* (Dial, 1988) and *Further Tales of Uncle Remus: The Misadventures of Brer Rabbit, Brer Fox, Brer Wolf, the Doodang, and other Creatures* (Dial, 1990).

Lindbergh, Reeve. *Johnny Appleseed: A Poem.* Ill. by Kathy Jakobsen. Little, Brown, 1990. [32]p. Poet.

In this beautifully written poem, readers learn about John Chapman, who left his native Massachusetts in the early 1800s to sow apple seeds in New York, Pennsylvania, Ohio, and Indiana. The intense folk-art illustrations show Johnny Appleseed in total harmony with nature, generously committing his entire life to bringing the valuable apple trees to the new frontier. This is a good read-aloud choice for young children. An author's note at the end of the book separates the legend from the real John Chapman.

Locker, Thomas. *Washington Irving's Rip Van Winkle.* Dial, 1988. [32]p. Folk.

Malotki, Ekkehart. *The Mouse Couple: A Hopi Tale.* Ill. by Michael Lacapa. Northland Pub., 1988. 56p. Folk.

This brightly illustrated authentic Hopi tale is well-suited as a read-aloud book. The illustrations are strong, stylized Hopi art forms showing the mouse couple as they seek a husband for their daughter so that they will be cared for in their old age. Young children will like the repetition of the story as the father mouse goes to the East, the West, the North, and the South in search of a suitable husband, only to find him living nearby. For older readers, the tale cites the problems of the elderly and of the younger generation.

McDermott, Gerald. *Arrow to the Sun: A Pueblo Indian Tale.* Viking, 1974. [32]p. Folk.

McDermott, Gerald. *Raven: A Trickster Tale from the Pacific Northwest.* Harcourt Brace Jovanovich, 1993. [32]p. Folk.

Raven, the shape-shifting trickster of Native American stories, is sad because the world is dark. He searches for the light and finds it coming from the house of the Sky Chief, where the sun is shut up in a box. By changing himself into a pine needle that is swallowed by the Chief's daughter, Raven becomes a child who demands to play with the box. He quickly resumes his form as Raven and flies off with the sun, bringing it to all the People. McDermott's colorful storytelling is poetic and charming, and the people and interiors are portrayed reflecting the arts of the Native Americans of the Northwest and Alaska. For another recent story about Raven, see Ann Dixon's *How Raven Brought Light to People* (McElderry, 1993).

McKissack, Patricia. *Flossie and the Fox*. Ill. by Rachel Isadora. Dial, 1986. [32]p. Folk.

A young black girl named Flossie Finley is sent by her grandmother to deliver a basket of eggs to a neighbor whose hens have stopped laying because of a terrorizing fox. Big Mama warns Flossie to beware of the fox and all along the way, the fox tries to outsmart Flossie and steal her eggs. In the end, Flossie is the wily one who chuckles to herself when Mr. McCutchin's hounds chase the fox into the woods. This timeless story was told to the author as a child by her grandfather.

McKissack, Patricia. *Mirandy and Brother Wind*. Ill. by Jerry Pinkney. Knopf, 1989. [32]p. Folk.

Set in a small town around 1906, this story of a black family and their way of life is told with pride and joy. Young Mirandy wants to win the cakewalk at the next village celebration, and she wants Brother Wind as her dance partner. Detailed, full-page illustrations add to the charm of this fanciful story and it is a good read-aloud choice for young children.

Mendez, Phil. *The Black Snowman*. Ill. by Carole Byard. Scholastic, 1989. [48]p. Folk.

Jacob Miller lives in a poor neighborhood and hates being black. When his younger brother puts an old kente cloth on the dirty snowman they have just built, the snowman magically comes to life. Telling and showing Jacob about his West African forebearers, the snowman succeeds in instilling courage and new-found pride in Jacob. Striking illustrations in brilliant hues help tell the story.

Musgrove, Margaret. *Ashanti to Zulu: African Traditions*. Ill. by Leo and Diane Dillon. Dial, 1976. [32]p. Non-fic.

The letters of the alphabet are the means to introduce readers to 26 African tribes in this Caldecott award-winning book. Stunning illustrations depict a custom important to each of the tribes, for example, farming to the Dogon, hair braiding to the Masai, and singing to the Tuareg. Readers will come to understand the rich variety of African peoples and cultures and will discover the many African traditions that have come to this country.

Osborne, Mary Pope. *American Tall Tales*. Ill. by Michael McCurdy. Knopf, 1991. 115p. Folk.

This oversized compilation of nine humorous "tall tales" is enhanced by Michael McCurdy's hand-colored woodcuts. From Paul Bunyan to Pecos Bill to Ann Thunder Ann Whirlwind, these stories present larger-than-life portrayals of some of the characters who carved the American frontier. The author also includes real people, such as Davy Crockett and Johnny Appleseed, and presents their human shortcomings, as well as their strengths. In the introduction and notes for each tale, the author explains the blend of history and fantasy, and how she adapted her sources. The stories will have to be read out loud for young children. Includes a detailed bibliography.

Osofsky, Audrey. *Dreamcatcher*. Ill. by Ed Young. Orchard, 1992. [32]p. Folk.

A young Ojibway baby of the Great Lakes region, tucked snugly in his cradleboard, spends the day sleeping and watching his mother hoe the garden, children at play, his sister drying berries, his grandmother weaving, and his father in his birchbark canoe. At night, when it is time to sleep, baby's older sister hangs a dreamcatcher on his cradleboard hoop. During the night, the dreamcatcher keeps out the bad dreams of the raggedy man, bears, and a mean owl, while letting in happy dreams of dancing, playing leapfrog, and sucking on maple sugar. Soft drawings accompany the lyrical text.

Oughton, Jerrie. *How the Stars Fell Into the Sky: A Navajo Legend*. Ill. by Lisa Desimini. Houghton Mifflin, 1992. [32]p. Folk.

After considering the sand and the sea, First Woman decides to write the laws in the sky so all the people can easily see them. Using her jewels, she carefully places the stars in patterns in the sky. But when she allows the wily Coyote to aid her in this task, he becomes impatient and randomly tosses First Woman's jewels into the sky. Unable to undo Coyote's actions, First Woman mourns that the people will never know why chaos and confusion will always dwell among them. Stylistic, brilliant illustrations accompany the simple text.

Rodanas, Kristina. *Dragonfly's Tale*. Clarion, 1991. [32]p. Folk.

Based on a Zuni tale, this is the story of the Ashiwi people who lived and prospered in the American Southwest. In order to boast of their plentiful corn harvest, the elders invited neighboring peoples and staged a mock battle with bread and batter. This waste so enraged the two Corn Maidens that they sent a drought which killed the village's corn harvest. When the Ashiwi leave their homes in search of food, a brother and sister are accidentally left behind and it is their good works and kind hearts, along with help from a magical insect, that save the village. Brilliant illustrations accompany the text.

San Souci, Robert D. *Larger than Life: The Adventures of American Legendary Heroes*. Ill. by Andrew Glass. Doubleday, 1991. 59p. Folk.

San Souci, Robert D. *The Legend of Scarface: A Blackfeet Indian Tale*. Ill. by Daniel San Souci. Doubleday, 1978. [32]p. Folk.

Born with an ugly scar on his cheek, Scarface is taunted throughout his life. He falls in love with the beautiful Singing Rains, and she with him, but she has made a promise to the Sun never to wed. Scarface then heads out to find the dwelling place of the Sun, beyond the Great Waters, and he is helped by the animals he meets on his way. This is a beautiful story of love, generosity, honesty, and goodness.

San Souci, Robert D. *Sukey and the Mermaid*. Ill. by Brian Pinkney. Four Winds, 1992. [32]p. Folk.

Based on folklore from the South Carolina islands, this picture book tells of young Sukey, an African-American girl, who is befriended by a beautiful mermaid named Mama Jo. Because Sukey is so unhappy, Mama Jo carries her down to the ocean world until Sukey, now a grown woman, wishes to return to the human world. On the eve of Sukey's wedding, tragedy strikes and Mama Jo asks Sukey to make a very difficult decision. The colorful, striking illustrations are crucial to the text, and an author's note tells the historical background of this folk tale.

San Souci, Robert D. *The Talking Eggs: A Folktale from the American South*. Ill. by Jerry Pinkney. Dial, 1989. [32]p. Folk.

This Creole story will remind children of fairy tales, such as Cinderella; indeed, the story shows the probable influence of the French immigrants. This tale concerns two sisters—a mean-spirited one called Rose and a kind-hearted one named Blanche. When they encounter a magical old woman, Blanche follows her directions, while Rose, overcome with greed, ignores them. The colorful illustrations, with Pinkney's remarkable attention to detail, are a beautiful portrayal of black people. The story-telling style is ideal for read-aloud and dramatizations.

Steptoe, John. *The Story of Jumping Mouse: A Native American Legend*. Lothrop, 1984. 40p. Folk.

A young mouse meets Magic Frog who gives him long strong hind legs so that he can jump far. As Mouse sets off to find the Far-Off Land, he meets a blind bison who is waiting to die. Mouse gives Bison his sight and then Bison escorts Mouse to the mountains. Here Mouse meets a wolf who also needs help. When Mouse meets Magic Frog again, he is told to jump as high as he can. He soars into the sky and, because of his unselfish spirit and compassion, he is renamed Eagle. The full-page, black-and-white drawings add much to this beautiful tale.

Stevens, Janet, reteller. *Coyote Steals the Blanket: A Ute Tale.* Holiday, 1993. [32]p. Folk.

Coyote is a proud braggart—the King of the Desert—who does and takes what he wants. When he spies a beautiful blanket draped over a rock in the middle of nowhere, Coyote takes it, despite Hummingbird's warning not to. From then on, Coyote is bedeviled by a large rock that chases him all over the desert. Mule Deer and Big Horn Sheep try to help Coyote, but it is only when he returns the blanket that his troubles end. Bright illustrations enhance this delightful story about a Native American trickster.

Van Etten, Teresa Pijoan de. *Spanish-American Folktales: The Practical Wisdom of Spanish-Americans in 28 Eloquent and Simple Stories.* August House Pubs., 1990. 127p. Folk.

Growing up on the San Juan Pueblo Reservation, the author tells the folk tales she recalls of her youth in New Mexico. This collection of 28 tales shows the character, shrewdness, customs, language, wit, persistence, and humor of the Spanish Americans in the United States. Animals, including wily coyote, grandparents, shepherds, children, rivers, thieves, and even postmen, are featured in stories that will appeal to readers of all ages. An author's note at the end of the book provides the origin and background for each story.

Williams, Julie Stewart. *And the Birds Appeared.* Ill. by Robin Yoko Burningham. University of Hawaii Press, 1988. [32]p. Folk.

This is the folk tale of Maui, the Hawaiian boy with magical powers, who could see what others could not. When a man from another island arrives and brags about how beautiful everything is on his home island, Maui calls forth the birds to sing and show themselves. Ever since that day, all the people can see and hear the birds. The simply told tale is beautifully illustrated with realistic full-color pictures of the people, birds, flowers, trees, and plants of the island.

Williams, Julie Stewart. *Maui Goes Fishing.* Ill. by Robin Yoko Burningham. University of Hawaii Press, 1991. [31]p. Folk.

Maui lives with his family on an island in the Pacific. He has three older brothers, and he loves to play tricks on them when they go out on their fishing boat every day. Fed up, the brothers refuse to let Maui join them until the day that Maui explains that the special fish hook he has made will help them catch all the fish they need. Instead of snaring a fish, Maui catches land and this delightful tale explains how the Hawaiian Islands came into existence. Brilliant illustrations accompany the text.

THE NEW NATION

❖ ❖ ❖ ❖ ❖ ❖ ❖ ❖

INTRODUCTION TO UNITS 4, 5, AND 6

In the next three units, "Exploring the New World," "New Villages in America," and "Revolution and New Nation," the learning activities and selected books develop the early history of the United States. In Unit 4, "Exploring the New World," the concept of location will be emphasized through activities about the discovery and exploration of North America by various people, such as the ancestors of the present-day Native Americans, the Vikings, and Christopher Columbus. Through expanding their library skills and comparing what is known about the discoveries of Columbus and the Vikings, children will be introduced to how we learn about the past. Children will also conduct a survey to learn about their own family history. Historical perspectives will be illustrated by recording the voyages and discoveries on the time line constructed in Unit 1.

Unit 5, "New Villages in America," will focus on the lives of the European colonists and the Native Americans. As children learn about the national origins of the European colonists, they will also seek to find out the national heritages of their own families. The origins of Thanksgiving will aid the children in identifying the reasons why colonists came to the unknown lands of America. Freedom of religion will be emphasized in this unit, then expanded in later units to include other freedoms guaranteed by the Constitution of the United States. Children will use dramatizations and comparisons to interpret the significant changes that took place during this period.

Unit 6, "Revolution and the New Nation," concentrates on everyday life in the late 1700s and some of the causes of the Revolutionary War. Children will compare their celebrations of the Fourth of July with the original Independence Day in 1776. They will identify George Washington as the leader of the new nation. Through writing, drawing, dramatizations, and comparisons, children will learn about the new nation and the U. S. Constitution as the foundation of our laws today.

UNIT
four

Exploring the New World

OBJECTIVES

1. Using maps of the world and of North America with the help of the teacher, children will trace the probable routes to North America of Asians moving into North America across the Bering Straits, of the Vikings, and of Christopher Columbus.
2. Using the time line constructed in Unit 1, children will record the voyages of the Vikings and of Columbus.
3. After the teacher or librarian guides the children through the use of the card catalog or online catalog, children will locate books about Columbus and the Vikings. Using these books, and with the help of the teacher or librarian, the children will deduce and list ways in which we learn about the past.
4. With guidance from the teacher or librarian, children will discover their personal histories by developing a list of questions about their family's history to be answered with the help of their parents, grandparents, or guardians.

LEARNING ACTIVITIES

1. Mapping the Routes to North America

Using a variety of references, such as *The Discovery of the Americas,* the teacher or librarian will help children trace and date the routes on the world map of the ancestors of Native Americans, of the Vikings, and of Columbus. Note how these people came from three different areas: Asia, northern Europe, and southern Europe. Ask children to list what they know about the ancestors of the Native Americans, the Vikings, and Columbus and his crew. Record their speculative answers for use with a later activity.

2. Compare the Travels of the Vikings and Columbus on the Time Line

Using the information from the previous lessons, record the travels to North America by the Vikings and Columbus on the time line. With the teacher's help, the children can count the years between the voyages of the Vikings and Columbus. With advanced students, enter on the time line the voyages of other people to North America as listed in *The Discovery of the Americas*.

3. A Mystery to Solve: How Do We Find Out About the Past?

Finding Information in the Library. The teacher or librarian should demonstrate the use of the card catalog or the online catalog. In small guided groups, the children will use the subject headings "Columbus" and "Vikings" to locate books and media for classroom use. In all probability, they will locate several books about Columbus and only a few books about the Vikings. For children with advanced library skills, search for books about the ancestors of the Native Americans. This topic will be very challenging because there will be many books about Native Americans from the 1600s to the 1900s, but few sources for children about earlier times.

Using Information from the Library. Read aloud from *The Discovery of the Americas* or tell the children about the early Asian people who became the ancestors of the Native Americans. Use the books about the ancestors of the Native Americans that were located in the previous activity. Now make another list of what children know about the ancestors of the Native Americans. Compare this list with the children's list from Activity 1 in this Unit. Try to deduce reasons why we know very little about these people of long ago. Help the children conclude that the early Asians did not write books about their experiences in the Americas. With older children, the role of the archaeologist in finding out about the past can be discussed.

Should We Celebrate "Viking Day"? Read aloud books or portions of books or use other media about the Vikings. Again have the children list important information, then compare the information with the children's recorded list from Activity 1. Ask the children to state reasons why they think Americans should or should not celebrate a "Viking Day" similar to "Columbus Day." Children of Scandinavian descent may indeed think we should celebrate Viking Day. There may also be discussion with other children, who are aware of the history of the Native Americans, as to whether Columbus Day should be celebrated at all.

Why Do We Know so Much About Columbus? Use the discussion of Viking Day and Columbus Day as an introduction to finding out more about

Christopher Columbus through books and other media. Have children expand and correct the list of information about Columbus they constructed in Activity 1.

Ask children to identify the ways in which we have come to know about his voyages. Look for evidence in the books and media from the days of Columbus, such as a replica of a map, a drawing, or a quote from a diary or journal. In the references about Vikings or early Asians, were there copies of drawings, maps, or diaries from those people? Why are there replicas from the days of Columbus, but none from the early Asians or from the Vikings?

How Do We Learn About the Past? With the children, list how they learn about events of the past: e.g., through both fiction and nonfiction books, movies, television, newspapers, and from other people, such as parents, teachers, and librarians. Have they solved the mystery of how we learn about the past? Why do we know more about Columbus than we do about the Vikings?

4. How Do We Learn About Our Personal History?

The children will develop a list of questions to be answered with the aid of their parents or guardians. Send a letter to the parents and guardians explaining the purpose of the questions and soliciting their cooperation. For young children, start with their own history. Suggested questions are as follows:

1. When and where was I born?
2. How did I get my name? Was I named for someone?
3. What were my first words? When did I start talking?
4. When did I begin to walk?
5. As a baby, a toddler, a school child, what were my favorite toys? Foods? Colors? Activities?
6. What are your favorite memories or stories about me before I started school?
7. What are your favorite memories or stories about me after I started school?
8. Have we lived in another town or home than where we now live?

With older children, construct questions about their family history in order to obtain information about other generations, parents or guardians, grandparents, other members of the family, and family friends. See also, Activity 3, "National Origins of Today's Americans" in Unit 5.

After the information has been gathered, the children as historians can share their answers in class. The teacher or librarian should answer the same list of questions about themselves as an additional way to show generational likenesses and differences.

BOOK LIST

Adler, David A. *A Picture Book of Christopher Columbus.* Ill. by John and Alexandra Wallner. Holiday, 1991. [32]p. Biog.

Benchley, Nathaniel. *Snorri and the Strangers.* Ill. by Don Bolognese. Harper & Row, 1976. [64]p. Fic.

In this "I Can Read" book, Snorri Thorfinnsson is the first white child to be born in America, early in the eleventh century. The son of Norwegian settlers who traveled from Greenland, Snorri grows up wanting to know about his homeland. When Snorri is a boy, strangers come to his home, Native peoples who have dark hair and who trade with the Scandinavians. However, an incident triggers hostilities and the Norsemen decide to leave the land because they know that killing these people is not the answer. This is one author's depiction of what might have been the experiences of the first European settlers in the New World.

Fradin, Dennis Brindell. *Hiawatha: Messenger of Peace.* Margaret K. McElderry, 1992. 40p. Biog.

The *real* Hiawatha, not Longfellow's mythical hero, was an Iroquois Indian who lived in the mid-1400s in what is present-day New York State. There was much fighting among the five tribes of the Iroquois when Hiawatha was growing up and he was familiar with the custom of "blood revenge." After his wife and daughters were killed by Ododarhoh, Hiawatha, instead of seeking revenge, left his village and lived as a hermit. Along with Degandawida, a man called the Peacemaker, Hiawatha developed a successful plan to unite the five tribes to form one government, called the Iroquois Federation, where all would be represented. The blood revenge custom ceased and murderers began to pay a price for their crimes. Includes photographs, drawings, a bibliography, and index.

Liestman, Vicki. *Columbus Day.* Ill. by Rick Hanson. Carolrhoda, 1991. [56]p. Non-fic.

The author begins this short volume by destroying the myth that Columbus "discovered" America, and continues to relate in detail how Columbus came to make his historic voyage in 1492. She explains how the Spanish treated the Native Americans harshly in their quest for riches and power. The book ends with the message that Columbus Day should be a day to celebrate not only Columbus's accomplishments, but also to remember the heritage of Native Americans and that when we explore, we must be good to the people we meet along the way.

Lowe, Steve. *The Log of Christopher Columbus: The First Voyage: Spring, Summer and Fall 1492.* Ill. by Robert Sabuda. Philomel, 1992. [32]p. Non-fic.

Maestro, Betsy. *The Discovery of the Americas.* Ill. by Giulio Maestro. Lothrop, 1991. 48p. Non-fic.

Columbus's "discovery" of America is put into a wider historical context as the Maestros tell of the Stone Age explorers who crossed the land bridge from Asia to North America, and of the Chinese seamen who may well have explored the western shores of South America before Vikings came to Greenland. Through clear text and brilliant, detailed drawings, children will learn about the periodic discoveries of the Americas by such explorers as John Cabot, Amerigo Vespucci, Leif Ericsson, and Vasco Núñez de Balboa. Includes many maps and a helpful Table of Dates.

Marzollo, Jean. *In 1492.* Ill. by Steve Bjorkman. Scholastic, 1991. [32]p. Poet.

The author uses the familiar rhyme "In fourteen hundred and ninety-two; Columbus sailed the ocean blue" to acquaint young children with the story of this famous voyage. The simple text is written in rhyming couplets and readers will learn that "Day after day they looked for land; They dreamed of trees and rocks and sand." The author writes with humor ("But 'India' the land was not; It was the Bahamas, and it was hot") and the brilliant blues, greens, and purples of Bjorkman's vivid illustrations help visualize this significant event for children.

Ortiz, Simon. *The People Shall Continue.* Ill. by Sharol Graves. Children's Book Press, 1988. 24p. Non-fic.

This is a succinct, yet epic story of the Native American Peoples, told from the creation through the present day. The People were in harmony with the earth, trading with their neighbors, caught up in the daily struggles for existence. From the 1500s to the 1800s, the People were at war with the Europeans in order to preserve their land and way of life. The defeat of the People was bitter, full of broken promises by the American government. However, in the present day, the People have become self-aware and unified and are struggling anew to tell their story and to instill in all peoples a sense of responsibility for life and the land. This excellent overview is presented from the Native American perspective.

Sis, Peter. *Follow the Dream: The Story of Christopher Columbus.* Knopf, 1991. [32]p. Biog.

This remarkable picture book tells the story of Columbus's life, beginning with his childhood dreams of adventure and ending with his landing in what he thought to be the Far East. The illustrations, reminiscent of Renaissance painting, range in color from dull grays and browns to brilliant blue, green, and rose hues. The pages overflow with details and this is a good read-aloud choice, although the simple text is suitable for independent readers.

Yolen, Jane. *Encounter.* Ill. by David Shannon. Harcourt Brace Jovanovich, 1992. [32]p. Fic.

A young Taino boy living on the island of San Salvador narrates this story of what might have been one of Columbus's first encounters with the Native peoples in 1492. The boy relates how his people were taken in by the pale men's gifts and false offers of friendship. As an old man, he mourns how his people gradually lost their lands, speech, clothing, culture and even their souls to the white men. This is a fascinating account told from the Native American viewpoint; an author's note explains the factual basis for the story. The full-page color paintings are captivating.

U N I T
five

New Villages in America

OBJECTIVES

1. After reading about the colonists from Europe, children will list reasons why Europeans left their homeland to settle in the New World.
2. After recording the new settlements and books about new settlements in the New World on the time line, children will locate the national origins of the colonists on the world map.
3. Children will ask their parents, guardians, and grandparents about the national origins of their family.
4. Children will demonstrate their understanding of the lives of the colonists and of their Native American neighbors through creative dramatizations of "A Day in the Life of. . ." or "How Our Lives Changed Forever."

5. As a class, in groups, or independently, children will construct Then and Now Charts to compare their own lives with the lives of a colonial child or a Native American child of the same time period.
6. Children will identify the origins of Thanksgiving.

LEARNING ACTIVITIES

1. Why Would Anyone Leave Their Homeland for a Wilderness?

Reasons for Seeking New Homes. After reading about the colonists, or listening to read-aloud books, children will list reasons why people from various European countries left their old homes and came to America. As a class or in small groups, the children will rank the importance of the colonists' reasons for coming to North America. Through this guided activity, children may begin to understand the significance of freedom of religion and having a voice in government.

Would We Move to an Unknown Land for the Same Reasons as the Colonists? Using the list of reasons for immigrating developed in the previous activity, have the children identify which reason(s) would be of most importance to them today. Perhaps they would select freedom of religion and having a voice in their government.

Freedom of Religion. Read portions of *The Jews of New Amsterdam* to the children to show how this group of people kept moving from country to country in search of religious freedom. Also read selections from *The Pilgrims of Plimoth* that tell about the Pilgrims' search for religious freedom.

In order to link the past with the present, look in the Yellow Pages of the phone book for a list of the religious groups and churches in your community. Do not ask children what religion they practice, but use the phone book as a source of evidence that there are many different religions in the United States and within their own community. Follow up this discussion in Unit 6, "Revolution and The New Nation," when learning about the Declaration of Independence, the Constitution, and the Bill of Rights.

Having a Voice in Government. Another major reason the early colonists left their homeland and came to America was to have a say in how they were governed. As evidence that Americans have a voice in their government, talk about the occasions when adults vote for representatives at the local, state, and national levels, and for questions about taxes. Make a list of the occasions when children vote on questions of concern in their classroom or school. If the school has a student council, have children from the later elementary grades explain what decisions the council makes, and how those decisions are made. Help children identify the opportunities they have to involve themselves in the responsibilities of democracy.

The phone book lists the local, county, state, and federal offices in your community, as well as the local offices of political parties. These lists can show children that government is indeed close to the people.

2. Colonies in North America

When, Where, and by Whom? Record the dates and names of the settlements of the new colonies on the time line. On the Outline Map of the United States constructed in Unit 1, place name, national origin, and date markers showing where the new settlements were located. Include the Spanish settlements of St. Augustine, Sante Fe, and the California missions on the West Coast, as well as other European colonies on the East Coast. The time line will help children see that the Pilgrims were only one of many groups of colonists and were not the first settlers in North America.

Writing Home. After reading about the colonists from Europe, choose one group from such books as *Spanish Pioneers of the Southwest* or *The Pilgrims of Plimoth*. Although most children had very little education during this period of history, ask children to assume they were among the educated few who could write. They should write postcards or letters to friends or family back in Spain, the Netherlands, or England, telling them about their new home and their celebrations.

Other children in the class can assume the role of the Wampanoag Indians in the *People of the Breaking Day*. These Native Americans had their own language but it was an unwritten language at that time. Ask children to pretend that they visited the colonists at the Thanksgiving celebration. Ask the children to write what they would have told their friends and families about their encounter with the colonists. Predict how the letters to Europe and the narratives of the Native Americans would be alike. How will they be different?

3. National Origins of Today's Americans

The Ancestor Hunt. Help the children construct a simple form asking parents, guardians, and grandparents about the national origins of their family and approximately when their ancestors came to the United States. Send a note home that explains the purpose of this homework and indicates that the United States is an appropriate national origin for Native Americans and others who do not know their ancestors' origins beyond the United States. For African-Americans, the continent of Africa is an appropriate origin if a specific nation is not known.

After the information has been returned to school, add markers to the world map showing the national origins, including the United States, of the ancestors of the children.

Writing to Ancestors. Children may wish to write a letter to their ancestors expressing their appreciation that the ancestors came to America and thanking them for bringing their traditions with them. Children of Native American and African-American ancestry could write to their forebearers in appreciation of their preservation of the traditions of their families.

4. "A Day in the Life of. . ." or "How Our Lives Changed Forever"

Creative Dramatizations by "Family" Groups. After reading about life in North America prior to European colonization, the colonists' journeys to America, and the early days in a colony, organize the students into small cooperative groups representing families of colonists or Native Americans. The family groups of children will use creative dramatizations or puppets to portray "A Day in the Life of. . ." or "How Our Lives Changed Forever." Any of these scenes may be simply portrayed with few props, or could become full-scale productions with elaborate puppets, costumes, and scenery. Keep in the mind the purpose is to help children understand how life was different from today, and that both the Indians and the colonists were involved in many new experiences that changed their lives forever.

Consider the following scenes for dramatization: packing for the journey; explaining to their old friends why they are going to the New World; life on board the ship; daily life in the Indian village; sighting the ships; landing at the site of the new colony; observing the white people; observing the Indians; building a new home in the Indian village; building a new home in the colonists' village; learning from the Indians how to plant and harvest food; learning from the colonists how to use tools new to the Native Americans; Indians explaining to their friends why they are helping the white people; and colonists and Indians celebrating the harvest with a Thanksgiving feast.

Dramatizations of Books. Several of the books featured in this unit would lend themselves to dramatization. A few examples are described here.

Small Wolf. Read *Small Wolf* to the class. Identify the characters of the story and list the events in the story in sequence. Then ask the children to hypothesize different endings to the story. What would happen if Small Wolf's people had not moved away? What would happen if the white people tried to be friendly to the Indians? What would happen if the white people or the Indians attacked the other people? Show how the lives of the colonists and the Indians changed. Dramatize the story with different endings and compare the outcomes.

Sarah Morton's Day and *Samuel Eaton's Day*. Using the companion books, *Sarah Morton's Day: A Day in the Life of a Pilgrim Girl* and *Samuel Eaton's Day: A Day in the Life of a Pilgrim Boy*, choose events in their days to dramatize. Or, suppose that Sarah, Thomas, and Small Wolf met, what would they say to each other? Would they be afraid? What would they have in common? What would their hopes for the future be? How are their daily chores like those of children today? How and why are they different?

Alternative to Dramatization. The scenes for dramatization may also be the content of scenes for a mural. Small groups or individuals may draw the various scenes to portray life in the early colonies and in the Native American villages of the 1600s.

5. Then and Now Charts: Comparing the Lives of Colonial Children, Native American Children of the 1600s, and Children of Today

The class as a whole, small groups, or individuals can construct Then and Now Charts comparing information from *Sarah Morton's Day*, *Thomas Eaton's Day*, *The Pilgrims of Plimoth*, and *People of the Breaking Day* with a day in the lives of the children in the classroom. Include the dates on the chart. Compare how the children of the past and present meet their daily needs for food, clothing, shelter, and education. Then, expand the comparison to include religious practices, recreation, or other important events.

| | THE 1600S | | THE 1990S |
	COLONIAL CHILDREN	NATIVE AMERICAN CHILDREN	CHILDREN TODAY
FOOD			
CLOTHING			
SHELTER			
EDUCATION			

CHART 4   Comparing the Lives of Children of the 1600s, and Children of Today

6. Tacos for Thanksgiving?

After reading *The Mission Bell* or *Spanish Pioneers of the Southwest*, plan a menu for the Thanksgiving dinner of the Spanish colonists. What foods would they have eaten instead of turkey and pumpkin pie? Would the Spanish settlers share their dinner with Native Americans as the Pilgrims of Plimoth did? What would the Native Americans contribute to the dinner? What would the Spanish settlers be thankful for?

As a follow-up activity to the dramatizations and discussions, have each child divide a large sheet of paper into four sections. Title the sections: The Pilgrims' Thanksgiving, Native Americans' Thanksgiving, A Colonial Spanish Thanksgiving, and My Thanksgiving. Using drawings, lists, or paragraphs, the children can compare these events.

BOOK LIST

Note: Starred (*) books are reviewed in a previous section or unit of this book.

Anderson, Joan. *The First Thanksgiving Feast.* Photographs by George Ancona. Clarion, 1984. [48]p. Non-fic.

In this black-and-white photographic essay, Anderson and Ancona collaborate to recreate the first harvest festival at Plimoth Plantation at the living history museum in Plymouth, Massachusetts. The story contains fictional dialogue by such people as Myles Standish, Elizabeth Hopkins, and John Alden, based on first-hand accounts of the original celebration. Children will learn about the ocean crossing, the first year in the settlement, the way in which the Wampanoag Indians helped the Pilgrims, and the celebration itself. A note at the end of the book tells of the Native American alternate celebration called the National Day of Mourning.

*Anderson, Joan. *Spanish Pioneers of the Southwest.* Dutton, 1989. Non-fic. (Unit 2, Sect. 4)

*Benchley, Nathaniel. *Small Wolf.* Harper & Row, 1972. Fic. (Unit 2, Sect. 4)

Costabel, Eva Deutsch. *The Jews of New Amsterdam.* Atheneum, 1988. 32p. Non-fic.

This picture book tells the story of the Jews who were expelled from Spain in 1492, how they made their way to Brazil, and later emigrated to New Amsterdam (New York City) in 1654. The Jews encountered difficulties in being accepted, but eventually they established their place in the community. Includes a glossary, source notes, and index.

Harness, Cheryl. *Three Young Pilgrims.* Bradbury, 1992. [38]p. Fic.

This picture book tells the story of a Pilgrim family who came to America in 1620. The three Allerton children, Mary, Remember, and Bartholomew, are accompanying their parents to the New World, but when Mrs. Allerton and the new baby die in the first year, the family has some adjustments to make. Life is hard in the new colony, but with the help of Samoset and other Native Americans, the colonists manage to survive and bring in a good first harvest. The softly colored illustrations are full of detail, including special pages devoted to the *Mayflower*, the new colony, the people of Plymouth, and the Native peoples.

Kroll, Steven. *Oh, What a Thanksgiving!* Ill. by S.D. Schindler. Scholastic, 1988. [32]p. Fic.

As his family is preparing to celebrate the Thanksgiving holiday, a twentieth-century boy named David imagines what it was like for the Pilgrims during the first Thanksgiving feast. While at the grocery store, David imagines hunting turkey in the woods with his father, and while walking the two blocks to Grandma's house, he pictures greeting Squanto and Samoset on the street in Plymouth Colony. In the end, David realizes that the thankfulness for home, family, and friends has not changed over the centuries.

McGovern, Ann. *If You Lived in Colonial Times.* Ill. by Brinton Turkle. Scholastic, 1964. 79p. Non-fic.

McGovern, Ann. *If You Sailed on the Mayflower.* Ill. by J.B. Handelsman. Scholastic, 1969. 80p. Non-fic.

Politi, Leo. *The Mission Bell.* Scribner's, 1953. 32p. Biog.

This book tells about one of California's earliest pioneers—Father Junípero Serra—who founded many missions in that state during the early 1700s. While the Spanish soldiers traveling with Father Serra wanted to use force to "civilize" the Indians, the Jesuit priest insisted on treating the Indians with love, patience, and kindness. This book will demonstrate the important contribution of the Spanish to American culture, since people like Father Serra were building villages in California at the same time that the New England colonies were still in their fledgling states.

Sewall, Marcia. *People of the Breaking Day.* Atheneum, 1990. 48p. Non-fic.

In this companion volume to *The Pilgrims of Plimoth*, Sewall tells the story of the Wampanoag Indians, a tribe living in Massachusetts at the time the Pilgrims arrived. Among the things discussed are the importance of the tribe and the family; the division of labor between the sexes; what

Wampanoag homes looked like; how the children played and helped their families; and what they ate and how they obtained their food. Sewall portrays the Wampanoag people as caring deeply for each other and as being in close harmony with nature. Includes a glossary of Indian words.

Sewall, Marcia. *The Pilgrims of Plimoth.* Atheneum, 1986. 48p. Non-fic.

This story of the early Pilgrims is divided into five sections: Pilgrims, Menfolk, Womenfolk, Children and Youngfolk, and the Plantation. Men, women, and children worked together to make the settlement prosper, and the author describes their homes, what they wore, what they ate, and how they spent their time. This factual and well-written book is an excellent introduction to the Pilgrims because it does not focus solely on the Thanksgiving feast as do many other children's books. Use in conjunction with Sewall's *People of the Breaking Day.*

*Waters, Kate. *Sarah Morton's Day: A Day in the Life of a Pilgrim Girl.* Scholastic, 1989. Non-fic. (Unit 2, Sect. 4)

Weisgard, Leonard. *The Plymouth Thanksgiving.* Doubleday, 1967. [64]p. Non-fic.

UNIT
six

Revolution and the New Nation

OBJECTIVES

1. After reading a book about everyday life in the late 1700s, children will construct story maps or charts that tell about the characters, events, and living conditions the books portrayed.
2. Children will compare and write about why they would like to have lived in a new colony in the 1600s or in a village in the late 1700s.

3. After reading about George Washington, children will list at least three of his accomplishments on the time line, and draw a picture representing George Washington as an important leader in the new nation.
4. After reading in the social studies textbook or other informational source, or participating in a discussion led by the teacher or librarian about the causes of the Revolutionary War, children will identify causes of the Revolutionary War and the significance of July 4, 1776.
5. Children will identify the need for rules and laws for the new nation and in their lives today. Children will identify the Constitution of the United States as the foundation of our laws.

LEARNING ACTIVITIES

1. Learning about Everyday Life in the 1700s

Make a Story Map. A story map is a chart that represents the main elements in a story: setting, characters, time and place, plot or problems to be solved, main events listed in chronological order, and the resolution of the plot or problem. Developing a story map with children allows them to record cause-and-effect relationships, sequential actions, character development, and comprehension of the plot. In small groups or with the whole class, read books from the book list and use them as the foundations for story maps of the everyday experiences of Americans in the late 1700s.

A story map can be a simple chart, as shown in Chart 5, or the chart may illustrated or shaped like an object representing the book. For example, *Obadiah the Bold* (see Unit 7) may be represented by a spy glass, and the story map for *Buttons for General Washington* may be recorded in the shape of a large button.

Life in the New Nation: Comparison Circles (Venn Diagrams). Draw two very large, overlapping circles. Label the circles, "Life in Colonies in the 1600s" and "Life in the New Nation in 1776." In each circle, list the ways the people who lived at these times fulfilled their basic human needs using the categories of food, shelter, and clothing. Note the changes and differences. List those aspects of life that did not change in the section of the diagram where the circles overlap. Use books listed for Unit 5, "New Villages in America," as references for the colonies, and the book list for this unit for the new nation. Help the children differentiate between having to produce or make everything that was needed by a family in the early colonies, and the availability of stores, goods, and services in 1776. *The Ox-Cart Man* tells about one way in which families were able to buy or barter for their needs.

Title: *OBADIAH THE BOLD*

Setting: Nantucket Island

Who: Obadiah Starbuck, about seven years old, and members of his Quaker family

When: 1798

Plot/Problem: After receiving a spy glass as a gift, Obadiah decides he would like to be a pirate. However, being a pirate is not acceptable in his Quaker family.

Main Events (in chronologial order):

Obadiah gets his spy glass.

He wants to be a pirate.

He has a very rough "pirate" play time with his brothers.

He learns pirates are not honorable.

He abandons his spy glass.

His father tells him about his brave grandfather who is a sea captain.

Resolution of Problem: Obadiah resolves to use his spy glass when he becomes a brave and honorable sailor like his grandfather.

CHART 5 Story Map for *Obadiah the Bold* by Brinton Turkle

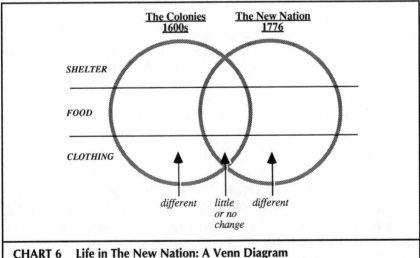

CHART 6 Life in The New Nation: A Venn Diagram

The Time Machine. Children can pretend they can program a time machine and explain why they would like to have lived in one of the early colonies or in the new nation. Children can write and draw about their own experiences or the experiences of book characters, when, through the time machine, they visited an early colony or a village in the new nation. Display the pictures and stories under these headings: "Life in the Colonies" or "Life in the New Nation."

Some children will find the following sentence starters helpful.

When I lived in the colony/village of _____, in the year of _____, our home was made of _____.

Every day we had to_____.

Our clothing was_____.

The hardest part of being a colonist/citizen of the new nation was

_____.

What I like best about being a colonial child/citizen of the new nation was _____.

2. The Life and Times of George Washington

Prior to reading *George Washington: A Picture Book Biography*, which includes an explanation of the source of the cherry tree story, make a list with the children of what they know (or think they know) about Washington. With the list posted, read about the life and accomplishments of George Washington. As children find out about his real life, revise and correct the list. Enter information about George Washington on the time line by listing at least three of his *greatest* accomplishments. In this context, children will learn that the cherry tree story is a legend and is not important when compared with his being a general in the Revolutionary War and first president of the United States.

3. Becoming an Independent Nation

Causes of the Revolution. After reading about George Washington and other leaders of the new nation, discuss with the children why the people of America went to war against Great Britain. Because there are few books for young children about the American Revolutionary War, the teacher or librarian will need to be the source of information. Refer back to the reasons why the colonists came to America in Unit 5. Review representation in the government as very important to the early settlers but lacking for the colonists.

Paul Revere's Ride, Buttons for General Washington, Deborah Sampson Goes to War, Samuel's Choice, Katie's Trunk, and *Phoebe the Spy* will give information about this period which must be expanded upon in order to tell the story of the War for Independence.

The Fourth of July, Then and Now. In small groups or in pairs, have children list or draw the activities of children celebrating the Fourth of July in the new nation in the late 1700s, and today. As each group tells about their lists or pictures, the teacher should record the activities under the headings "Children Celebrate the Fourth of July in the New Nation" and "Children Celebrate the Fourth of July in the United States Today." Conclude this chart by identifying the activities in both lists that are similar.

4. Laws for the New Nation

Review the classroom and school rules with the children. Have the children speculate about what would happen if there were no rules. Relate this discussion to the new nation and its need for laws that would be fair to everyone. Read aloud portions of *A More Perfect Union: The Story of Our Constitution* or *Shhh! We're Writing the Constitution.* Next, use the many examples and illustrations from Peter Spier's *We the People: The Constitution of the United States of America* to show children how the Constitution is a part of their rights and responsibilities today. Emphasize the Bill of Rights.

Have children write or draw about one of their rights and one of their responsibilities as young citizens of the United States. Post these pictures and paragraphs under the title "Children Are Citizens with Rights and Responsibilities," or make a class book to share with others.

BOOK LIST

Note: Starred (*) books are reviewed in a previous section or unit of this book.

Benchley, Nathaniel. *Sam the Minuteman.* Ill. by Arnold Lobel. Harper & Row, 1969. 62p. Fic.

In this "I Can Read History Book," the story of the Battles of Lexington and Concord in 1775 is told through the eyes of a very young Minuteman named Sam Brown. Accompanying his father to the confrontation with the British, Sam is scared, especially when Minutemen die in Lexington, but anger soon replaces fear and Sam is proud to follow his father to Concord. The British viewpoint is told in Benchley's companion volume, *George the Drummer Boy* (Harper & Row, 1977).

Berleth, Richard. *Samuel's Choice.* Ill. by James Watling. Albert Whitman, 1990. [40]p. Fic.

Fourteen-year-old Samuel, a slave in New York City, has no great regard for the white men who have enslaved him. In 1776, Samuel does not place much faith in the Declaration of Independence either. During the Battle of Long Island, Samuel must decide whether or not to help the retreating American troops and eventually comes to a realization of what freedom really means. Includes a map.

Brown, Drollene P. *Sybil Rides for Independence.* Ill. by Margot Apple. Albert Whitman, 1985. 48p. Non-fic.

At the age of 16, Sybil Ludington, at the request of her father, a colonel in the Continental Army, rides through the countryside, gathering his men in order to fight the approaching British. Although frightened, Sybil rides all night, successfully carrying out her mission, and also fulfilling her dream to do something important in her country's struggle for independence.

Ferris, Jeri. *What Are You Figuring Now?: A Story of Benjamin Banneker.* Ill. by Amy Johnson. Carolrhoda, 1988. 64p. Biog.

This is a simplified biography of Benjamin Banneker, a free black man who lived in colonial Maryland and who was a farmer and a self-taught mathematician, astronomer, and surveyor. Among his accomplishments were helping to survey the new capital of Washington, D.C., authoring an accurate and popular almanac, and predicting eclipses of the sun and moon. This is a good read-aloud story about a fascinating individual.

Fritz, Jean. *And Then What Happened, Paul Revere?* Coward, McCann, 1973. 48p. Biog.

Fritz, Jean. *Shhh! We're Writing the Constitution.* Ill. by Tomie dePaola. Putnam, 1987. 64p. Non-fic.

Taking the Constitutional Convention from beginning to end, Fritz shows readers that the founding fathers were beset by a myriad of obstacles as they struggled to create a better form of government. The delegates come alive as the reader learns about their heights and weights, gastronomical problems, irritating habits, and the way in which they spent their leisure time. This book, written with considerable humor, is an excellent introduction to the U.S. Constitution.

Fritz, Jean. *What's the Big Idea, Ben Franklin?* Ill. by Margot Tomes. Scholastic, 1976. 48p. (4-6) Biog.

Gauch, Patricia Lee. *This Time, Tempe Wick?* Ill. by Margot Tomes. Coward, McCann, 1974. [47]p. Fic.

In this story, part fact and part legend, a resourceful New Jersey colonial girl named Temperance Wick resorts to desperate measures during the winter of 1781. When two soldiers harass Tempe as she is riding on her horse, Bon, she is forced to hide the horse inside the house for days so that the British will not steal the animal. This story points out the different kinds of battles that take place during wartime, and how factual events sometimes grow into legend.

Giblin, James Cross. *Fireworks, Picnics, and Flags: The Story of the Fourth of July Symbols.* Ill. by Ursula Arndt. Clarion, 1983. 90p. Non-fic.

Giblin, James Cross. *George Washington: A Picture Book Biography.* Ill. by Michael Dooling. Scholastic, 1992. 48p. Biog.

Griffin, Judith Berry. *Phoebe the Spy.* Scholastic, 1977. 48p. Non-fic.

Based on real events, this story tells of a 13-year-old black girl named Phoebe Fraunces whose father sends her to work in General Washington's headquarters while he is quartered in New York City in 1776. Sam Fraunces has heard that someone on the General's staff is going to kill him, and so he sends his daughter undercover to find out what she can. This tale will show readers that even children played an important role in the American Revolution.

Gross, Ruth Belov. *If You Grew Up with George Washington.* Ill. by Jack Kent. Scholastic, 1981. 63p. Non-fic.

Jacobs, William Jay. *Washington.* Scribner's, 1991. 42p. Biog.

Illustrated with many photographs and reproductions of paintings, this book presents Washington as a *real* person—a willful man hungry for power, but one who also treasured his privacy at his beloved Mount Vernon. Washington's childhood years are covered, although the majority of the book focuses on his military and political career. Includes a bibliography and index.

Longfellow, Henry Wadsworth. *Paul Revere's Ride.* Ill. by Ted Rand. Dutton, 1990. [40]p. Poet.

Maestro, Betsy, and Giulio Maestro. *A More Perfect Union: The Story of Our Constitution.* Lothrop, 1987. 48p. Non-fic.

This easy-to-comprehend picture book reveals what happened after the American Revolution—how the new states were not cooperating with each other and how the government had no way to raise funds. The authors portray the Constitutional Convention of 1787 as an occasion of conflicts, personal sacrifices, and great compromises, but the delegates' hard work came to fruition when New Hampshire became the ninth state to ratify the document on June 21, 1788. Includes a simple summary of the Articles of Confederation and the amendments to the Constitution.

McGovern, Ann. *If You Lived in Colonial Times.* Ill. by Brinton Turkle. 79p. Scholastic, 1964. Non-fic.

Phelan, Mary Kay. *The Fourth of July.* Ill. by Symeon Shimin. Crowell, 1966. [40]p. Non-fic.

The historic events behind the birthday of the United States are explained in this simple story. Beginning with the settlement of the new continent, the author relates how the Declaration of Independence came to be written and why its signing is celebrated each year. Although the United States is one of the newest nations, its independence celebration is one of the oldest in the world. The author examines the ways in which this oldest of our national holidays has been celebrated over the years.

Provensen, Alice. *The Buck Stops Here: The Presidents of the United States.* Harper & Row, 1990. 55p. Non-fic.

This interesting account of the lives and accomplishments of the presidents of the United States, from George Washington to George Bush, is written on a primary level. The picture-book format presents each man surrounded by headlines, events, symbols, posters, and other materials highlighting the main occurrences of his presidency. Occasionally, information is given about the First Ladies, if they played a notable role in the administration. The short verses describing each president are sometimes funny, sometimes piercing. For example: "Number Five is James Monroe./ He told the world where not to go." The author includes additional information about the leaders at the end of the book.

Rappaport, Doreen. *The Boston Coffee Party.* Ill. by Emily Arnold McCully. HarperCollins, 1988. 63p. Fic.

In Boston, during the Revolutionary War, a greedy merchant named Mr. Thomas decides to charge much more than the average rate for the precious commodity of sugar. When Boston's matrons discover that Mr. Thomas is hoarding 40 barrels of precious coffee in his warehouse, in order to sell it expensively in case of a shortage, they decide to take action and teach this unpatriotic man a lesson. A large group of angry women and girls kidnap Mr. Thomas until he gives them the key to his warehouse. An author's note tells of the actual event that inspired this "I Can Read" book.

Roop, Connie and Peter. *Buttons for General Washington.* Ill. by Peter E. Hanson. Carolrhoda, 1986. 48p. Fic.

As a Quaker, 14-year-old John Darragh is not permitted to fight in the Revolutionary War. However, John's parents are spying on General Howe in Philadelphia, and John carries the information, sewn into his coat buttons, to Washington's camp. One day, John loses one of the special buttons and is arrested as a spy. An author's note gives a brief history about the Darragh family and the importance of espionage during the struggle.

Spier, Peter. *We the People: The Constitution of the United States of America.* Doubleday, 1987. [48]p. Non-fic.

In the first four pages of this book, Spier succinctly furnishes an historical overview of the writing of the U.S. Constitution. From there he provides illustrations for each phrase of the Constitution. Sixteen pictures depict the phrase "insure domestic tranquility;" 40 illustrate "promote the general welfare;" and 16 show examples of establishing "justice." The details in the pictures will give young readers much to study. Numerous maps are included, along with the full text of the document.

Stevens, Byrna. *Deborah Sampson Goes to War.* Ill. by Florence Hill. Carolrhoda, 1984. 48p. Biog.

A dedicated patriot, Deborah Sampson so longed to fight for the independence of her country that she disguised herself as a man, Robert Shurtleff, at the age of 21 and joined the Continental Army. After three years and several serious wounds, Deborah's identity was discovered. At the end of the story, the author recounts what happened to Deborah after she was honorably discharged in 1783.

Tripp, Valerie. *Meet Felicity: An American Girl.* Ill. by Dan Andreasen. Pleasant Company, 1991. 69p. Fic.

This "American Girl" is an energetic tomboy named Felicity who lives in Williamsburg, Virginia, in 1774. In this opening book, Felicity is angry with the abusive owner of a horse she loves and she makes a courageous decision to try and help save the horse. Felicity's father owns a mercantile and readers will get a flavor for life in colonial Williamsburg, especially after reading the historical notes appended to the story. There are numerous other titles in the "Felicity" series.

Turner, Ann. *Katie's Trunk.* Ill. by Ron Himler. Macmillan, 1992. [32]p. Fic.

In this story, the Revolutionary War is seen from the viewpoint of a young girl named Katie Gray. Although she does not fully understand, Katie hears the word "Tory" hissed whenever she walks by and her friend Celia Warren no longer plays with her. When rebels come to attack their house, the Grays hide in the woods—all except for Katie, who is so angry at the unfairness of having her home mistreated, that she rushes back to the house before the men come. Hiding in her mother's trunk, Katie experiences the hatred of war first-hand. Soft illustrations, full of detail, depict the action in the story, which is based on a true incident.

THE WESTWARD MOVEMENT, SLAVERY, AND CIVIL WAR

❋ ❋ ❋ ❋ ❋ ❋ ❋

INTRODUCTION TO UNITS 7 AND 8

The changes in the United States from the mid-nineteenth century to the present day are many and complex. Two topics are developed in Unit 7, "The Nation Grows: The Westward Movement and Immigration." While many European immigrants joined in the Westward Movement, there were also those who stayed in the cities of the east coast. Asian immigrant workers were brought to the west coast and Africans were brought to the Americas as slaves. The stories of the immigrants and of the Westward Movement are among the most appealing to children because these were the adventures of many of the children's ancestors. Previous activities about family history will be reviewed. The relationships among the various Native American tribes and between Native Americans and the various peoples who settled the western United States are emphasized.

Unit 8, "Slavery and the Civil War," looks at the changes in the United States as regionalism and the differing views of slavery brought about the destruction of war. Through the children's literature about this period, children will see the effects of slavery and warfare. They will begin to comprehend the devastation and sorrow of this tumultuous time through writing from the viewpoint of children during the Civil War era. The African-American folk tales and other literature relate the heroism and bravery of the slaves, the abolitionists, and Abraham Lincoln's leadership in freeing the slaves and preserving the Union.

UNIT
seven

The Nation Grows:
The Westward Movement and
Immigration

OBJECTIVES

1. After reading or listening to several books about pioneer settlers and Native Americans west of the original 13 states, children will record the Westward Movement by marking the settings and the dates of the events in the books on the Outline Map of the United States, and on the time line.

2. In small groups, or as a class, children will list in sequence a family's process of deciding to move, packing for the journey, the journey itself, and establishing a new home.

3. Children will differentiate between wants and needs as they pack the covered wagon for their journey to Ohio, Nebraska, Oregon, or other places west of the original 13 states. In Activity 8, students will pack their trunks for their imaginary immigration to America.

4. While reading a book depicting the journey west, children will draw and date the route taken by the story-book family on the Outline Map of the United States. In Activity 8, students will draw and date the route taken by a story-book immigrant family on the world map.

5. After reading or listening to several books about pioneer settlers and Native Americans, children will identify the home territories of the Native Americans on the Outline Map of the United States.

6. When reading about settlers and others moving into the western part of what is now the United States, children will portray through dramatization the reasons why Native Americans decided to move away from the new settlers, fight them, or learn to live with them.

7. The teacher or librarian will provide information about the way in which the territory in the southwest became part of the United States. On the map, children will locate the southwestern states that were settled by the Spanish and people from Mexico. With help, they will identify Spanish place names in the southwestern United States.

8. Children will identify place names in their home state, and make deductions about origins of the settlers in their state and the influence of the Native Americans in their state and other regions.

9. Through reading, mapping, comparisons, and decision making, children will identify the experiences of immigrants from Europe, Africa, and Asia.

10. Children will locate the continent of Africa on the globe or world map and describe how and why African men, women, and children were brought to the United States and other nations in the Americas.

11. Children will locate the continent of Asia on the globe or world map and describe how and why Asian men came to the west coast of America.

12. After reviewing activities in previous units related to family history, children will seek information about the origin of their home community.

13. Children will summarize the information in this unit by writing about the lives of the people involved in the Westward Movement and immigration to the United States.

LEARNING ACTIVITIES

Before beginning this unit, review the following units and activities: Unit 2, "Comparing Families of the Past and Present"; Unit 4, "Exploring the New World," Activity 3, A Mystery to Solve: How Do We Find Out About the Past? and Activity 4, How Do We Learn About Our Personal History?; and Unit 5, "New Villages in America," Activity 2, Writing Home and Activity 3, National Origins of Today's Americans.

Although the Westward Movement and the large waves of immigration overlap in time, the learning activities explore the Westward Movement first, then immigration.

1. Mapping the Westward Movement

Throughout this unit, children will be recording the books they read on the time line and the Outline Map of the United States. Children will read books set in the early phases of the Westward Movement into the areas west of the Appalachian Mountains, books about Native Americans, living both east and west of the Mississippi River, and books about moving west of the Mississippi River, across the plains and mountains to the Pacific Ocean.

Have the children make a small flag or use a 3" x 5" index card to record the book title, author, time and place of the setting, and the main characters. If possible, name the nationality of the book characters.

2. Planning to Move Westward

Decisions, Decisions! As a class, in groups, or independently, make a list of the decisions a family had to make before, during, and after their westward journey. This list can be based on one story-book family, such as the family in *The Josefina Story Quilt*, the Ingalls family in the *Little House* books, or other families. The first item on the list should identify why the story-book family chose to move. What did they hope to accomplish? The list can become quite detailed as children deduce the story-book family's decisions from their reading. With younger children, develop a story map or list the sequence of decisions the story-book family had to make in order to achieve their goal of moving to the West.

Packing for the Westward Journey. Write several headings on the chalkboard or on chart paper: Father, Mother, teenagers, elementary children, preschoolers, and babies. Mark an area in the classroom or library about the size of the interior of a station wagon or van to illustrate the size of the covered wagon. Ask children to name items that they would pack for their journey. As they name an item, have the children designate which member(s) of the family would most likely pack the item. Accept all suggestions.

When the lists have five to ten items for each family member, go through the lists item by item and discuss whether this item is appropriate for the time and whether it is a want or a need for the pioneer family. Draw a line through the wants, and remove the inappropriate items. Review the remaining list of needs. Have the children planned to meet the family's basic needs of food, clothing, shelter, and love? What should be added to the needs lists? Review the list of wants. Will there be room in the wagon for a few wants? Is the family dog a want or a need? What books will the family pack?

This activity can become a complex decision-making lesson for advanced students, or a simple activity for younger children in which they differentiate between wants and needs.

Conclude this activity by having the children write a paragraph about a "want" appropriate to the period that they would like to take with them on their journey to a new home. How would they convince their parents to make room for this non-essential item, such as Josefina, Faith's pet chicken in *The Josefina Story Quilt*?

3. Mapping a Family's Journey

While reading *The Josefina Story Quilt,* or other books about a family's journey westward, draw the family's route on the Outline Map. If possible, record the dates or number of days necessary for the trip. Compare the Outline Map of the United States with the wall map showing natural features and regions. Display pictures of mountains, plains, rivers, forests, oceans, and deserts to help the children visualize both the hazards and the beauty of the journey.

4. The Homeland of Native Americans

Where did the Native Americans Live? On a map, show the homelands of various groups of Native Americans: the Eastern Woodlands, Southeastern, Plains, Southwestern, California, Northwest Plateau, or Northwest Pacific Coast. *Keepers of the Earth* shows where the Native Americans lived in 1600.[1] Many children will be surprised to see that Native Americans were living throughout the area of North America that we now know as the United States before Europeans arrived.

Help the children identify the local place names with Indian names, and the names of the tribes who used to live in the children's home state and who currently live in the state. Children will find that Native Americans live throughout the United States today.

Land and Lifestyles. As a way to contrast the different lifestyles of various tribes, read several books from the book list for this unit that are set in different regions of the United States. The illustrations and the stories, which contrast homes, climate, environment, clothing, and lifestyles, will help to eliminate the stereotypes that all Indians live in tipis.

5. Decisions to Stay or Move, Fight or Be Peaceful

Role Playing Conflicts. After reading or listening to books about how the settlers and the Native Americans related to one another, help children use role playing of book characters to identify the Native Americans' reasons for moving away from the new settlers, fighting them, or learning to live with them. Books especially well-suited for this activity are *Little Yellow Fur,* *Wagon Wheels,* and *Death of the Iron Horse.*

Understanding Conflicts Through Story Maps. After reading aloud books about families moving west *and* about Native Americans in the West, as a whole class, in small groups, or independently, develop story maps about

---

[1.] Michael J. Caduto and Joseph Bruchac, *Keepers of the Earth: Native American Stories and Environmental Activities for Children* (Golden, Colorado: Fulcrum, Inc., 1988).

the books. See Unit 6 for an example of a story map. Develop the plot/ problem and the resolution carefully so that the problems and changes in the lives of the Indians and the settlers are revealed.

6. The United States Expands to the Southwest

Mapping Settlements of Hispanic Pioneers. Using road maps of the southwestern states, help the children find Spanish place names. Ask the children to hypothesize why many communities have Spanish names. Teachers and librarians should note that the history of Hispanics in the southwestern United States is not well represented in children's literature; however, *The Mission Bell, The Bell Ringer and the Pirates*, and *Spanish Pioneers of the Southwest* will provide limited information about settlers of Hispanic origin.

Refer to the Outline Map and time line for the date and place of the Spanish settlement of Sante Fe. Locate the settings of these books on the outline maps.

Acquiring the Southwest Territories. After establishing the time frame of the Spanish settlements, the teacher or librarian should provide information about the United States' acquisition of the southwestern territories. *Susannah of the Alamo* provides an interesting picture of the white settlements in Texas, the fighting at the Alamo, and the bravery of a young white woman who, along with Mexican women, survived the battle.

7. American, Native American, and Other Place Names

Make a list of the communities children can name in their state. Help the children identify the origins of the names. In Michigan, Holland is a name from the Netherlands; White Pigeon and Kalamazoo are Native American names; Charlevoix is a French name; Yankee Springs is from American sources. Use road maps of the students' home state to add to the list. What deductions can they make about the settlers in their state? What deductions can they make about the influence of Native Americans in their state?

Examine maps of other states and regions for place names that tell who settled there.

8. The Immigrant Experience

Mapping Immigration. As children read books about immigrants from Europe, Asia, and Africa, they will place flags or 3" by 5" cards on the Outline Map, as described in Activity 1.

Planning to Immigrate. As described in Activity 2, discuss and list the decisions the immigrants had to make before they left their homes in Europe,

Asia, or Africa. How were the decisions different for the immigrants from each of these continents?

Packing to Move. Immigrants from Europe might have packed one large trunk or box for the family, plus small bundles for each family member. What wants and needs will they be able to pack? What family pictures will the immigrant family bring with them?

Contrast the experiences of nineteenth-century immigrant families from Europe with the experiences of the early Spanish settlers, the people who can as slaves from Africa, and with the Asian men and boys who immigrated to work on the railroads and in the mines.

Mapping the Family's Journey. By reading *Meet Kirsten: An American Girl, The Long Way to a New Land,* and *Watch the Stars Come Out,* children will learn about some of the experiences of European immigrants. Find Kirsten's European home on the globe or the world map, then find her American home. Show Kirsten's journey on the world map and the Outline Map of the United States.

9. Immigrants from Africa

Help children locate the continent of Africa on the world map, noting with them its many different nations, natural regions, and climates. The teacher or librarian should describe how African men, women, and children were captured by other Africans and by Europeans and sold to slave ship captains who took them across the Atlantic Ocean and sold them to the owners of very large farms called plantations in the islands of the Caribbean, in South America, and in the United States. Draw the journey of the Africans to the Americas on the Outline Map.

10. Immigrants from Asia

Help children locate Asia on the world map, noting with them the many different nations , natural regions, and climates of this huge land mass. *Pie-Biter* by Ruthanne Lum McCunn is one of the few stories for young children about nineteenth-century Asian immigrants who came to the west coast of America for jobs on the railroad and in the mines. Teachers and librarians will need to fill in the history of the Asian immigrants, including the enduring importance of family life for Asian Americans and the Asian Exclusion Acts. Draw the journey of the Asians to North America on the Outline Map.

11. Our Community's History

With the help of the teacher, librarian, or other resource persons, children can list and seek answers to questions about their community's history. The following are examples of questions to be answered:

1. Did Native Americans live in this area of our state/community before other settlers came? If so, which tribe(s) lived here in the past? Do Native Americans live here today?
2. When did non-Native American settlers start a community here? Who were those people and where did they come from?
3. Why did people, Native Americans and others, decide this was a good place to live?
4. How did our community get its name?
5. How did the people who settled this community make a living?
6. Where was the first school? The first store? The first industry?

12. Residents, Immigrants, and Pioneers

Writing Home. Role playing as a European or Asian book character or as an immigrant ancestor, children will write to their grandparents or friends in their nation of origin telling them about their trip, what they are seeing, the hardships, hard work, excitement, happy times, and their hopes for the future.

Telling the Story. As an African book character or an African-American ancestor, children will write the story they would have told about their forced trip to America, the hardships, hard work, the sense of community among the African Americans, and their hopes for the future. The teacher should make clear to the children that a real African-American slave would not have been able or allowed to write home.

Drawing the Story. As a Native American book character or Native American ancestor, children will draw a series of pictures that tells about their lives before and after encounters with European explorers or settlers, as well as their hardships, hard work, and hopes for the future.

Writing a Chapter in the Lives of Residents, Immigrants, and Pioneers. Summarize the differences among immigrants from European nations, Asian nations, and African nations. What choices did the immigrants have who were forced to immigrate? This last question leads into Unit 8, "Slavery and the Civil War."

As a group project or independent creative writing activity, children will write and illustrate an experience of an ancestor's family or extend the experiences of a story-book family as they immigrated or as they were part of the Westward Movement.

BOOK LIST

1. The Nation in the 1790s-1830s

Note: Starred (*) books are reviewed in a previous section or unit of this book.

Anderson, Joan. *The Glorious Fourth of July at Prairietown.* Photos. by George Ancona. Morrow, 1986. [46]p. Fic.

The year is 1836 and the Carpenter family is moving by Conestoga wagon from Pennsylvania to Illinois. Disappointed not to be celebrating the Fourth of July in their hometown, the Carpenter children are delighted when they arrive in Prairietown, Indiana, just in time to participate in the festivities. There is a parade, hoop rolling contests, a shooting match, music, dancing, and special foods. The story is set and photographed at the Conner Prairie Pioneer Settlement near Indianapolis, Indiana. A similar book by Anderson and Ancona, set at Fort New Salem, West Virginia, around 1800, is *Pioneer Children of Appalachia* (Clarion, 1986).

Coerr, Eleanor. *The Bell Ringer and the Pirates.* Ill. by Joan Sandin. Harper & Row, 1983. 64p. Fic.

Set in California's San Juan Capistrano Mission in 1818, this is the story of a young Ahachmai Indian boy. Pio attends school and has daily chores, but he is preoccupied because there have been rumors that pirates are going to attack his mission home. Based on stories from the archives of the San Juan Capistrano Mission, this book instructs young readers in what life on the Pacific coast might have been like in the early nineteenth century.

Costabel, Eva Deutsch. *A New England Village.* Atheneum, 1983. 42p. Non-fic.

de Paola, Tomie. *An Early American Christmas.* Holiday, 1987. Fic. [323] p.

*****Hall, Donald.** *Ox-Cart Man.* Viking, 1979. Fic. (Unit 1)

Jakes, John. *Susannah of the Alamo.* Ill. by Paul Bacon. Harcourt Brace Jovanovich, 1986. [32]p. Non-fic.

Susannah, her daughter, and Mexican women and children have taken refuge in the old mission known as the Alamo while General Santa Anna's troops are gathering to force the Americans out of Texas in 1836. At the close of the struggle, with over 200 Mexicans and 188 Americans dead, Santa Anna charges Susannah with the task of carrying his letter to Sam Houston telling the Texas rebels what has just taken place at the Alamo. Jakes' description of the actual events focuses on Susannah's fears and bravery.

Lydon, Kerry Raines. *A Birthday for Blue.* Ill. by Michael Hays. Albert Whitman, 1989. [32]p. Fic.

A pioneer boy named Blue spends his seventh birthday traveling westward in a covered wagon with his family along the Cumberland Road in the early 1800s. He is given two presents: a song hummed by his mother, and, at the end of the day, his father plants seven saplings around a tree and carves "BLUE 7" into the trunk, leaving a natural legacy in honor of his son. An author's note gives information about the Cumberland Road and its importance in the opening of the West.

McCurdy, Michael. *Hannah's Farm: The Seasons on an Early American Homestead.* Holiday, 1988. [323]p. Fic.

Mitchell, Barbara. *Cornstalks and Cannonballs.* Ill. by Karen Ritz. Carolrhoda, 1980. 46p. Non-fic.

Based on an historical event, this story will show readers how the small town of Lewes, Delaware, was able to dupe the British Navy during the War of 1812. When the British, who had bottled up the harbor, ran out of food and the citizens of Lewes refused to help the enemy, the navy began to shell the city. The author explains how the town of Lewes has been telling this story for nearly 200 years and how it has evolved into legend.

Roop, Peter, and Connie Roop. *Ahyoka and the Talking Leaves.* Ill. by Yoshi Miyake. Lothrop, 1992. 60p. Non-fic.

This beginning reader book, illustrated with black-and-white drawings, tells the story of the efforts of the Cherokee Indian Sequoyah, and his daughter, Ahyoka, to create a written alphabet for the Cherokee language in the early 1800s. After being ostracized by their family, father and daughter devoted many years to the very difficult task of creating a written language for a spoken language. Eventually Sequoyah succeeded, creating a Cherokee alphabet with 86 characters, and children will be amazed at how Sequoyah and Ahyoka accomplished this significant goal. An epilogue explains the factual basis for the story, and a brief bibliography is appended. A simplified biography of Sequoyah is David Peterson's *Sequoyah: Father of the Cherokee Alphabet* (Children's Press, 1991).

*Sanders, Scott Russell. *Aurora Means Dawn.* Bradbury, 1989. Fic. (Unit 2, Sect. 4)

Spier, Peter. *Erie Canal.* Doubleday, 1970. [32]p. Non-fic.

Spier, Peter. *The Star-Spangled Banner.* Doubleday, 1973. [55]p. Non-fic.

Turkle, Brinton. *Obadiah the Bold.* Viking, 1965. [36]p. Fic.

After receiving a spyglass as a gift, a young Quaker boy named Obadiah Starbuck decides he wants to be a pirate. After some rough "pirate" play with his brothers and sisters, Obadiah decides maybe pirating is not such a desirable thing. When Obadiah's father tells him about his sea-faring grandfather, Obadiah decides to save his spy glass for the time when he goes to sea. Other books by Turkle include *Thy Friend, Obadiah* (Viking, 1969), *The Adventures of Obadiah* (Viking, 1972), and *Rachel and Obadiah* (Dutton, 1978).

2. The Nation in the 1840s-1890s

Note: Starred (*) books are reviewed in a previous section or unit of this book.

Ackerman, Karen. *Araminta's Paint Box.* Ill. by Betsy Lewin. Atheneum, 1990. [32]p. Fic.

In 1847, young Araminta Darling is traveling by covered wagon from Boston to California. Along the way she loses her treasured paint box, which is found by a farmer, accidentally put on a Mississippi steamboat, picked up by a bride going west to meet her husband, acquired by a Mormon family, and eventually ends up in the hands of an old gold prospector. Soft watercolor drawings add much to the story and a map on the title page routes the journey of both the Darling family *and* the paint box.

Alter, Judith. *Growing Up in the Old West.* Franklin Watts, 1989. 64p. Nonfic.

Children growing up in the West during the second half of the nineteenth century are the focus of this book. Among the topics discussed are the prairie home, food and clothing, children's and family work, entertainment, recreation and holidays, schooling, and dangers on the frontier. The author uses good comparative descriptions to help young readers understand, for example, likening the size of a covered wagon to an area not much bigger than a double bed. The many illustrations and photographs help set the scene. This volume is shorter and simpler than Russell Freedman's *Children of the Wild West.*

Bedard, Michael. *Emily.* Ill. by Barbara Cooney. Doubleday, 1992. [38]p. Fic.

In the 1800s in a yellow house in Amherst, Massachusetts, lives a lady called the Myth, for she has not left her home in 20 years. The young girl who lives across the street is fascinated with the Myth, who is actually Emily Dickinson, and when the girl has the chance to visit the yellow house, she encounters a lady dressed in white who gives the girl a poem of her own. An afterword tells about Dickinson's life and this beautifully illustrated picture book not only tells about one of the most famous poets of the nineteenth century, but also about small town life in the 1800s.

*Brenner, Barbara. *Wagon Wheels*. Harper & Row, 1978. Fic. (Unit 2, Sect. 4)

Coerr, Eleanor. *The Josefina Story Quilt*. Ill. by Bruce Degan. Harper & Row, 1986. 64p. Fic.

As her family is traveling in 1850 by covered wagon to California, young Faith is piecing together quilt squares that describe the various events of the crossing. Along the way, Faith's pet hen, Josefina, dies, and upon reaching their new home, Faith and her mother piece the quilt together and it becomes her Josefina Story Quilt. The story shows how people often documented family events in their quilts.

DeClements, Barthe. *The Bite of the Gold Rush: A Story of the Alaskan Gold Rush*. Ill. by Dan Andreasen. Viking, 1992. 56p. Fic.

Fradin, Dennis B. *Pioneers*. Childrens Press, 1984. [48]p. Non-fic.

Clear text, accompanied by photographs, illustrations, and maps, discusses who pioneers were, why they left their homes, ancient pioneers traveling by land and by sea, pioneers in America, and a few well-known pioneers, including Eric the Red, Leif Ericsson, Marcus Whitman, and Daniel Boone. The book closes with a discussion of pioneering in space. Includes a glossary and index.

Gunby, Lise. *Early Farm Life*. Crabtree Pub. Co., 1983. 80p. Non-fic.

Harvey, Brett. *Cassie's Journey: Going West in the 1860s*. Ill. by Deborah Kogan Ray. Holiday, 1988. [32]p. Fic.

Based on true accounts, such as those in Lillian Schlissel's *Women's Diaries of the Westward Journey*, the story of Cassie's family moving from Illinois to California is told in journal format. Cassie describes the children's jobs, the boredom, and the hazards of the trip, but the feelings of shared accomplishments and mutual support among the travelers also shine through.

Harvey, Brett. *My Prairie Year: Based on the Diary of Elenore Plaisted*. Ill. by Deborah Kogan Ray. Holiday, 1986. [32]p. Biog.

Based on the reminiscences of Elenore Plaisted, this picture book vividly depicts the everyday life of Dakota homesteaders in the 1880s. As the oldest child, Elenore had many responsibilities, and the author includes descriptions of how pioneer children contributed to the family's subsistence. The seasons of the year include both hard labor and recreation, surviving a tornado and a prairie fire, and bring the realization that home is now on the plains. Follow this story with Harvey's *My Prairie Christmas* (Holiday, 1990) which portrays the family's first Christmas celebration in their new home.

Hayes, Wilma Pitchford. *Little Yellow Fur.* Ill. by Richard Currari. Coward, McCann, 1973. 48p. Fic.

This book contains five short stories based on the author's recollections of her girlhood spent homesteading in South Dakota in the early years of the twentieth century. The homestead was close to the Rosebud Indian Reservation where Susannah befriends some of the Sioux Indians. Red Cloud explains how drastically the Indian way of life changed when Indians were put on reservations, and eventually Susannah's family gains a greater understanding of their Native American neighbors. A companion volume is *Yellow Fur and Little Hawk* (Coward, McCann, 1980).

Kalman, Bobbie. *Early Pleasures and Pastimes.* Crabtree Pub. Co., 1983. 95p. Non-fic.

Using archival photographs and illustrations from the late nineteenth and early twentieth centuries, the pleasures and pastimes of America are described. There is good humor in the text, which is addressed to children, and which aids in directing attention to the amusing details of the illustrations. Most examples are from the Victorian era, appropriate to rural or town settings, and some illustrations are specific to frontier times.

Kudlinski, Kathleen. *Night Bird: A Story of the Seminole Indians.* Ill. by James Watling. Viking, 1993. 54p. Fic.

Night Bird is an 11-year-old Seminole Indian girl living with her family in the Florida Everglades around 1840. Her tribe is preparing for its annual Green Corn Ceremony when her cousin, Little Mouse, and her family arrive in the village after having escaped a slave plantation. When white men come and tell the Indians that they must move to the Oklahoma Territory, Night Bird faces a very difficult decision about the future course of her life. The bond of family is very strong, especially between Grandmother and Night Bird, and this simple story tells about the plight of Native Americans as white settlers encroached upon their lands. An author's note explains the fate of the Seminoles.

Levine, Ellen. *If You Traveled West in a Covered Wagon.* Ill. by Charles Shaw. Scholastic, 1986. 80p. Non-fic.

Levinson, Nancy Smiler. *Snowshoe Thompson.* Ill. by Joan Sandin. HarperCollins, 1992. 64p. Fic.

This "I Can Read Book" is based on fact and tells the story of John Thompson, a Norwegian immigrant who went to California in the 1850s in search of gold. Thompson was among the first Scandinavian immigrants to introduce skis to the American people, and he volunteered to ski across the perilous Sierra Nevada Mountains in winter, carrying mail packs on his back that sometimes weighed 100 pounds. Young Danny O'Reily is glad when Snowshoe Thompson is able to deliver a letter to his father in time for Christmas, helping to make Thompson's feats of endurance a legend in the Gold Rush days.

*MacLachlan, Patricia.** *Three Names.* HarperCollins, 1991. Fic. (Unit 2, Sect. 2)

Martini, Terri. *Indians.* Ed. by Margaret Friskey. Childrens Press, 1982. 48p. Non-fic.

This brief introduction to the Native American tribes of the United States discusses Indians of the Northwest Coast, Plains, Southwest, and the Northeast Woodlands. The author does a good job of distinguishing between the different tribes and explaining how the environment influenced the ways in which Indians obtained their food, what they used for clothing, and what materials they used for their homes. The book is illustrated with drawings, photographs of Indian artifacts and art objects, and reproductions of historical photographs and paintings.

*Ortiz, Simon.** *The People Shall Continue.* Children's Book Press, 1988. Non-fic. (Unit 4)

Patterson, Lillie. *Booker T. Washington: Leader of His People.* Ill. by Anthony D'Adamo. Chelsea House, 1991. 80p. Biog.

This easy-to-read biography begins with Washington's childhood as the son of a slave. As he grew, he worked at many different jobs and attended school part-time. He worked as a janitor at the Hampton Institute for three years, before leaving to teach black children. After he returned to the Hampton Institute, where he taught Native Americans, he was chosen to organize a school at Tuskegee, Alabama, where African Americans could learn to become teachers or study industrial arts. Tuskegee, which stressed self-respect and economic independence, became one of the leading institutions for blacks in America. Washington's role as a teacher and leader is well served in this interesting biography.

Stein, R. Conrad. *The Story of the Golden Spike.* Ill. by Tom Dunnington. Childrens Press, 1978. 31p. Non-fic.

The joining of the Union Pacific and Central Pacific Railroads is presented in detail in this book. The author discusses how railroad fever swept the nation and the importance of the railroad for both the transportation of people and goods. With the Union Pacific centered in the Great Plains and the Central Pacific in California, the stage was set for a great rivalry that kept the country enthralled for over three years. This well-written, informative nonfiction book touches on the competition between the Chinese and Irish railroad workers.

Stein, R. Conrad. *The Story of the Homestead Act.* Ill. by Cathy Koenig. Childrens Press, 1978. 31p. Non-fic.

*Turner, Ann. *Dakota Dugout.* Macmillan, 1985. Fic. (Unit 2, Sect. 4)

Van Leeuwen, Jean. *Going West.* Ill. by Thomas B. Allen. Dial, 1992. [48]p. Fic.

Seven-year-old Hannah narrates the journey her family made by covered wagon west to the prairie. She recounts the crowding in the wagon, crossing rivers, terrible storms, and getting stuck in the mud. Mama finds the prairie lonesome, but the family works together to build a cabin, plant a garden, and prepare the fields. In winter, the snowbound children work on their lessons while Mama sews her quilt. By summer, the homestead is a farm and Hannah delights in the green cornfields. Muted illustrations depict this pioneer family during the first year in their new home.

Whelan, Gloria. *Hannah.* Ill. by Leslie Bowman. Knopf, 1991. 63p. Fic.

A farming community in northern Michigan in the late 1880s is the setting for this story about nine-year-old Hannah, who is encouraged by the new teacher to attend school despite her visual handicap. "Poor" Hannah, as she is called, longs to attend school, although her mother is fearful. Whelan sensitively portrays the adjustments both at school and at home, including Hannah's determination to overcome her disability. Illustrated with black-and-white drawings.

Whitman, Walt. *I Hear America Singing.* Ill. by Robert Sabuda. Philomel, 1991. [32]p. Poet.

Although not a children's poet, Walt Whitman's poem from the *Leaves of Grass* is presented in this picture book as a celebration of the working people of mid-nineteenth-century America. Sabuda's double-page spreads dynamically portray mechanics, stonemasons, housewives, washgirls, carpenters, rivermen, hatters, and shoemakers hard at work in the forests, valleys, towns, rivers, and prairies of the United States.

3. Immigrants Arrive on America's Shores in the 1800s

Note: Starred (*) books are reviewed in a previous section or unit of this book.

Coerr, Eleanor. *Chang's Paper Pony.* Ill. by Deborah Kogan Ray. Harper & Row, 1988. 64p. Fic.

Chang, a young Chinese immigrant living during California's Gold Rush days, longs for a pony more than anything. Working hard with his grandfather in a gold-mining camp kitchen, and with some help from his miner friend, Big Pete, Chang is able to realize his dream. The author includes a brief note at the end of this "I Can Read Book" about the historical setting of the story.

Cohen, Barbara. *Molly's Pilgrim.* Ill. by Michael J. Deraney. Lothrop, 1983. [32]p. Fic.

The daughter of Russian immigrants, Molly finds it difficult to adjust to life in the United States at the turn of the century. The children in Molly's third-grade classroom make fun of her and she is afraid that she will never feel at ease. In the end, Molly's little Pilgrim doll, dressed like a European immigrant, helps her classmates understand that all kinds of pilgrims, at different times in American history, settled the United States and helped to make it a good country.

*Harvey, Brett. *Immigrant Girl, Becky of Eldridge Street.* Holiday, 1987. Fic. (Unit 2, Sect. 4)

Jacobs, William Jay. *Ellis Island: New Hope in a New Land.* Scribner's, 1990. 34p. Non-fic.

The use of captivating period photographs, along with a simply written but well-researched text, recreate the arrival and processing of immigrants at Ellis Island in the early 1900s. The history of Ellis Island is related, from its opening in 1892 to its closure in 1954, a time that saw 17 million new Americans come through its portals. The closing chapters discuss present-day immigrants and the current restoration of Ellis Island as a national museum. Includes an index.

Kroll, Steven. *Mary McLean and the St. Patrick's Day Parade.* Ill. by Michael Dooling. Scholastic, 1991. [32]p. Fic.

New Irish immigrant, Mary McLean, wants nothing more in life than to ride beside Mr. Finnegan in New York's big St. Patrick's Day parade in 1850. Mr. Finnegan tells Mary she must find the perfect shamrock in order to do so, but where in snowy New York will she find one? This story tells of Irish immigrants in the mid-nineteenth century, including an import from the old country—the leprechaun. An author's note tells about Irish Americans, St. Patrick, and the tradition of St. Patrick's Day parades in America.

Leighton, Maxinne Rhea. *An Ellis Island Christmas.* Ill. by Dennis Nolan. Viking, 1992. 31p. Fic.

When she is six years old, Kyrsia Petrowski leaves Poland with her mother and two brothers to join their father in America. After a difficult crossing, filled with sea-sickness and bad food, the Petrowski family arrives at Ellis Island on Christmas Eve. The size of the Great Hall and the number of people overwhelm Krysia, but she is delighted to see the large decorated Christmas tree and visit by Saint Mikolaj, Santa Claus. The impressionistic illustrations help convey the fears, wonder, hardships, and joys of the trip and the eventual reunion with Papa. An author's note at the end of the book tells more about the immigrant experience in America.

Levine, Ellen. *...If Your Name Was Changed at Ellis Island.* Ill. by Wayne Parmenter. Scholastic, 1993. 80p. Non-fic.

In the familiar question-and-answer format, Levine answers many questions about the immigrants who came to the United States, especially in the late nineteenth and early twentieth centuries. Beginning with a description of Ellis Island, children will learn the reasons why people left their homelands, modes of travel, what people brought with them, what people did all day on the voyages, what happened when people arrived at Ellis Island, what kinds of tests people were subjected to, what happened if people were detained or rejected, and how long the immigrants stayed on Ellis Island. Illustrations accompany the simple text. This book would make a good introduction to a unit on immigration.

Levinson, Riki. *Watch the Stars Come Out.* Ill. by Diane Goode. Dutton, 1985. [32]p. Fic.

Brother and Sister depart for the New World alone since their parents and older sister have already traveled to America. The ship's conditions are poor, many people get sick, and after 23 days the children are delighted to spy the Statue of Liberty. After a joyous family reunion, Younger Sister is happy in their top-story townhouse apartment since she can look out the window and see the stars come out. Suitable for reading aloud, this picture book is an excellent introduction to the immigrant phenomenon in the United States.

Maestro, Betsy, and Giulio Maestro. *The Story of the Statue of Liberty.* Lothrop, 1986. 46p. Non-fic.

McCunn, Ruthanne Lum. *Pie-Biter.* Ill. by You-shan Tang. Design Enterprises of San Francisco, 1983. [34]p. Fic.

This is the story of a young man named Hoi who comes to America from China in the 1860s to work on the transcontinental railroad. Hoi loves to eat pies and as he gets older, he becomes very strong. Upon completion of the railroad, Hoi remains in the United States for 15 years, but at the close of the story he returns to China to get married. This humorous story depicts the role of the Chinese in railroad construction and the illustrations are a skillful blend of Asian and western art forms.

*Polacco, Patricia. *The Keeping Quilt.* Simon & Schuster, 1988. Fic. (Unit 2, Sect. 3)

Sandin, Joan. *The Long Way to a New Land.* Harper & Row, 1981. 63p. Fic.

Following the "hunger years" of 1868 and 1869 in Sweden, Carl Erik's parents make the difficult decision to leave their home and join Uncle Axel in America. Selling their belongings and saying good-bye to family and friends is extremely difficult. Upon their arrival in New York City, the family is happy to receive word from Uncle Axel welcoming them to their new home. This is a good choice for discussing the topic of immigration to this country. Continue the discussion with Sandin's sequel to Carl Erik's story, *The Long Way Westward* (Harper & Row, 1989).

Shefelman, Janice. *A Peddler's Dream.* Ill. by Tom Shefelman. Houghton Mifflin, 1992. [32]p. Fic.

At the turn of the century, Solomon Joseph Azar comes to America from Lebanon, hoping to own his own store. He starts out as a peddler, carrying a pack of household items. After he is robbed by thugs, a farm family takes him in as a hired hand. He then gets a job at the store in town where he eventually becomes a partner, then the owner. Solomon's story is that of the American dream. The illustrations provide details about life in an urban community.

Shaw, Janet Beeler. *Meet Kirsten: An American Girl.* Ill. by Renée Graef. Pleasant Co., 1986. 59p. Fic.

In 1854, Kirsten Larson's family is traveling from their home in Sweden to start a new life in Minnesota. During their long and arduous journey, the immigrants suffer many hardships and Kirsten's young friend dies. There is great joy, however, when the Larsons are reunited with Uncle Olav and his family, and when the Larson's build their own log cabin and clear the land. There are numerous other books in the "Kirsten" series.

Winter, Jeanette. *Klara's New World.* Knopf, 1992. [32]p. Fic.

In the mid-1800s, Klara's family makes the difficult decision to emigrate from Sweden to the United States in order to make a better life for themselves. Throughout the winter the family prepares and in the spring they say good-bye to relatives and friends and journey for many weeks across the Atlantic. The simple text and vibrant illustrations combine to give young readers a clear sense of the stresses and joys of the move to America. In the end, Klara's family joins friends in Minnesota who help them start their new life. An author's note at the end of the book provides additional information about immigration in the late 1800s.

UNIT
eight

Slavery and the Civil War

OBJECTIVES

1. Based on information from various story-books, reference sources, and text-books, children will compare life in the northern states and the southern states in the middle 1800s.
2. Children will identify reasons why slavery violated human rights and could not be allowed to continue in the United States.
3. Children will trace the routes of the Underground Railroad and identify the bravery and heroism of slaves and the abolitionists.
4. After reading American folk tales and singing songs stemming from the days of slavery and reviewing the activities in Unit 3, "Folktales and Songs of America," children will identify how the slaves and other people used stories and music to help them cope with their condition.
5. Through a variety of activities based on the books read, children will identify the causes and effects of the Civil War.
6. Children will record on the time line events in the life of Abraham Lincoln that show his leadership in keeping the nation intact.

LEARNING ACTIVITIES

1. Making a Living in the North or the South

If possible, locate a map showing the United States in the 1850s and 1860s. Note how many cities were located in the northeastern states, and how few cities were in other states. Help children determine how people living in cities in the 1850s and 1860s made their living providing goods and services, sometimes to people of other regions. *Mary McClean and the St. Patrick's Day Parade* and *Watch the Stars Come Out* tell about immigrants living in cities. How did people make a living if they did not live in a city? Did all the white people in the South own plantations and slaves? How did people in the South who did not own plantations make a living?

2. Contrasting Working for Pay and Working as a Slave

Read *Nettie's Trip South* to the class. Discuss with the children the difference between hired helpers, such as cooks, house cleaners, farm workers, or child caretakers who work for the person(s) who *pay* them, and slaves who also did all these jobs for the person(s) who *owned* them. What decisions can hired helpers make about the money they earn? They can decide to move, to change jobs, to spend the money for food, clothing, shelter, and other things. What decisions can slaves make? They get food, shelter, and clothing, but have few if any choices about these things. They do not get any money for their work. They cannot change jobs or move to another place unless they and members of their families are sold to someone else. The events in *Nettie's Trip South* may disturb young children, but will help them understand why slavery was cruel and inhumane and could not be allowed to continue.

3. The Underground Railroad

Many people believed that slavery was wrong and they worked to help slaves run away to freedom in states were slavery was illegal. The hidden routes and secret stopping places were called the Underground Railroad.

Sojourner Truth. Read aloud *Walking the Road to Freedom: A Story About Sojourner Truth*. Record Sojourner Truth's life on the time line along with information about her bravery in helping slaves escape to freedom. Make a story map based on this book. Emphasize the problems for slaves and the ways that Sojourner Truth tried to resolve those problems.

Mapping the Underground Railroad. Using *If You Traveled on the Underground Railroad* as a reference, help children estimate how far slaves had to walk to freedom. Mark important rivers and boundaries on the Outline Map. How did they know where to go and when they had reached a free state? Why were these routes called the "Underground Railroad?"

The Drinking Gourd. Show the children a picture of the constellation, the Big Dipper, and point out its relationship to the North Star. If possible bring a large gourd to class and show how it could be hollowed out to be a dipper for water or a "drinking gourd." Read *Follow the Drinking Gourd* and teach children the song. The words and music are included in this book. Have small groups of children pantomime the story as the class sings the song. After the pantomime, have the children tell about their trip to other characters they meet in the North. Remind children that many slaves were forbidden to learn to read and write, so story telling and singing were important and intelligent ways to secretly share information and feelings.

4. Folk Tales and Songs of the Civil War

Review Unit 3, "Folk Tales and Songs of America," Activities 1-5. Apply these activities to stories and songs of the Civil War. Be sure to include the Brer Rabbit stories; sing the Union song, "When Johnny Comes Marching Home"; the song of the Confederates, "Dixie"; and songs of the slaves, such as "Swing Low, Sweet Chariot" and "The Drinking Gourd."

5. Learning About the War Years

The following books will help children learn about the events and impact of the Civil War on both the North and the South, but will not convey the specific campaigns and battles. Other sources will provide that information.

The Tin Heart. In this story, two girls who are good friends, live on opposite banks of the Ohio River, which became the boundary between the Union and the Confederacy. When the war erupts, each girl keeps half of a tin heart necklace to remind them of their friendship. The conflict between the two families may be highlighted through developing a story map of the events.

Writing as one of the girls or their brothers, have children write to their friend on the opposite bank of the Ohio telling about their family's experiences and about their hopes for the future. Divide the class so that half will write from the South and half from the North. Children can then exchange and answer letters. With younger children, this may be done as a whole class activity with children dictating the content of the letters from the North and the South.

Thunder at Gettysburg. The battle, as seen by a 14-year-old girl, was a Union victory and a turning point of the war, but had heavy losses on both sides. Find Gettysburg, Pennsylvania, on the map. Note how close this battle was to Washington, D.C., the capital of the Union. If Confederate General Robert E. Lee had won this battle, the Confederacy might have won the Civil War and changed the history of America. Record Gettysburg and Robert E. Lee on the time line.

The Gettysburg Address. Read or restate portions of Lincoln's Gettysburg Address, especially the beginning and the ending where Lincoln emphasizes that this nation stands for liberty for all because our government is "of the people, by the people, and for the people." Help children identify present-day examples of government of, by, and for the people by reviewing Unit 6, "The New Nation," Activity 4, Laws for the New Nation.

Cecil's Story. Read aloud the simple but moving text. Sharing the illustrations of Cecil's Story will bring home to children that the soldiers on both sides were members of families: fathers, brothers, uncles, and husbands.

Reading the story and sharing the pictures may unwittingly stimulate discus-sion among children about their fears of loss of a family member and how they would learn to cope.

Memorial Day. Record the beginning and the end of the Civil War on the time line. After the Civil War, which left 600,000 people dead, Decoration Day originated as a day to honor those who had lost their lives. The book, *Memorial Day*, describes how Decoration Day became Memorial Day in the twentieth century as a national holiday in honor of everyone who has died at any time for our country.

Help children research their school and community for memorials in the form of statues, monuments, names of schools and other buildings, street names, and special events. Perhaps there is a plaque in your school telling about the person for whom it is named. Is there a memorial monument or sign in your community that lists the names of people who have died for our country? Did they die in the Civil War or at some other time?

Ask children to speculate about what kind of memorial they would design in honor of people who have died to help our country. What are the ways in which a monument built of stone honors people? How would a park honor people?

Wagon Wheels. One aftermath of the Civil War was the exodus of freed slaves from the South. Some of these African Americans became "Exodusters," those freed slaves who traveled west of the Mississippi to homestead land and become independent farmers. *Wagon Wheels* is based on the true story of exodusters who emigrated to Kansas. Locate Kansas on the map. How far did this family have to travel before they homesteaded their new home? How far did the boys walk by themselves when they followed their father's map?

6. Abraham Lincoln

There are many biographies of Abraham Lincoln. Two books that are especially interesting are *If You Grew Up With Abraham Lincoln* and *Abraham Lincoln and the End of Slavery*. After reading aloud all or portions of these or other biographies of Lincoln, record Lincoln's life and accomplishments on the time line. Also have each child write a sentence or paragraph about Abraham Lincoln's great contributions to America. Some children may wish to illustrate their writing. Post all the writings and pictures on a bulletin board. Relate this bulletin board to Activity 5, *Memorial Day*, described above. In what ways are the children remembering and honoring Lincoln?

BOOK LIST

Note: Starred (*) books are reviewed in a previous section or unit of this book.

Ackerman, Karen. *The Tin Heart.* Ill. by Michael Hays. Atheneum, 1990. [32]p. Fic.

Flora and Mahaley live on opposite sides of the Ohio River, but they visit nearly every day since Mahaley's father operates a river ferry. The girls each wear one half of a tin heart around their necks—a gift to each other symbolizing their eternal friendship. When the Civil War comes, open river crossings come to an end, but their true friendship remains intact despite the dissension going on around them.

Adler, David A. *A Picture Book of Harriet Tubman.*Ill. by Samuel Byrd. Holiday, 1992. [32]p. Biog.

*Brenner, Barbara. *Wagon Wheels.* Harper & Row, 1978. Fic. (Unit 2, Sect. 4)

Ferris, Jeri. *Go Free Or Die: A Story About Harriet Tubman.* Ill. by Karen Ritz. Carolrhoda, 1988. 63p. Biog.

In this short book, Ferris tells the story of Harriet Tubman—how she was born in 1820 to a slaveholder in Maryland, how she was mistreated in her early life, and how at the age of 24 she ran away in search of her freedom. With the help of Quakers and other people on the Underground Railroad, Tubman traveled alone until she reached freedom in Philadelphia. Readers will get a clear idea of the injustices and sorrows of slavery and will admire this strong woman, nicknamed "Moses," who dedicated the rest of her life to helping black people escape slavery. Includes black-and-white drawings and a map.

Ferris, Jeri. *Walking the Road to Freedom: A Story About Sojourner Truth.* Ill. by Peter E. Hanson. Carolrhoda, 1988. 64p. Biog.

An author's note gives the historical context for the life of the woman named Isabelle Hardenberg, who became Sojourner Truth. Born into slavery in the late 1790s, she won her freedom in 1827 when all New York slaves were freed. Truth then began working with the Quakers and other abolitionists on behalf of her people, traveling over much of the United States and making speeches. This is a moving biography with stirring depictions of slavery and the anti-slavery movement that will touch all who read it. Black-and-white drawings enhance the text and a map is included.

Gauch, Patricia Lee. *Thunder at Gettysburg.* Ill. by Stephen Gammell. Putnam, 1990. (Reprint of 1975 ed. pub. by Coward, McCann) 46p. Fic.

Excited about having the war come so close to her Gettysburg home, 14-year-old Tillie Pierce discovers the dark side of war when she inadvertently becomes caught in the thick of this momentous campaign. After risking her life by helping wounded soldiers, Tillie experiences first-hand the horror and confusion of battle. Black-and-white drawings accompany the poignant text, which is based on Tillie Pierce Alleman's account of the Battle of Gettysburg published in 1889.

Hopkinson, Deborah. *Sweet Clara and the Freedom Quilt.* Ill. by James Ransome. Knopf, 1993. [32]p. Fic.

Eleven-year-old Clara is sent away from her mother to another plantation to be a field slave. Aunt Rachel, a house slave, teaches Clara to sew and become a seamstress. Saving bits of cloth, Clara slowly makes a quilt that is a map to freedom beyond the Ohio River. When she and her friend, Young Jack, run away, she leaves the quilt behind for others to use as a map north. The well-told story is richly enhanced by Ransome's full-page illustrations. This is an excellent choice for reading aloud.

Kunhardt, Edith. *Honest Abe.* Ill. by Malcah Zeldis. Greenwillow, 1993. [32]p. Biog.

This simply written biography of Abraham Lincoln will appeal to young children as will the brightly colored, folkstyle illustrations by Zeldis. The major events in Lincoln's life are described in an easy-to-understand manner. The text for the Gettysburg Address and a chronology of Lincoln's life are included.

*Lester, Julius. *The Tales of Uncle Remus: The Adventures of Brer Rabbit.* Dial, 1987. Folk.(Unit 3, Sect. 2)

Levine, Ellen. *If You Traveled on the Underground Railroad.* Ill. by Richard Williams. Scholastic, 1988. 63p. Non-fic.

Lyon, George Ella. *Cecil's Story.* Ill. by Peter Catalanotto. Orchard, 1991. [32]p. Fic.

Set in the 1860s, this timeless story is told from the viewpoint of a young boy whose father has gone to fight in the Civil War. He expresses his fears, such as Papa might get hurt, or worse, that he might not come home at all, and then who would take care of his mother, do the chores, and plow? The book could easily be used with children dealing with a separation caused by service in wartime, although the pictures are of the Civil War era.

McGovern, Ann. *If You Grew Up With Abraham Lincoln.* Ill. by Brinton Turkle. Scholastic, 1966. 72p. Non-fic.

Porter, Connie. *Meet Addy: An American Girl.* Ill. by Melodye Rosales. Pleasant Co., 1993. 63p. Fic.

Set in North Carolina in 1864, where the Emancipation Proclamation could not be enforced during the war, this is the beautifully written story of nine-year-old Addy Walker and her family, African-American slaves hoping and planning for freedom. The ordeal of slavery is seen when Poppa and Addy's 15-year-old brother are sold, and Addy and her mother run for Philadelphia, leaving one-year-old Esther behind. This outstanding and poignant story illustrates the devastation of bondage, the ties among African Americans, and the endurance of the human spirit. The illustrations show not only the characters, but also the details of the setting. A historical essay at the end of the book presents an excellent, concise description of the lives of slaves and their survival strategies. Other books in the "Addy" series follow this one.

Ringgold, Faith. *Aunt Harriet's Underground Railroad in the Sky.* Crown, 1992. [32]p. Fic.

A young African-American girl named Cassie Louise Lightfoot and her brother, Be Be, are flying among the stars when they discover a railroad train in the sky. The conductor is a little woman named Harriet Tubman, and when Cassie and Be Be, are separated, Cassie has to make the journey from slavery to freedom that some of her ancestors made. Running away from a plantation, Cassie visits some of the numerous stops on the Underground Railroad until she reaches Canada and is reunited with Be Be. The brilliant, stylistic illustrations reveal Cassie's fears as she undertakes this difficult trip. An author's note provides additional information about Harriet Tubman and the Underground Railroad. The book also includes a bibliography.

Scott, Geoffrey. *Memorial Day.* Ill. by Peter E. Hanson. Carolrhoda, 1983. 48p. Non-fic.

Scott's simple yet thoughtful nonfiction book tells of the Memorial Day holiday that began after the Civil War and describes the ways in which "Decoration Day" was celebrated in a small town in 1878. The book explains how Memorial Day evolved into a national holiday in 1971—a day to commemorate those who have died in the wars of our nation.

Shorto, Russell. *Abraham Lincoln and the End of Slavery.* Millbrook Press, 1991. [32]p. Biog.

Turner, Ann. *Nettie's Trip South.* Ill. by Ronald Himler. Macmillan, 1987. [32]p. Fic.

This moving story is told in letter format by 10-year-old Nettie to her friend Addie. In the late 1850s, Nettie accompanies her brother and sister on a trip down South where Nettie witnesses slaves working in the fields, their poor living conditions, and a slave auction. The author deals sensitively with the topic of slavery on a level that will be understood by young children.

Whittier, John Greenleaf. *Barbara Frietchie.* Ill. by Nancy Winslow Parker. Greenwillow, 1992. 32p. Poet.

John Greenleaf Whittier's famous poem is presented for children in this illustrated picture book. Barbara Fritchie, a 95-year-old resident of Frederick, Maryland, proudly flew the Union flag in September 1862, when Generals Lee and Jackson marched through her hometown on their way to meet McClellan's troops at Sharpsburg. Moved by her loyalty, Stonewall Jackson vowed that she was not to be harmed for her actions. The illustrator gives background information on the poem, Stonewall Jackson, and John Greenleaf Whittier.

Winter, Jeanette. *Follow the Drinking Gourd.* Knopf, 1988. [48]p. Fic.

In this brilliantly illustrated picture book, children will learn about the Underground Railroad and how it enabled runaway slaves to reach freedom. An abolitionist named Peg Leg John would travel throughout the South, teaching a song to slaves called "Follow the Drinking Gourd." Hidden in the lyrics were directions for following the Underground Railroad, and in this story, five runaways manage to find their way to safety in the North.

THE TWENTIETH CENTURY: THE NATION CHANGES

❀ ❀ ❀ ❀ ❀ ❀ ❀ ❀

INTRODUCTION TO UNITS 9, 10, 11, AND 12

The twentieth century is divided into four units: Unit 9, "Inventions and Technology"; Unit 10, "Conflicts and Cooperation Among Nations"; Unit 11, "Human Rights"; and Unit 12, "Everyday Life in the United States." Throughout these units, the themes of the twentieth century provide a link to the past, present, and future. In Units 10 through 12, the quest for human rights is a prominent theme that relates the Bill of Rights, the Constitution, and the United Nations Declaration of the Rights of the Child to the present day. The units end by reiterating the concepts from Units 1 and 2, with another look at the ways in which human rights and responsibilities are part of the everyday life of Americans, past, present, and future.

In Unit 9, "Inventions and Technology," the role of technology and invention in our lives links the nineteenth and the twentieth centuries and extends into the future. The changes in everyday life brought about by various inventions will be examined through the time line, Then and Now Charts, dramatizations, and the creation of new inventions to fulfill a want or need.

In Unit 10, "Conflicts and Cooperation Among Nations", the conflicts and cooperation among nations accentuate the role of the United States as a significant leader in our world. America's connections, conflicts, and cooperation with other nations highlight the universal concerns for human rights, for solving environmental problems, and for maintaining peace. Children will read about and survey the wars of the twentieth century through mapping, interviewing people who recall first-hand experiences, reviewing the purpose of Memorial Day, identifying and illustrating an understanding of their own rights based on the Bill of Rights and the United Nations Declaration of the Rights of the Child, and identifying ways in which people can cooperate with one another.

Children will read about the problems, the leaders, and the changes brought about through the Civil Rights Movement in Unit 11, "Human Rights." They will dramatize examples of their rights and responsibilities and write letters of appreciation to the leaders.

Unit 12, "Everyday Life in the United States," reviews concepts from earlier units about ancestors, families, land use, immigration, the Constitution and the Bill of Rights, and how these concepts apply to the present day. Through several culminating activities, children will review their understanding of their rights, their responsibilities, and their own place in American history.

UNIT
nine

Inventions and Technology

OBJECTIVES

1. Children will record inventions, inventors, and the changing technologies of the nineteenth and twentieth centuries on the time line.
2. In order to identify the impact of technology on our lives, children will develop Then and Now Charts and dramatizations comparing everyday life before and after an invention or a technological change.
3. Children will record inventions and technological changes on a mural that includes a section on the future for their predictions.
4. Children will invent machines that can help fulfill a want or a need in their lives.
5. Children will distinguish between the functions of machines and the importance of human relationships.
6. Children will select an invention or technological change and write about how this invention makes their life happier, safer, healthier, or more interesting.

LEARNING ACTIVITIES

1. Connections

Throughout this unit, children will place inventors' lives and inventions on the time line as they read about them. Note what other events were occurring at the same time. For example, what was happening in the United States when the railroads were built across the nation? How did the railroads help the Westward Movement? Help children make the connections among events at a given time.

2. How Did People Live without Electricity, Telephones, and Other Technology?

Comparisons. After reading *Tin Lizzie* and *Flight: The Journey of Charles Lindbergh*, make Then and Now Charts illustrated with the children's drawings and pictures from magazines comparing the automobile of 1909 with automobiles of today in looks, performance, and usage, and comparing Lindbergh's airplane with airplanes of today in looks, performance, and purpose. *Sally Ride, Astronaut: An American First* could be included in order to contrast flight and space travel. Record Henry Ford, the Wright Brothers, Charles Lindbergh, Sally Ride, and other significant Americans connected with changes in transportation on the time line.

The Good Old Days? Have children select several inventions that are commonplace in their lives, such as electricity, automobiles, and telephones. Pantomime situations in which the technology is essential, then replay the situation without the technology. For example, pantomime making breakfast consisting of scrambled eggs, toast, and orange juice using electricity, then without electricity. Call Grandmother who lives in another city on the telephone to tell her about something important. How will she know the news without using the telephone? What will children do after school without television?

The progress in medical technology has in many ways improved life for everyone. Consider a child's life before and after there were antibiotics to treat infections and vaccinations against measles, mumps, whooping cough, tetanus, and polio; before and after the invention of attractive eyeglasses and the development of hearing aids; before and after the development of ways to protect and preserve teeth; before and after the invention of protective clothing for various sports; and before and after the invention of child car seats and seat belts.

3. Changes Over Time

As a research project, have children record on pictorial, time-line murals the changes in transportation and communication within American history beginning with Native Americans before the arrival of European colonists. Cooperative groups may select land, water, or air transportation to research and depict on their murals. Be sure to include horses and horse-drawn vehicles *after* the Spanish explored and settled in North America.

Other groups may research and illustrate various forms of communication, including mail delivery, newspapers, telegraph, telephone, television, and computers. The murals could include a section for predictions of future changes in transportation and communication.

4. Be an Inventor

Review wants and needs with children. As children think about food, shelter, and clothing, ask them to list all the machines they know that help to provide each need. These lists may take the form of concept webs or flow charts. For example, farm machinery, cereal processing factories, and George Washington Carver's experiments with plants help provide food; a saw mill, a cement mixer, and hammers help to build a house; looms that make cloth, sewing machines, and needles help to make clothing.

After reviewing the lists, brainstorm with the students about what new inventions would help to provide our needs or wants. Have children draw a new invention and write a description of how this invention would help provide a need or a want.

5. Machines or People?

Challenge the children to create an invention that will fulfill an identified want. Perhaps children want to have more fun on the playground. They might invent new games and playground equipment. Challenge the children to create an invention that will help everyone play the games by the rules. Children may want to be able to do their school work more easily, or play a new computer game. They can easily determine that a new computer program can help provide those wants, but challenge the children to determine whether people or machines developed the programs. Help children distinguish between the functions of machines and the importance of human innovations and relationships.

6. My Favorite Invention

Children will select one real invention or technological change and write about how this invention makes their lives happy, safe, healthy, or interesting. They may wish to draw a picture of themselves using this invention. Display the stories and pictures, or make a large illustrated book of the stories and pictures, titled "Our Favorite Inventions."

BOOK LIST

Behrens, June. *Sally Ride, Astronaut: An American First.* Childrens Press, 1984. 30p. Biog.

Burleigh, Robert. *Flight: The Journey of Charles Lindbergh.* Ill. by Mike Wimmer. Philomel, 1991. [32]p. Non-fic.

The brilliant illustrations and simple text in this picture book tell the story of Charles Lindbergh, the 25-year-old aviator who dared to fly alone across the Atlantic Ocean in May 1927. Young readers will get a real sense of the stress, excitement, fright, loneliness, and physical adversities experienced by this pioneer pilot who became a world hero following the landing of his plane, the *Spirit of St. Louis*, in Paris after nearly 34 hours in the air.

Epstein, Sam, and Epstein, Beryl. *George Washington Carver: Agricultural Scientist.* Dell Yearling, 1991. 80p. Biog.

This is a simply written biography of the man who made 300 products out of the peanut. The Epsteins depict Carver's youth and recount his many intriguing experiments with plants that led to the beginning of scientific farming in the American South.

Gibbons, Gail. *Deadline: From News to Newspaper.* Crowell, 1987. [32]p. Non-fic.

Lewis, Cynthia Copeland. *Hello, Alexander Graham Bell Speaking: A Biography.* Dillon Press, 1991. 64p. Biog.

Spier, Peter. *Tin Lizzie.* Doubleday, 1975. [32]p. Fic.

The "Tin Lizzie," produced in 1909, was the first of Henry Ford's assembly-line automobiles; it revolutionized transportation in America. Purchased by a merchant in 1909, this Tin Lizzie goes through several owners before falling into disrepair; it is eventually restored as an historic car in the present day. Spier's illustrations are full of details about life at the turn of the century.

Towle, Wendy. *The Real McCoy: The Life of an African-American Inventor.* Ill. by Wil Clay. Scholastic, 1992. [32]p. Biog.

This is a brief biography of Elijah McCoy, the black engineer who overcame numerous obstacles to become a famous inventor in the late 1800s and early 1900s. Born of fugitive slaves in Canada in 1844, McCoy went to Scotland at the age of 16 to study engineering. Settling in Michigan, McCoy worked for the Michigan Central Railroad and in 1872 he patented a lubricating device that would automatically drip oil. When others tried to imitate his invention, people began asking for the "real McCoy." McCoy was a prolific inventor and in 1916 he patented the graphite lubricator, his proudest achievement. This is an excellent picture-book biography of a persistent black man who was able to succeed in the white man's world.

Van Rynbach, Iris. *Everything from a Nail to a Coffin.* Orchard, 1991. [48]p. Fic.

A commercial establishment in Glastonbury, Connecticut, called the Goodrich General Store is the focus of this picture book. Built in 1874, this building over the years served as a general store, pharmacy and soda fountain, hardware store, grocery, gas station, and garden center. The author discusses events, such as World War I, the Great Depression, the local flood of 1936, and the advent of suburbia and how these occurrences affected the town's development. The full-page illustrations are overflowing with details about American life. This fascinating piece of local history should motivate children to research some of the buildings in their own communities.

U N I T
ten

Conflicts and Cooperation Among Nations

OBJECTIVES

1. After reading about World War I, children will locate the major nations involved on the Outline Map and record World War I on the time line.
2. After a presentation of information about the Second World War, and reading about World War II, students will locate on the world map Germany, Italy, Great Britain, France, Hawaii, Japan, and Russia and other nations formerly part of the USSR, and note the relationship of the United States to these areas.
3. Children will read about everyday life in the United States during the Second World War and will interview a resource speaker about the Second World War.
4. Children will review the book *Memorial Day*, and Activity 5, from Unit 8. Students will apply this information as they read about the Vietnam Veterans Memorial and identify local memorials for Americans who have died in wars in the twentieth century.
5. The children will review Activity 4, Laws for the New Nation, from Unit 6. The Bill of Rights and the United Nations Declaration of the Rights of the Child will then be discussed and illustrated by the children.

6. After illustrating their understanding of their rights in Activity 5, children will identify ways in which people, including children, cooperate with one another.

LEARNING ACTIVITIES

1. Where and When Was the First World War?

The books for young children to read about conflicts among nations are few in number and mainly portray the homefront. Nationalism and other causes of the First World War may be difficult for young children to understand; however, some of the books cited in the book lists for grades four through eight, Part 2, Unit 9, will be of value as references and read-aloud books. Use reference books and textbooks as sources of information so that children can locate the continent of Europe and the major nations involved in World War I on the Outline Map. When children see that many nations on several continents were involved in the war, they will understand why this conflict was call a world war. Record World War I on the time line.

Many children will have found these nations earlier as they traced their ancestors. Help children understand that while their ancestors may have immigrated from a nation that was an enemy of the United States at some point in our history, they and their family are now Americans.

Hero Over Here, set during World War I, tells how a child became a homefront hero during the influenza epidemic of 1918. Relate this book to the changes in medical technology since 1918 found in Unit 9. People still get flu, but compared to 1918, few die because of antibiotics and other medical improvements.

2. The Second World War

The Scope of World War II. Record the Second World War on the time line from the late 1930s to the middle 1940s. As children read about World War II in reference books, textbooks, and fiction, including books from Part 2, Unit 12, they will locate Germany, Italy, Great Britain, France, Russia and other nations formerly part of the USSR, Hawaii, and Japan on the world map. List the nations according to the Allied and the Axis Powers. They will see that the Second World War was even more widespread than the First World War. Children will see how far away Europe, Japan, and the islands of the Pacific are from mainland United States.

The War in Europe. With the help of the teacher or librarian, children can understand Nazi Germany's role in causing the Second World War— Nazi aggression against other countries and Adolf Hitler's evil plan to exterminate millions of innocent people. *Rose Blanche* is the moving story of a German child who discovers a concentration camp near her home and secretly takes food to the starving Jews held prisoner there. This book reveals only one aspect of the war and is best understood within the context of the war in Europe. This somber book is an important one because it shows the compassion and human decency afforded to the oppressed by a child. It also depicts the results of fanatical intolerance.

The War in the Pacific. Children will have determined from the previous activities that Japan was an ally of Nazi Germany when Japanese aircraft attacked the United States' naval base at Pearl Harbor. For vivid descriptions of the attack on Pearl Harbor, read aloud portions of Kathleen V. Kudlinski's book, *Pearl Harbor Is Burning: A Story of World War II*, (see Part 2, Unit 12). Hawaii was annexed by the United States in 1898 and became the fiftieth state in 1959.

The war in the Pacific does not excuse the United States government for punishing loyal Japanese Americans for having Japanese ancestors. As a read-aloud, *The Journey* (see Part 2, Unit 12), tells the story of Japanese Americans who were held in relocation camps during the Second World War.

3. What Did You Do During the Second World War? Homefront and Eyewitness Accounts

My Daddy Was a Soldier: A World War II Story, *When Mama Retires*, and *All Those Secrets of the World* portray family life in the United States when fathers became soldiers. These books, plus *Cecil's Story*, set in the Civil War, view warfare from the American children's perspective, as children worry about parents and deal with shortages and extra work for all members of the family on the homefront. These books will help children understand that while the Second World War did not destroy cities (other than Pearl Harbor) and homes within the United States, there were some changes and hardships for American families.

These books set the stage for interviewing a resource person to speak about the Second World War. With the children, make a list of questions to be asked of the resource person when he/she comes to the classroom. Questions to be asked may include some of the following:

1. How old were you during the war?
2. What did you do during the war?
3. In what ways was your job important?
4. How was your life changed by the war?
5. Were you afraid? If so, of what or of whom?
6. Did anyone you know die in the war? Where and how?
7. What things about everyday life were different during the war? After the war?
8. Did the war help anyone? If so, in what ways?

4. Remembering Vietnam

While the Vietnam War remains vivid in the memories of many adults, the conflict is past history for elementary children. Three books will aid children in understanding this difficult chapter in our history. *A Wall of Names: The Story of the Vietnam Veterans Memorial* presents a concise history of the war and the construction of the Vietnam Veterans Memorial. *Everett Alvarez, Jr.: A Hero for Our Times* is the biography of a Mexican American pilot who was shot down and became a prisoner of war. After nine years, Alvarez and other prisoners were released, and Alvarez continued to serve his country. *The Wall* is a moving story of a child and his father who visit the Memorial to find the grandfather's name among those who died in the war.

Review the purpose of Memorial Day, then note how each book in its own way pays tribute to those who were involved in the Vietnam War and how the Vietnam Veterans Memorial honors those who died in that conflict.

5. Cooperation Among Nations

The United Nations. The teacher or librarian will tell the children about the organization of the United Nations following the Second World War for the purpose of encouraging cooperation among nations. Read aloud and discuss the illustrations of the United Nations' Declaration of the Rights of the Child as depicted in *Children's Chorus: Celebrating the 30th Anniversary of the Declaration of the Rights of the Child* (see Unit 11, "Human Rights"). Post the list of rights.

United Nations Declaration of the Rights of the Child[1]

The right to affection, love and understanding.

The right to adequate nutrition and medical care.

The right to free education.

The right to full opportunity for play and recreation.

The right to a name and a nationality.

The right to special care, if handicapped.

The right to be among the first to receive relief in times of disaster.

The right to be a useful member of society and to develop individual abilities.

The right to be brought up in a spirit of peace and universal brotherhood.

The right to enjoy these rights, regardless of race, color, sex, religion, national or social origin.

[1.] "The International Year of the Child and You," *Childhood Education* (January 1979), 130-131.

Use Activity 4, Laws for the New Nation, from Unit 6 to review the Bill of Rights. Discuss each right from the United Nations Declaration of the Rights of the Child. Help children find the similarities between these two important documents. Ask each child to select a right from the Bill of Rights or from the Declaration of the Rights of the Child, and then draw a picture to illustrate that right, or write a poem or story about the right. Make classroom books of the illustrations, poems, and stories about the Bill of Rights and the Declaration of the Rights of the Child.

Examples of Cooperation Among People. From the anthology, *The Big Book for Peace*, read aloud and discuss several selections. Ask the children to be looking for examples of cooperation among people throughout the day. At the end of the school day, ask for specific examples of cooperation that the children have implemented or observed. Post a list of these experiences. The teacher or librarian can also cite examples. Keep adding to the list. Some of the following experiences may be observed:

• Greg, the crossing guard, helped Christianna, Frank, and Hannah cross the street.

• Sara Ellyn and Diego passed out books and picked up papers.

• The ladies in the cafeteria—Gail, Marta, Ann, and Debbie—worked together to make our lunch.

• The playground supervisors helped the class have fun at recess.

• Everyone listened as Sarah explained the directions for the math assignment.

• Matthew helped Rachael learn her spelling words.

• At home, Jim set the table for supper while his sister, Susan, folded laundry, Dad cooked supper, and Mom fed the baby, Nora.

BOOK LIST

Ackerman, Karen. *When Mama Retires.* Ill. by Alexa Grace. Knopf, 1992. [38]p. Fic.

The home front during World War II is the setting for this simple picture book. When Mama talks about retiring from housework in order to work at the local war plant, she decides to teach her three boys about taking care of the house. With Dad away fighting overseas, Charley, Henry, and Will remember their promise to pitch in and they learn about doing laundry, sweeping the carpet, cleaning their rooms, using the ration books, and dusting the furniture. Softly colored illustrations show an American family at home during the war in this timeless story.

The Big Book for Peace. Ed. by Ann Durrell and Marilyn Sachs. Dutton, 1990. 120p. Non-fic. Fic. Poet.

This valuable collection of 17 stories and poems, which highlights the good sense of peace and the waste of war, is written by such noted children's authors as Milton Meltzer, Jean Fritz, Myra Cohn Livingston, Katherine Paterson, and Steven Kellogg. Some of the illustrators include Maurice Sendak, Paul Zelinsky, and Leo and Diane Dillon.

Bunting, Eve. *The Wall.* Ill. by Ronald Himler. Clarion, 1990. [32]p. Fic.

A young boy and his father visit the Vietnam War Memorial in Washington, D.C., to find the name of the boy's grandfather, George Muñoz, who died in the war. Written in simple words and illustrated with soft, watercolor drawings, this book will help even young readers understand the sadness and waste, but also the honor, of war. Use in conjunction with Judy Donnelly's *A Wall of Names.*

Clinton, Susan Maloney. *Everett Alvarez, Jr.: A Hero for Our Times.* Children's Press, 1990. 30p. Biog.

Everett Alvarez, a Navy pilot in the Vietnam War, was shot down in 1963 and became the first American prisoner of war in North Vietnam. Thoughts about his home, family, and his religious beliefs helped him survive nine years of harsh treatment as a POW. The focus is on Alvarez as a real person who supports his country, and the photographs emphasize his family and the strength he gained from them.

Donnelly, Judy. *A Wall of Names: The Story of the Vietnam Veterans Memorial.* Random, 1991. 48p. Non-fic.

Houston, Gloria. *But No Candy.* Ill. by Lloyd Bloom. Philomel, 1992. [32]p. Fic.

During World War II, seven-year-old Lee knows there is a war going on because there is no candy at her father's store. The men listen to the news on the radio, and mother is eager to hear from Uncle Ted who is in the army. This simply told story describes the home front by measuring the days without candy at the store for Lee and her brother, Tommy. When Uncle Ted eventually comes home, he brings Hershey chocolate bars and Lee knows the war is really over.

Innocenti, Roberto, and Christophe Gallaz. *Rose Blanche.* Creative Education, 1985. [32]p. Fic.

Rose Blanche lives in a small German town during the Second World War. She and the other children enjoy watching the soldiers' activities, and one day, when she sees a young boy being taken away, she follows the truck.

Rose Blanche discovers a Jewish concentration camp, and for months she brings food to the starving people. One day, in a dense fog, Rose Blanche is mistaken for the enemy and shot dead. The somber-colored, almost full-page illustrations are graphically real and full of detail.

Kudlinski, Kathleen V. *Hero Over Here.* Ill. by Bert Dodson. Viking, 1990. 54p. Fic.

The American home front during World War I is the focal point of this story. While his father and brother fight "over there," 10-year-old Theodore becomes a different kind of hero when the influenza epidemic of 1918 strikes Teddy's mother and sister. With his father away, Teddy must shoulder the heavy responsibility of caring for his patients, which he manages to do for several weeks before Mama and Irene get better.

Morimoto, Junko. *My Hiroshima.* Viking, 1987. [32]p. Non-fic.

In this simply told story, the author recalls growing up in her hometown of Hiroshima, Japan, during World War II. She relates, in moving words and graphic drawings, the "Flash" and how the inhabitants of Hiroshima suffered death, pain, and devastation following the dropping of the atomic bomb on August 6, 1945. This powerful book is a testament to peace and the occasional use of archival photographs strengthens the message.

Ray, Deborah Kogan. *My Daddy Was a Soldier: A World War II Story.* Holiday, 1990. [32]p. Fic.

The United States is at war with Germany and Japan, but the war does not significantly touch Jeannie's life until her father is drafted in 1943. Mama takes a day job to support the family and Jeannie is lonely and worried. Jeannie's third-grade class sponsors a scrap drive, and Jeannie feels she is helping Daddy in the war effort. Ration books and Victory gardens are discussed as are other hardships that families endured during the conflict.

Say, Allen. *The Bicycle Man.* Houghton Mifflin, 1982. [32]p. Fic.

A small rural school in Japan is the setting for this story out of the author's Japanese childhood. It is Sportsday and the children are competing in athletic games, enjoying picnics with their parents, and laughing at the adult competitions. When two tall American soldiers, one black and one with carrot-red hair, arrive on the playground, the children are astounded. World War II has not been over for long and most of them have never seen an American. The black man asks permission to ride the principal's bicycle and delights the crowd with amazing riding feats. The black soldier is awarded the biggest prize and good will abounds.

Scholes, Katherine. *Peace Begins with You.* Ill. by Robert Ingpen. Sierra Club Books, 1990. [40]p. Non-fic.

Children reading this book will learn what peace is, and how it means different things to different people. The author celebrates the diversity in the world, but also teaches that we are all dependent on each other, regardless of where we live. Alternate ways of handling conflict are discussed and the illustrations make this a truly universal book. Although well written, the teacher will probably need to lead the discussion after reading this story to the class.

Stevenson, James. *Don't You Know There's a War On?* Greenwillow, 1992. [32]p. Non-fic.

In this picture book, the narrator, 10-year-old James Stevenson, recalls the home front during World War II. He recalls his brother entering the Navy, no candy bars, gas and food rationing, Victory gardens, collecting scrap tin, and blackouts so the enemy would not see their house at night. The boy remembers eating lots of Spam and kale, trying to learn enemy planes, dreaming of fighting in the army, and the desolation and worry he felt when his father went off to war. Many of the reminiscences are quite humorous and young readers will get a vivid sense of what life was like for children during this conflict.

Yolen, Jane. *All Those Secrets of the World.* Ill. by Leslie Baker. Little, Brown, 1991. [32]p. Fic.

The narrator recounts an episode from her childhood when her father left home to fight in World War II. Four-year-old Janie's life changed dramatically after her father's departure as she and her young cousin, Michael, now living near Chesapeake Bay, attempt to understand the "secrets of the world" as they watch the warships sailing for Europe. Soft, delicate watercolor illustrations recreate a stressful time in our nation's history and a family drama that continues to be played out.

* * * * * * * * *
UNIT
eleven
* * * * * * * * *

Human Rights

OBJECTIVES

1. After reviewing the rights of children from Unit 10, "Conflicts and Cooperation Among Nations," children will identify and list the violations of these
   rights after reading and discussing several books from this unit, and will list the
   actions taken to guarantee the rights for all.
2. After reading about prominent leaders in the Civil Rights Movement, the
   children will record these leaders and their accomplishments on the time line.
3. Children will write a letter of appreciation to one leader in the Civil Rights
   Movement, and then, assuming the identity of one of the leaders, will write a
   letter about their work and accomplishments.
4. Children will interview a resource person about how the rights of people have
   been improved in the past 30 years in the United States.
5. Children will list and role play their rights and responsibilities.

LEARNING ACTIVITIES
1. The Bad Old Days

Read aloud from *Three Cheers for Mother Jones!*, *Rosa Parks and the Montgomery Bus Boycott*, *Teammates*, *A Long Way to Go*, *César Chávez and La
Causa*, or one of the many books about Martin Luther King, Jr. In these books,
children will learn about the "bad old days" when children worked in factories
and mines, when athletic teams were either black or white, when women had
few rights and could not vote, and when some immigrants, Mexican Americans, and African Americans had few rights and were not treated as citizens.
As children discover these violations of the rights of people, list these events
and the actions people took to guarantee human rights for all.

VIOLATIONS OF RIGHTS	ACTIONS FOR HUMAN RIGHTS
children worked in factories	Child Labor Laws forbid children to work in factories
black children attended poorer schools than white children did	court decisions state that children of all races will attend school together
women could not vote	19th Amendment of Constitution

CHART 7   Actions for Human Rights

2. Our Heroes!

Children will read about the real people who worked to achieve rights for all people. *If You Lived at the Time of Martin Luther King* is especially well-suited to help children understand the ways in which King and others worked for civil rights. The other books listed in Activity 1 and in the book list cite people who worked for the rights of all. Record these leaders and their accomplishments on the time line.

3. Writing to Our Heroes!

After completing Activities 1 and 2, the teacher or librarian will write the names of the human rights leaders on small slips of papers, duplicating the names so that several children can randomly draw the same leader's name. The list of leaders should be based on the books read and other information known by the children. Leaders included in the book list for this unit are Martin Luther King, Jr., Mary Harris Jones (Mother Jones), Rosa Parks, Jackie Robinson, PeeWee Reese, César Chávez, and Susan B. Anthony. Books about additional leaders will be found in the library. Have each child write a letter to the person whose name they have drawn and express appreciation for that person's work for human rights.

When children finish their letters, group the children according to the leader they have addressed. Each group will list on a chart their reasons for appreciation of that leader.

Collect all the letters, then redistribute them so that every child gets a letter of appreciation addressed to a leader other than the one she or he wrote to. Each child will, as that leader, answer the letter telling about their work, their motivations, and their accomplishments. A child may have written a letter to Jackie Robinson, then answer a letter in the role of Susan B. Anthony telling about her work. Regroup the children according to their second letter. The children who wrote a letter as Susan B. Anthony will make a chart, this time listing what Anthony wrote about her work. The letters and charts will serve to identify many leaders in human rights, their work, and why they are appreciated today.

This activity can be pursued as a whole class experience by having the class contribute to the letters of appreciation, the letters from the leaders, and the summarizing charts.

4. What Was It Like Then?

With the help of the teacher or librarian, children will prepare questions for a resource speaker about working for social change through nonviolent actions. Ask the speaker to talk about the rights that were denied, the ways in which the speaker and others worked, and how rights were gained. Children need to know that schools and other public places were segregated in the past, and that they cannot be segregated today; that positive changes have taken place; and that ordinary people, like members of their own families, have worked to guarantee rights for all.

5. What Can Kids Do?

The class, with the help of the teacher or librarian, can list and role play the rights and responsibilities of children. Be very specific with young children by citing the rights and responsibilities that they have in the classroom and the school, then go to the bigger picture. Have children role play such rights and responsibilities as the following:

- All children have a *right* to use the drinking fountains and bathrooms.
- All children have the *responsibility* to follow the classroom rules about when and how to use the drinking fountain and bathroom.

- All children have the *right* to use the same doors to the school.
- All children have the *responsibility* to follow the procedures for lining up at the doors.

- All children have the *right* to use of the same textbooks.
- All children are *responsible* for taking care of the textbooks, and following assignments to use the textbooks.

- All children have the *right* to be called by their real names.
- All children are *responsible* for avoiding use of insulting names for others.

- In the United States all children have the *right* and the *responsibility* to attend schools so that they can learn.

BOOK LIST

Note: Starred (*) books are reviewed in a previous section or unit of this book.

Adler, David A. *A Picture Book of Martin Luther King, Jr.* Ill. by Robert Casilla. Holiday, 1989. [32]p. Biog.

Bethell, Jean. *Three Cheers for Mother Jones!* Ill. by Kathleen Garry-McCord. Holt, 1980. 47p. Fic.

The focus of this book is Mary Harris Jones's famous "March of the Mill Children" from Philadelphia to Oyster Bay, New York, in the summer of 1903. The march dramatized the plight of child laborers in the United States. The story is told from the viewpoint of a 10-year-old boy named James, and is a good introduction for young children to the American labor movement. An author's note gives some background information on Mother Jones and her efforts on behalf of working people.

Celsi, Teresa. *Rosa Parks and the Montgomery Bus Boycott.* Millbrook Press, 1991. [32]p. Non-fic.

This is a first-rate depiction of both Rosa Parks and the civil rights movement of which she was a part. The courageous refusal of this rather ordinary woman to vacate her seat on the bus inaugurated a year-long boycott of the Montgomery, Alabama, bus system by blacks. Page-long inserts explain related issues, such as the Ku Klux Klan, boycotts, and segregated schools. After reading this story, children will understand the relationships between people and events. Includes many period photographs and an index.

Children's Chorus: Celebrating the 30th Anniversary of the Declaration of the Rights of the Child. Dutton, 1989. [26]p. Non-fic.

In this 30th anniversary tribute, 11 of the world's most noted children's book illustrators bring to life the 10 principles of the United Nations' Declaration of the Rights of the Child. A text of the Declaration is appended and the book includes double-page illustrations by such artists as Helme Heine, Paul O. Zelinsky, Satoshi Kitamura, Anastasia Arkhipova, and Stepan Zavrel.

Codye, Corinn. *Vilma Martinez.* Ill. by Susi Kilgore. Raintree Publishers, 1990. 32p. Biog.

Born into a poor Mexican-American family in San Antonio, Texas, in 1943, Vilma Martinez overcame enormous obstacles to earn her law degree from Columbia Law School in 1967. This brief biography highlights Martinez' career as an attorney and civil servant, working for the rights of Mexican Americans and other minorities. She was instrumental in helping to pass the Voting Rights Act in 1975 and in securing the right for bilingual education for non-English-speaking children. The text, presented in English and Spanish, is well-written and Martinez will serve as an inspiring role model for all children.

Golenbock, Peter. *Teammates.* Ill. by Paul Bacon. Harcourt Brace Jovanovich, 1990. [32]p. Non-fic.

This book centers on the racial prejudice experienced by Jackie Robinson in the late 1940s when he joined the Brooklyn Dodgers—the first black man to play in the Major Leagues. For daring to cross into the white arena, Robinson was ostracized, scorned, taunted, and threatened by fans, other ball players, and even by his own teammates. Early in the season, when the Dodgers were in Cincinnati playing the Reds, the jeering of the crowd was so horrendous that Pee Wee Reese, the Dodgers shortstop, boldly decided to take a stand and support his teammate before the whole world. Photographs and other illustrations help depict this breakthrough in baseball history.

Levine, Ellen. *If You Lived at the Time of Martin Luther King.* Ill. by Beth Peck. Scholastic, 1990. 72p. Non-fic.

McKissack, Patricia, and Fredrick McKissack. *Ida B. Wells-Barnett: A Voice Against Violence.* Ill. by Ned O. Enslow Pubs., 1991. 32p. Biog.

This is a concise biography of Ida B. Wells-Barnett, the journalist and reformer who advocated civil rights for African Americans and condemned violence and lynchings. In the 1890s, when she was in her 30s, she left the South and went to New York City where she wrote for the *New York Age*, taking her case to the public and even the president. Photographs and drawings accompany the simple text, and the book includes a glossary and index.

McKissack, Patricia, and Fredrick McKissack. *Marian Anderson: A Great Singer.* Ill. by Ned O. Enslow Pubs., 1991. 32p. Biog.

Oneal, Zibby. *A Long Way to Go.* Ill. by Michael Dooling. Viking, 1990. 54p. Fic.

Eight-year-old Lila's grandmother is a suffragette in New York City in 1917. Lila believes in and is proud of her grandmother, and is very happy when she convinces her father to allow her to march in the suffragist parade. This book presents the women's suffrage movement in the United States and the feelings and events are taken from actual fact. The author includes a two-page synopsis of the suffrage movement at the end of the book.

Patrick, Diane. *Martin Luther King, Jr.* Franklin Watts, 1990. 64p. Biog.

Patterson, Lillie. Booker T. Washington: Leader of His People. Chelsea House, 1991. Biog. (Unit 7)

Roberts, Naurice. César Chávez and La Causa. Childrens Press, 1986. 32p. Biog.

César Chávez's childhood and family life are portrayed through photographs, including the story of how the family lost their store and became migrant workers. After serving in World War II, Chávez became an advocate for migrants and in 1962, he founded the National Farm Workers Association. The union is now called United Farm Workers and continues to work today for social change through nonviolent methods. The simple but effective writing style, along with many photographs, make this a high-interest story.

UNIT
twelve

Everyday Life in the United States

OBJECTIVES

1. Individually or as a whole class activity, children will read books about everyday life in the United States, past, present, or future, and make story maps about the books.

2. After reviewing Activity 4 in Unit 2, "Comparing Families of the Past and Present," children will identify in the books they read in Activity 1, above, examples of environmentally sound land and resource use.

3. Children will identify books about twentieth-century immigrants.

4. After reviewing Unit 6, Activity 4, and Unit 11, children will identify the ways in which the Bill of Rights and the United Nations Declaration of the Rights of the Child are implemented in the lives of the book characters.
5. Each child will draw a self-portrait that shows the child pursuing a favorite activity or responsibility.

LEARNING ACTIVITIES

1. Reading About Americans

These culminating activities will integrate reading and American history while reviewing the themes of the various units. Independently or as a whole class activity, children will read about the everyday life of Americans. The teacher and librarian can guide children in their selection of books that are realistic in content. Include books about recent immigrants, environmental concerns, and ones that demonstrate the application of human rights in everyday life. Individually or as a whole class activity, the students can make story maps for each book on large sheets of paper, using about half of the page. The other half of the chart will be used in Activities 3-5.

TITLE:

STORY MAP:
Setting
Who
When
Plot/Problem
Main Events
Resolution
  of Problem

Use of Land
and Resources:

Rights and
Responsibilities:

Twentieth-Century
Immigrants:

CHART 8   Books about Americans

2. "This Land Is Your Land, This Land Is My Land:" A Picture Quilt of Our Nation

Sing Woody Guthrie's song "This Land Is Your Land," found in many collections of American songs. Make a collage of pictures from magazines or of the children's own drawings to illustrate the words to this song. The pictures or drawings may be arranged on the bulletin board to form paper quilt blocks set together with a lattice of cookie cutter shapes of boys and girls, implying all the people of the United States. The children will color the individual shapes to look like themselves, including their own sex and race.

3. Use of the Land and the Resources

For the books read for Activity 1, have each child include on their story maps how the book characters made use of the land and the resources. Some children will have to speculate about this concern as not all the books read will include this content.

4. Twentieth-Century Immigrants

Identify the books read in Activity 1 about recent immigrants and make story maps of the books. Use the story maps to review how the recent immigrants resolved their problems of living in a new country.

5. The Rights and Responsibilities of Americans

Review Unit 6, Activity 4, and Unit 11, "Human Rights." Independently or as a whole class activity, children will list on their story maps from Activity 1 the ways in which the Bill of Rights and the United Nations Declaration of the Rights of the Child are implemented in the lives of the book characters. For example, the loving family in *The Year of the Perfect Christmas Tree* celebrates Christmas, thus illustrating freedom of religion and rights to affection, love, and understanding. *Lee Ann: The Story of a Vietnamese-American Girl* illustrates the first five rights in the Declaration of the Rights of the Child. *Hattie and the Wild Waves: A Story from Brooklyn* especially illustrates the right to be a useful member of society and to develop individual abilities. *Hannah* illustrates the right to develop individual abilities, the right of special care if handicapped, freedom of religion, and the right to affection, love, and understanding.

6. "We Are Americans . . ."

Each child will draw a portrait that shows him or her doing a favorite activity or pursuing a responsibility. Post the portraits under the title, "We are

Americans in _____Grade, Room _____, [name of school], [community], [state]. We have the right to enjoy these rights and responsibilities, regardless of race, color, sex, religion, national or social origin."

If there are immigrant children or children from another nation in the class, they can be included by changing the beginning of the title of their portraits to " We are Children in _____Grade, ..."

If the pictures drawn for Activity 4 of Unit 6 have been preserved, compare the content and the understanding of rights and responsibilities portrayed by the children. In this culminating activity, the children are identifying them-selves in their pictures as citizens with rights and responsibilities.

BOOK LIST

Note: **Starred (*) books are reviewed in a previous section or unit of this book.**

Allen, Thomas B. *On Granddaddy's Farm.* Knopf, 1989. [40]p. Fic.

The Tennessee hills during the Depression are the setting for the author's reminiscences of childhood summers spent with his cousins at their grand-parents' farm. Grandpa was a brakeman for the L & N Railroad and was gone for days at a time. Before leaving, he assigned chores to the children, including weeding the garden, watering the animals, and fetching for Granny. The cousins also found time to jump in haystacks, play basketball, swim in the pond, and go to church. Softly colored illustrations help evoke the feeling of love, unity, and contentment in this farm family.

Anzaldúa, Gloria. *Friends From the Other Side: Amigos del Otro Lado.* Ill. by Consuelo Mendéz. Children's Book Press, 1993. [32]p. Fic.

Prietita, a young Mexican-American girl living in South Texas, befriends a boy named Joaquín, an illegal immigrant who has crossed the border from Mexico. When Prietita's friends taunt and scare Joaquín, she steps in on his behalf, and the two become friends. When *La Migra* (immigration border patrol) appears one day, Prietita and the herb woman hide Joaquín and his mother. Written in both English and Spanish, this simply told story tells of the dilemmas facing immigrants who enter the United States without papers and of the goodness and friendship of people.

Baylor, Byrd. *The Best Town in the World.* Ill. by Ronald Himler. Scribner's, 1983. [32]p. Fic.

A father reminiscences in this book about life in the small Texas town where he grew up—the *best* town in the world. The town had the best cooks, craftsmen, blackberries, melons, builders, swimming creeks, and neighbors, as well as the smartest dogs. Papa's thoughts transport readers to life in a small town around the turn of the century—a quiet life where people knew each others' names and created their own homemade toys. Nostalgic drawings accompany the text.

Brown, Tricia. *Lee Ann: The Story of a Vietnamese-American Girl.* Photos. by Ted Thai. Putnam, 1991. 48p. Non-fic.

Third-grader Lee Ann, born shortly after her parents were forced to flee Vietnam, is the focus of this photographic essay. Lee Ann loves America— eating hot dogs and popcorn, learning English at school, video games, and jumping rope—but she also values her Vietnamese heritage, including the foods, music, and festivals of her other country. The photographer, himself a Vietnamese refugee, captures the spirit of a young girl who celebrates being a part of two cultures. This is a commendable introduction to one of America's more recent immigrant groups. A similar story about a boy named Hoanh Anh is Diane Hoyt-Goldsmith's *Hoang Anh: A Vietnamese-American Boy* (Holiday, 1992).

Bunting, Eve. *How Many Days to America?: A Thanksgiving Story.* Ill. by Beth Peck. Clarion, 1988. [32]p. Fic.

Fleeing harsh military rule in their Caribbean country, a mother and father decide they and their two children must find a new home. Leaving all their possessions behind, they leave their island home on a small boat that only holds 16 people. They run out of food and water, people are sick, and then the small boat is attacked by thieves. Despite the adversities, the small family never loses the hope of reaching America. They arrive on American shores to find it is the Thanksgiving holiday, which the Americans are happy to share with the refugees. Soft illustrations help depict the refugee experience.

Cooney, Barbara. *Hattie and the Wild Waves: A Story from Brooklyn.* Viking, 1990. [38]p. Fic.

Life for young Hattie of Brooklyn, New York, in the early 1900s is good. Her wealthy parents have a lovely summer home on the ocean and Hattie especially loves to hear the waves crashing on shore. Hattie's dream is to become a painter and, not content to do fine needlework or become someone's wife, teen-aged Hattie enrolls in art school. Hattie is based on the author's mother and the beautiful illustrations reveal many details about life at the turn of the century.

*Crews, Donald. *Bigmama's.* Greenwillow, 1991. Fic.(Unit 2, Sect. 3)

Cross, Verda. *Great-Grandma Tells of Threshing Day.* Ill. by Gail Owens. Albert Whitman, 1992. [40]p. Fic.

Greenfield, Eloise. *Night on Neighborhood Street.* Ill. by Jan Spivey Gilchrist. Dial, 1991. [32]p. Poet.

This is a wonderful collection of 17 poems that deal with the daily concerns of African-American city children, among them a lonely boy who gazes at the moon while waiting for his friend; a young girl who tries to cheer up her jobless father; a mother playing a trumpet in the night; childrens' rejection of a drug seller; and a newborn baby girl who cries. Subtle shades of lavenders, pinks, greens, and blues, coupled with the golden brown of the characters, make for a visual treat.

Hewett, Joan. *Hector Lives in the United States Now: The Story of a Mexican-American Child.* Photos. by Richard Hewett. Lippincott, 1990. 44p. Nonfic.

Ten-year-old Hector Almaraz, a fifth-grader in Los Angeles, is Mexican by birth. He likes to play soccer, read comic books, and collect baseball cards. School is a challenge he values, and at home he speaks Spanish with his family. Although they miss Mexico, Hector's parents decide to become American citizens in order to give their children a better life. This well-written book, liberally illustrated with black-and-white photographs, celebrates Mexican heritage and customs. Includes a bibliography and a note on the 1986 Immigration Reform and Control Act.

Houston, Gloria. *My Great-Aunt Arizona.* Ill. by Susan Condie Lamb. HarperCollins, 1992. [32]p. Fic.

This is a beautiful tribute to Gloria Houston's Great-Aunt Arizona, a native of the Blue Ridge Mountains who became a teacher in the early 1900s and whose teaching career spanned 57 years. Arizona brought excitement and life to her one-room school, teaching her students about many interesting places in the world, but also about the wonders of home. The soft illustrations show the different generations of students taught by the industrious and very special Great-Aunt Arizona.

Houston, Gloria. *The Year of the Perfect Christmas Tree.* Ill. by Barbara Cooney. Dial, 1988. [32]p. Fic.

Young Ruthie Green lives a peaceful life with her parents in the Appalachian Mountains of North Carolina until her father is called away to serve in World War I. Ruthie and her mother struggle to maintain themselves, and especially to provide their village church with the perfect Christmas tree for the annual celebration. The blues, greens, and warm earth tones of the stunning illustrations help evoke a true picture of life in the mountains in the early decades of the twentieth century.

*Howard, Elizabeth Fitzgerald. *Chita's Christmas Tree.* Bradbury, 1989. Fic. (Unit 2, Sect. 4)

Hoyt-Goldsmith, Diane. *Totem Pole.* Photos. by Lawrence Migdale. Holiday, 1990. 32p. Non-fic.

Through the employment of color photographs, the author tells the story of a young Tsimshian Indian boy living in Washington State who watches his father carve a new totem pole. The entire process—from selecting the 40-foot cedar tree, to selecting the figures to be carved, to painting the faces, to the ceremony accompanying the raising of the new pole—is depicted in this well-crafted book that informs readers about Native American traditions in the Northwest.

Hudson, Wade, selector. *Pass It On: African-American Poetry for Children.* Ill. by Floyd Cooper. Scholastic, 1993. 32p. Poet.

Each of the 19 poems in this collection reflects the black oral tradition and represents a special aspect of the rich African-American experience. A wide variety of authors, including Langston Hughes, Eloise Greenfield, Countee Cullen, and Lucille Clifton, provide poems about love, family, play, going to sleep, slavery, prejudice, and foods. Cooper's beautiful illustrations show African Americans in all facets of life in this excellent introduction to poetry for children.

*Keegan, Marcia. *Pueblo Boy: Growing Up in Two Worlds.* Cobblehill Books, 1991. Non-fic. (Unit 2, Sect. 4)

Kuklin, Susan. *How My Family Lives in America.* Bradbury, 1992. [32]p. Non-fic.

This photo essay focuses on three children who are multi-ethnic and who have at least one parent who was not born in the United States. Sanu's father is from Senegal, Eric's father and grandparents were born in Puerto Rico, and both of April's parents are Taiwanese. Each of the children shares how, in addition to a common American heritage, their parents teach them about customs and foods from their home countries. Bright color photographs accompany the text and the author includes a recipe from each of the children's families.

Lewis, Claudia. *Long Ago in Oregon.* Ill. by Joel Fontaine. Harper & Row, 1987. 55p. Poet.

This compilation of 17 poems relates a year's events in the life of a young girl growing up in a small town in Oregon in 1917. The poems evoke an image of a place where the sound of saws and sawmills rang in the air, of Christmas and Decoration Day celebrations, of visits to the farm, and of ladies who wore long skirts that touched the ground when they walked. Despite its relative isolation, World War I touches the community and in November 1918 the whole town celebrates Armistice Day. Soft, black-and-white drawings accompany the poems. Also of interest is Claudia Lewis's *Up in the Mountains: And Other Poems of Long Ago* (HarperCollins, 1991) that tells of a little girl living at the turn of the century.

Little, Lessie Jones. *Children of Long Ago.* Ill. by Jan Spivey Gilchrist. Philomel, 1988. [32]p. Poet.

Based on this African-American author's recollections of her childhood in the rural South of the early 1900s, this collection of 17 poems creates a sense of children's lives "long ago." The poems describe getting dressed in "Sunday" clothes for church, asking Grandma to read a story, Papa chopping wood, playing with paper dolls, going barefoot, and taking care of the chickens. Soft pastel watercolor illustrations complete the mood of the beautiful poems.

*Lomas Garza, Carmen. *Family Pictures/Cuadros de Familia.* Children's Book Press, 1990. Non-fic. (Unit 2, Sect. 4)

Luenn, Nancy. *Nessa's Fish.* Ill. by Neil Waldman. Atheneum, 1990. [32]p. Fic.

Nessa, an Inuit girl, and her grandmother are out together on an ice-fishing expedition. When Grandmother becomes ill from something she ate, Nessa must use courage, wits, and the lessons learned from her parents and grandfather to defend their catch from the wolves and bears and to keep Grandmother safe. The soft blues, lavenders, pinks, and yellows of the illustrations help convey the setting of the story.

McDonald, Megan. *The Potato Man.* Ill. by Ted Lewin. Orchard, 1991. [32]p. Fic.

Two grandchildren listen with great interest as Grampa recounts his childhood, a time when horse-drawn carts dominated East Street. Grampa particularly remembers the Potato Man, Mr. Angelo—a food peddler with a frightening face who lost an eye in the Great War. The neighborhood boys taunted him by throwing cinders and name-calling, but three times Mr. Angelo's actions brought bad luck to Grampa. The softly colored illustrations provide readers with many details about life in the early 1900s. The story of the Potato Man continues in *The Great Pumpkin Switch* (Orchard, 1992).

Mora, Pat. *A Birthday Basket for Tía.* Ill. by Cecily Lang. Macmillan, 1992. [32]p. Fic.

As a Mexican-American family makes its preparations for a surprise party for Tía's ninetieth birthday, young Cecilia thinks about what she will give her beloved great-aunt. Cecilia takes a large basket and fills it with things that remind her of Tía, including their favorite book, flowers, a red ball they play with, and a pretty flowerpot. Each item speaks of Cecilia's love for Tía and there is a fine family celebration at the end of the book. The author based the book on her childhood experiences in the Mexican-American community in El Paso, Texas.

*O'Kelley, Mattie Lou. *Moving to Town.* Little, Brown, 1991. Fic. (Unit 2, Sect. 4)

Paek, Min. *Aekyung's Dream.* Children's Book Press, 1988. 24p. Fic.

After six months in the United States, Aekyung is very unhappy. At school nobody seems to know anything about her native Korea, her classmates call her "Chinese eyes," and she is convinced that even the birds sing in English. But one night the Great Korean King, Sejong, appears to her in a dream and tells her the secret to surviving in her new country. In this timeless tale, brilliantly colored illustrations accompany the Korean and English text.

Pinkney, Gloria Jean. *Back Home.* Ill. by Jerry Pinkney. Dial, 1992. [40]p. Fic.

Based on the author's childhood experiences, this book tells of eight-year-old Ernestine, a northern black girl who travels by train to Lumberton, North Carolina, to visit the place where her mother grew up. Ernestine is delighted with the verdant landscape and with everything on her uncle's farm. Everything, that is, except for her cousin Jack who teases her about her "citified" ways. The combination of rich text and detailed illustrations helps evoke a strong sense of time, place, and deep family love.

Surat, Michele Maria. *Angel Child, Dragon Child.* Ill. by Vo-Dinh Mai. Raintree Publishers, 1983. 35p. Fic.

Vietnamese-born Nguyen Hoa hates her new school in the United States. Because of her native dress, the red-haired boy named Raymond calls her "Pajamas" and he constantly teases her. Hoa's mother was not able to come with the rest of the family and Hoa misses her terribly. When Raymond and Hoa get into a fight, the principal makes the two children work out their differences and they devise a fund-raising effort to help pay the cost of the passage to America for Hoa's mother. Softly colored drawings accompany the simple text in this excellent picture book about the immigrant experiences of the Vietnamese in the United States.

Williams, Sherley Anne. *Working Cotton.* Ill. by Carole Byard. Harcourt Brace Jovanovich, 1992. [32]p. Fic.

This picture book relates a day in the life of a migrant African-American family as they pick cotton in California. The bus comes early in the morning, when it is still dark, and takes the entire family to the fields. Too young to pick cotton, Shelan helps with her younger sister and piles the cotton for her mother to bag. After a lunch break, the family goes back to work, now in the heat of day. The family leaves when it is almost dark, having put in a full day. The story is based on the author's childhood recollections and shows the deplorable reality of child labor. Vivid illustrations show a family who deeply cares for each other as they labor together.

*Yolen, Jane. *Letting Swift River Go.* Little, Brown, 1992. Non-fic. (Unit 2, Sect. 1)

PART
2

Intermediate and
Middle School:
Grades 4 through 8

LOOKING AT
AMERICA'S HISTORY

❈ ❈ ❈ ❈ ❈ ❈ ❈ ❈ ❈

INTRODUCTION TO UNIT 1

Unit 1, "Researching the Past," will introduce students to American history and to the methods of the historian. The learning activities introduced in this unit will be carried over into the succeeding units. Through children's literature and the associated historical accounts found in textbooks and reference books, students will identify the problems faced by people during various eras. By employing research strategies, including reading for information, students will pursue the methods of the historian by gathering, observing, and analyzing the data, and then drawing conclusions.

Some of the learning activities about time and space perspectives and chronology, such as the time line and the mapping of places and events, will be extensions from the primary grades into grades 4 through 8. Through the various activities, the learners will come to understand relationships and the continuum of events, multiple causation, and the effects of events over time. Many of the learning activities will be suitable for whole-class, teacher-directed instruction, or can be employed as cooperative learning or independent learning activities.

As in Part I, teachers and librarians will need to make decisions about which children's books will be read aloud, utilized for independent reading, or other uses. For the varying reading abilities found within any classroom, books may be selected from the primary book lists, books designated for grades 4 through 6, or for grades 6 through 8. The books designated for the middle school readers, grades 6 through 8, are advanced in both reading level and content, but may serve as read-alouds for younger children.

UNIT
one

Researching the Past

OBJECTIVES

1. Students will construct a survey to gather information about their own lives and the lives of adults. Students will select an activity or problem from their own lives and determine through research whether this activity or problem is unique to their own generation, and how and why it is different or the same as other generations.

2. As appropriate, students will plot the data from the survey on time lines and graphs, and make inferences about cause and effect relationships and changes over time.

3. Based on the data gathered, students will map where they, their parents, and their grandparents have lived, and list reasons why people move to other locations.

4. Students will begin their History Journals by writing about an activity or problem identified in Objective 1 as though they were the youngsters of a prior generation, either a real-life child or a fictional child from a book they have read.

5. Students will identify a family or community artifact or document and conduct an oral history interview with an adult who can provide information about the artifact and the people connected with it.

6. Through observation and analysis, students will interpret the content of archival photographs and other pictures, including family pictures.

7. From among the learning activities and data collected in this unit, students will select one that told them the most about their family or about their community. They will cite this activity and the data in their History Journals, and explain why or how these data helped them learn about their family or community.

LEARNING ACTIVITIES

1. What, When, How, and Why: The Generational Survey

The students will become historians who ask questions and gather information. Construct a simple survey form to be used by the students to gather data about their own lives and from adults they know. Have students complete their answers to the survey before collecting data from adults. Then give each student two or more copies of the survey. The students will gather data from adults of their parents' and grandparents' ages. Obtaining data from adults of two different generations will add depth to the survey. Young children may wish to use only one or two questions in their survey, while older students may use several questions, such as some of the following:

Generational Survey

_____   _____

(name of researcher)   date

1. How old are you?_____   Students: state your age:_____
   Adults, check one: ___20-29 years old; ___30-39; ___40-49; ___50-59;
   ___60-69: ____70 or older, please list age.
2. ____Female; ____Male.
   When you were my age:
3. What was your favorite game?
4. What was your favorite toy?
5. What was your favorite sport?
6. What was your favorite television program?
7. What was your favorite subject in school?
9. What was the biggest problem in your community?
10. What invention could you not live without?
11. Where did you live when you were my age? Please name the community, state, and nation. How large was the community?
12. Did you live on a farm or in town?
13. If you lived somewhere other than in this community, why did you or your family move to this community?
14. How old were you when you moved to this community?

The complexity of the content of the survey may vary with the learning levels of the students. However, keep the questions simple to answer and few in number so that the results can be tabulated. Be sure to retain the data sheets for use throughout this unit. For this sample survey, graph the results so that data can be compared by age and gender.

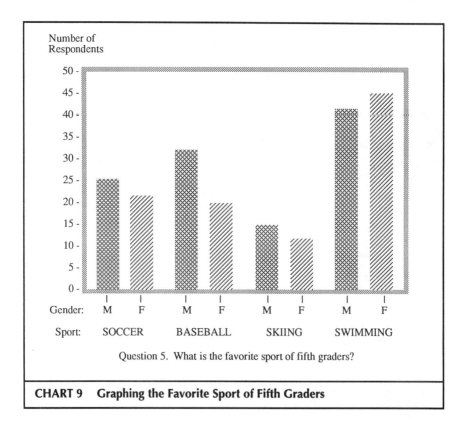

Question 5. What is the favorite sport of fifth graders?

CHART 9   Graphing the Favorite Sport of Fifth Graders

The graph could be duplicated for each age group surveyed, showing the names of the favorite sports by genders. Then the numbers of responses can be compared. What conclusions can be drawn? In what ways are the generations alike or different in their answers? In what ways are the interests of boys and girls more alike now than for boys and girls 30 years ago? Why? What factors influence the data? For example, electronic games may be favorites among many girls and boys, but were not childhood favorite games for their grandparents. Why are there generational differences?

For advanced students, data can be mathematically analyzed by finding the percent of respondents whose answers were alike, or finding the ratio of males to females who liked certain games. Also, advanced students may wish to construct their own survey questions.

2. A Time Line Comparison of Generations

A time line can be constructed showing decades from 1920 to the present. For the decades of the 1990s or 2000s, list the students' answers to some or all of the survey questions. The students will need to calculate the years when each age group they surveyed was 10-14 years old, and then record the answers for those generations on the time line for the appropriate dates.

Compare answers among the decades. Find evidence of changes and try to determine why these changes took place.

At another time, the students will construct a large time line to use in recording American history.

3. Our Old Home Town

Make a large outline map of the United States, or of the world, if data collected in the survey extend beyond the United States. Using data collected by question 11 of the Generational Survey, have each student mark on the classroom Outline Map or on individual maps where his/her respondents lived. If making individual maps, the students will make a record of where their own families have lived. By using this data from the survey, students will have a visual record of the home towns of older generations, possibly including immigrants.

Ask students to observe the distribution of the home towns of their respondents, then list reasons why they think people came to the students' home town. Make a composite list of these reasons from the survey. Draw conclusions about why people move.

In the next unit, students will construct large outline maps on which to record places and events associated with American history.

4. When I Was a Child in . . .

Throughout the year, students will write in their History Journals, often from the viewpoint of a person their age living during another era or past event. For this opening writing activity, students will write from the viewpoint of a grandparent after selecting data from one question on their survey sheets. For example, a student may choose the data about inventions, and the viewpoint of a grandparent who was 10 years old in 1945. The student may need to obtain more information from references and from the grandparent before writing. The journal entry will relate why this invention was important, how the writer in the role of the grandparent felt about it when he or she was a child, and what changes the invention made in his or her life. Advanced students will include additional information about the time frame, while the younger students may respond in a more superficial manner.

As an alternative to writing from the viewpoint of one of their respondents, students may wish to select a book character from another time in America's history and write from that person's perspective. In order to carry out the theme of a youngster's perspective, the student may have to deduce the book character's viewpoint.

5. Artifact or Junk?

Check with your local library or museum to obtain artifacts for use in your classroom. Bring to the classroom an outdated, everyday artifact, preferably unbreakable. Ask the students to speculate as to its use. If you brought a buggy whip to class, students would probably recognize it as some sort of whip. Ask them if they would like to invest in its manufacture. To whom would they sell this item? When would the buggy whip factory have been profitable? What are the changes that have made buggy whips an uncommon item today? The changes may simply be discussed or they may be listed on a chart in chronological order.

6. Attic and Community Treasures

Family Artifacts and Documents. Ask the students to locate some family object, such as a photograph album, quilt, or kitchen gadget that was used or owned by a previous generation, or documents, such as letters, newspaper clippings, or a scrapbook that tells about the family in some way. Then interview a family member who can provide information about the artifact or the document and the people connected with it. If possible, provide tape recorders or video recorders to be used for the oral history interviews. Conduct a few practice interviews in class to model the procedures before students conduct their own interviews. If tape recorders or video recorders are not available, the oral history interview can become a writing project, with the student taking notes during the interview, then presenting the information in written or oral form.

Most students will find that an outline or list of questions to be asked will help them obtain sufficient information about the artifact. They will also find that many people will be eager to talk to an interested listener. *Like It Was: A Complete Guide to Writing Oral History* and Chapter Five: "Exploring the Past" in *Do People Grow on Family Trees?* will provide many guidelines for this oral history research project.

Among the information to be gathered, try to include the following:

1. When and where is the interview being conducted?
2. Who is the interviewer and the interviewee?
3. What is the artifact or document? Describe it.
4. When and where was is used?
5. Who were the people who probably used this object?

6. What relationship do they have to the interviewee and the interviewer?
7. Is this artifact or document still being used? Why or why not?

Community Treasures. Using *Who Put the Cannon in the Courthouse Square?: A Guide to Uncovering the Past* as a reference and guide, plan an investigation of the history of some local monument, building, or the school building. This could become a long-term project for the advanced students, or result in inviting a resource person to the classroom for the younger students. Either approach will get at some of the investigative procedures of the historian.

7. A Picture Is Worth a Thousand Words

Photos of the Past. While seeking artifacts to use in the classroom, also check at your local library or museum for archival photographs and pictures that tell of another time period. Black-and-white photographs that are sharp in detail can be photocopied for classroom use. Colored photographs, colored prints of paintings, and other colored pictures may be photocopied, or perhaps they can be borrowed for the classroom.

Your local museum may have a photograph of Main Street in 1910 or of a famous person from your community. *New Providence: A Changing Cityscape* will give the students background for becoming more visually literate as they list observable details in archival pictures. In the picture of Main Street, note the names of the buildings. Are any of these buildings still on Main Street? Are there people in the picture? What are they doing? How are they dressed? Would the students want to dress like that? What do the students think they are saying to each other? Where are they going? What is the condition of the street? Cement? Mud? What things have changed since this scene was photographed? Why did these changes take place?

Interpretation of pictures can be a whole-class discussion activity. Photocopy the pictures and photographs so that each student can use the photocopies as worksheets to directly record their observations and deductions.

Portrait Gallery, Reading Family Pictures. The teacher or librarian will construct a display with pictures from their own family. Include the "snapshots" from various generations. Put captions on the pictures telling about the content: who, when, where, and perhaps why. Following this model, the students will seek to find family pictures to interpret.

Keep in mind that some children have no photographs of themselves or members of the family except those that may be taken at school. As an alternative to family pictures, provide photocopies of archival pictures of people and places from the community.

8. Historians at Work

After reviewing the various activities from this unit, students will individually select the activity that told them the most about their family or about their community. In their History Journals, they will explain how this activity helped them learn about their family or community. Take time to compare the students' answers, thus emphasizing that the work of historians takes many different forms.

BOOK LIST

Note: Starred (*) books are reviewed in a previous section or unit of this book.

Anderson, Joan. *From Map to Museum: Uncovering Mysteries of the Past.* Photos. by George Ancona. Morrow, 1988. 63p. (4-8) Non-fic.

This fascinating black-and-white photographic essay accompanies Dr. David Hurst Thomas, Curator of Anthropology at the American Museum of Natural History, on an archaeological expedition to St. Catherines Island, off the coast of Georgia, as he searches for an ancient Spanish mission. The text and illustrations trace the historical artifacts over a 15-year period: from planning the expedition; to uncovering, restoring, and researching the artifacts; to displaying the artifacts in the museum. A closing note explains the fields of anthropology and archaeology in terms children will understand.

Brown, Cynthia Stokes. *Like it Was: A Complete Guide to Writing Oral History.* Teachers and Writers Collaborative, 1988. 129p. (4-8) Non-fic.

Cooper, Kay. *Who Put the Cannon in the Courthouse Square?: A Guide to Uncovering the Past.* Ill. by Anthony Accardo. Walker, 1985. 70p. (4-8) Non-fic.

This concise and clearly written volume explains how to conduct research, especially in local communities. Students will learn how to focus their research; what questions to ask; sources of information; how to use their local libraries, museums, and historical societies; tips on how to interview people; and how to put the final story together. The author has included several examples of children's written projects, a useful directory of information sources, and an index.

Levin, Betty. *The Keeping Room.* Greenwillow, 1981. 247p. (6-8) Fic.

Hal Woodruff's social studies assignment leads him to investigate the history of a deserted farm in his hometown of Westwick, near Boston. He interviews and becomes friends with elderly neighbors, searches through the ruins of the ancient farm homestead, and eventually discovers the bones of a young girl named Hannah who disappeared in 1838. This complex, well-written story includes interesting information about rural existence in nineteenth-century America and about the life of the "mill girls" in Lowell, Massachusetts.

Loeper, John J. *The House on Spruce Street.* Atheneum, 1982. 81p. (4-6) Fic.

A colonial house on Spruce Street in Philadelphia is the protagonist in this unusual book that tells our nation's story through means of a dwelling. Built in 1772, the house had approximately 12 owners in its 200-year history— people who lived through events such as the Revolution, Civil War, waves of immigration, and the Depression. Each owner put his or her stamp on the house. Children will learn not only about historical events, but also many interesting architectural facts. The short chapters make this book suitable for reading aloud. Includes a bibliography.

*Mango, Karin N. *Map Making.* Julian Messner, 1984. (4-6) Non-fic. (Part 1, Unit 1)

Perl, Lila. *The Great Ancestor Hunt: The Fun of Finding Out Who You Are.* Ill. by Erika Weihs. Clarion, 1989. 104p. (4-8) Non-fic.

A large majority of present-day Americans had ancestors who were immigrants to this country, whether they arrived by ship in the 1700s, by steamer in the late 1800s, or by airplane in the last several decades. This high-interest, low-vocabulary book explains how to begin to trace your family's history, including information on how to gain access to public records. Includes an index.

Von Tscharner, Renata, and Ronald Lee Fleming, and the Townscape Institute. *New Providence: A Changing Cityscape.* Ill. by Denis Orloff. Harcourt Brace Jovanovich, 1987. [32]p. (4-8) Non-fic.

Six full-color, double-page illustrations depict the development of the fictional town of New Providence, from 1910 to 1987. The city's center is the focus, but development in the outlying areas is also depicted. As people and times change, so does the city—the Depression shows New Providence in need of repairs; in 1955, postwar prosperity is shown, although the downtown area is depressed; 1970 shows the central park converted into a pedestrian mall; and by the close of the book in 1987, New Providence is exhibiting signs of urban renewal. This wonderful book reflects, in the changing facade of a city, how the urbanization process in the United States affected cities and towns.

Weitzman, David. *My Backyard History Book.* Ill. by James Robertson. Little, Brown, 1975. 128p. (4-8) Non-fic.

Written in language that children will understand, this book explains the origins of surnames, how to construct family trees, how to conduct oral histories, the wealth of information found in old graveyards, how to re-search the history of your hometown, and a host of other activities and projects that bring family history within easy reach of most children. The book is illustrated with many fascinating drawings that will motivate readers to investigate their own family histories.

Wolfman, Ira. *Do People Grow on Family Trees?: Genealogy For Kids and Other Beginners: The Official Ellis Island Handbook.* Ill. by Michael Klein. Work-man Publishing, 1991. 179p. (4-8) Non-fic.

Children and adults alike will be fascinated with this book which explains where our ancestors came from, how they came to this country, how to find information and documents about your family, the history and meaning of names, and where to find libraries to help in research. The book is filled with facsimile reproductions and with archival photographs of immigrants and living conditions at the turn of the century. The section on Ellis Island is especially valuable. This is an excellent resource to share with children.

FROM
EXPLORATION TO
YOUNG NATION

✹ ✹ ✹ ✹ ✹ ✹ ✹ ✹

INTRODUCTION TO UNITS 2, 3, AND 4

In Unit 2, "Exploring and Settling the New World," students will find out about the European discovery and exploration of the Americas. Through mapping and time line activities, the students will record the ways in which the voyages of exploration expanded the world known to the Europeans and provided the means for informal exchange of plants and animals. Through reading about the relationships between explorers and Native Americans, students will identify the changes that took place through exploitation, cooperation, and the impact of European settlements. Journal writing activities will seek to view this period of American history from both the European and the Native American perspectives.

While there are many well-written recent books about Columbus, teachers will need to examine their library resources for additional titles about other explorers and early settlements. For this unit, the social studies and history textbooks will be needed to fill in the chronology of events.

In Unit 3, "Colonial Period," students will learn about the varied ethnic populations of the colonies and how the early settlements established in the exploration period gradually shifted from a precarious frontier existence to established towns and cities. Out of diverse peoples and communities emerged the roots of the American Revolution and the establishment of a new democratic nation. As students become "tour guides" for the various colonies in the late 1600s and early to mid-1700s, they will discover the colonies' strengths and weaknesses.

Unit 4, "Revolution and the Constitutional Period," will identify the people and the problems associated with the colonists' revolt against Great Britain. The students will develop a constitution for their classroom as a way to discover the difficulties and benefits of a democracy, and as a way to identify the relevance of the United States Constitution in their lives today.

UNIT
two

Exploring and Settling the New World

OBJECTIVES

1. After reading books about explorers, the students will construct charts summarizing the explorers' contributions, both positive and negative.
2. Using recent, well-researched nonfiction books as references and guides, the students will analyze the sources of information they have used in Objective 1, and predict how the discovery of new information might change the content of their charts.
3. The routes of the explorers will be placed on the Outline Map of the Western Hemisphere along with the locations of various Native American peoples.
4. Based on the charts constructed in Objective 1, the students will make composite lists of the positive contributions of the European explorers to America, along with the contributions of the Native Americans to Europe.
5. Students will write in their History Journals from the viewpoint of an explorer, a Native American, or an early European colonist, focusing on the changes that occurred in that person's life because of the interaction with the other people.
6. The explorers and early settlements will be recorded on the time line.
7. European settlements in America will be recorded on the Outline Map.

LEARNING ACTIVITIES

1. How Did Europeans Learn About America?

After reading general information from textbooks and other reference sources, the students will make a list of explorers to research. This list may have a few explorers to be researched by all members of the class, or, if resources are available, many explorers to be researched by individuals or small groups.

Develop an outline to be used with available reference resources so that comparable information will be obtained for each explorer, such as the following:

Explorers of the Americas

Name of explorer: Country of origin:

Dates of exploration:

Where did exploration take place?

What did the Europeans learn from this exploration?

What did the explorers and the Europeans learn from the Native Americans?

What were the positive effects that resulted from this exploration?

What were the negative effects that resulted from this exploration?

2. And Now for the Rest of the Story

The students will list the sources of information they have used in Activity 1, including the dates of publication. They will probably list encyclopedias, history textbooks, and some library books. Encourage the students to check these references for bibliographies and footnotes that tell the sources of the author's information.

The resources used in recent, well-researched books, such as *Discovering Christopher Columbus: How History Is Invented*, will then be listed, noting the use of original or primary documents, such as maps and journals from the time of the explorer. After comparing the two lists, the students will note the differences and predict how the discovery of new information could change the content of their charts.

Look for examples of how new information about topics and people change what we think is historically accurate. Suppose Columbus and other explorers had believed the accounts of the world being flat: how might civilization in the Americas have developed? Suppose we only credited Columbus with his failure to find a route to India; would we still celebrate Columbus Day? Note how the explorers' accounts of their expeditions are far different from Native American accounts of meeting the Europeans. Explain that each group applies its own historical bias to descriptions of the same events. See *Morning Girl* by Michael Dorris for an example of this kind of bias in historical accounts.

Search the newspapers of today for reports of how new information about the past "changes" or clarifies historical accounts. Accounts of retrieving the contents of ships sunken in the Caribbean Sea tell us about how people lived both in Europe and in the Caribbean at the time the ship was sunk. A related example would be finding the site of an ancient Indian village in Michigan where a new highway is to be built. The highway may be delayed or changed because of this discovery, which changes current knowledge about human habitation and land use in that part of the United States.

3. Mapping the Native American Residents and the European Exploration of North America

With the help of the opaque projector or an overhead transparency, the students will draw a large outline map of North America to be used for the remainder of the school year. Using the information from the charts in Activity 1 and other references, students will map and date the routes of the explorers on the Outline Map of the Western Hemisphere. They will also record the locations of various Native American peoples on the Outline Map. Both the explorers and the residents of North America should appear on the same map. To show only the routes of the European explorers implies that the Americas were uninhabited.

4. Gifts To and From America

Pictorial Chart. Based on the charts constructed in Activity 1, and with the use of additional references, the students will make a pictorial chart showing the positive contributions of the European explorers to America, such as the introduction of the horse. The pictures may be drawn by the students, cut from magazines, or photocopied and assembled.

Teachers will need to consider how to include the introduction of Christianity to the Native Americans. From the Christian point of view, this was a positive change. From the perspective of the Native Americans, who had their own religions, was this a positive or negative change?

Food Webs. To list the contributions of Native Americans to Europeans and to Americans today, try developing food webs. List foods that are native to America, such as corn, tomatoes, beans, and potatoes, then identify the foods we eat today that stem from those foods.

Check the labels of foods for more uses of corn. You will be surprised to find corn in cookies, ice cream, and other favorites.

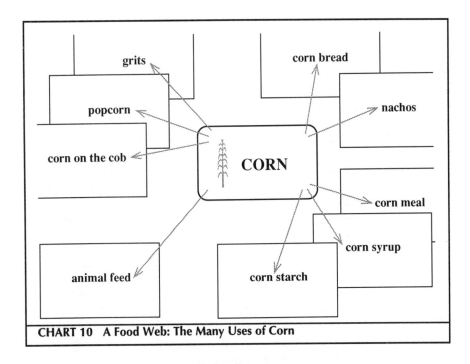

CHART 10   A Food Web: The Many Uses of Corn

5. Opposing Viewpoints

As a follow-up to the learning activities about explorers, early European colonists, and Native Americans, students will write two opposing viewpoints in their History Journals, then draw conclusions about the relationships of the persons. Following are some viewpoints to consider:

Explorers/Native Americans. Students will select an explorer and the location of the exploration. They will write two viewpoints, then draw conclusions about how the explorers and the Native Americans related to one another.

1. If you had been a member of the explorer's expedition, what would have been most memorable about this trip?
2. If you had been a member of the Native American community visited by this explorer, what would have been most memorable about the visit?
3. How do you think the explorer and the Native American got along together? How did they show respect or lack of respect for one another? How did they help or harm each other? Why did they help or harm each other?

Colonists/Native Americans. Based on their reading about such early settlements as Roanoke, Jamestown, Plymouth, or Sante Fe, students will write a journal entry, deducing the colonists' reasons for immigration, and whether they achieved their goals. Have some students respond to this journal entry based on a successful colony and some based on an unsuccessful colony. Specifically select the colonies and identify the Native Americans who were living nearby. When drawing conclusions, compare the colonists' viewpoints with the Native Americans' perspectives.

1. As a colonist in [name the colony], what did you think about the [name the Native Americans] who lived near your village? In what ways did they help or harm you? In what ways did you help or harm them?

2. As a Native American of the [name tribe or nation] what did you think of the European settlers near your village? In what ways did they help or harm you? In what ways did you help or harm them?

3. As a colonist, tell why you immigrated. In what ways were you successful in reaching your goals? In what ways were you unsuccessful?

4. As a Native American, tell why you stayed near the European village, fought the Europeans, or moved away. Were you successful in reaching your goals?

5. As a colonist living in a successful village, how are your views about America, immigration to America, and Native Americans the same or different from those of colonists living in an unsuccessful village?

6. As a Native American living near a successful village of European settlers, how are your views similar or different from those of Native Americans living near an unsuccessful European settlement?

6. Time Line

On a long roll of paper, students will construct a large time line starting with the year 1000 and extending to the year 2000. Divide each century into 25- or 50-year segments, leaving room to record historical events and people for the rest of the school year. Record the explorers and early settlements on the time line.

7. Mapping the European Settlements

Add the European settlements to the Outline Map. Include the date of settlement and the colonists' nations of origin. Discuss why settlers of certain European nations settled in certain parts of the Americas.

BOOK LIST

Note: Starred (*) books are reviewed in a previous section or unit of this book.

Alper, Ann Fitzpatrick. *Forgotten Voyager: The Story of Amerigo Vespucci.* Carolrhoda, 1991. 80p. (4-6) Biog.

*Anderson, Joan. *Spanish Pioneers of the Southwest.* Lodestar Books, 1989. (4-6) Non-fic. (Part 1, Unit 2, Sect. 4)

Baker, Betty. *A Stranger and Afraid.* Macmillan, 1972. 161p. (6-8) Fic.

This story relates what might have been one of the first encounters between the Spanish and the Native Americans of the Southwest in the first half of the sixteenth century. Sopete, a Wichita Indian, is captured along with his younger brother, Zabe, in a raid by the Cicuye Indians, a Pueblo people. Sopete's unhappy life is forever changed when Spaniards make contact with the Indians, riding huge beasts called horses that scare the Cicuyens. The author's knowledge of Native American culture is evident in this unusual story about a topic not often covered in children's literature.

Barden, Renardo. *The Discovery of the Americas.* Greenhaven Press, 1989. 112p. (4-8) Non-fic.

Part of the "Great Mysteries: Opposing Viewpoints Series," this book dispels the myth that Columbus "discovered" America in 1492. The author not only places Columbus's explorations in historic context, but also explores the Irish and Welsh legends surrounding the American continent, Viking wanderings and the *Icelandic Sagas*, historical and archaeological evidence supporting Viking visits, and other possible visitors to the Americas, including prehistoric sailors. Barden's presentation of information allows readers to make up their own minds on the questions. The liberal use of photographs, period paintings, and maps enhances the text. Includes a bibliography and index.

Bragg, Bea. *The Very First Thanksgiving: Pioneers on the Rio Grande.* Ill. by Antonio Castro. Harbinger House, 1989. 57p. (4-6) Fic.

Based on an actual event, this story tells of an expedition led by Don Juan de Oñate that left Mexico in 1598 with 400 people and 7,000 animals to settle in what is present-day Texas. Two orphaned brothers, 14-year-old Manuel and 12-year-old Fernando, leave their home to take part in this exciting adventure, hoping to find riches. Instead, they encounter hardship, hunger, thirst, blistering heat, snakes, dust storms, and wild coyotes. Upon reaching the Rio Grande near El Paso, the weary Spanish travelers held a great feast of celebration with the local Native peoples to celebrate their safe arrival. An author's note tells the historical background of the event; the book includes a glossary and pronunciation guide.

Conrad, Pam. *Pedro's Journal: A Voyage with Christopher Columbus: August 3, 1492-February 14, 1493.* Ill. by Peter Koeppen. Caroline House/dist. by St. Martin's, 1991. 80p. (4-6) Fic.

Pedro de Salcedo, one of the ship's boys on board Columbus's flagship, the *Santa María*, presents the events of this dramatic voyage in a journal. Pedro comments on the sailors' discontent with Columbus, the questionable way in which the Native Americans are treated, and his shame that these people are allowed to believe that some of the Spaniards are gods. An author's note explains the factual basis for the story, although Pedro was not a real person. This succinct book is a good read-aloud choice for the classroom. Two other similar stories about ship's boys worth reading are Susan Martin's *I Sailed with Columbus: The Adventures of a Ship's Boy* (Overlook Press, 1991) and Miriam Schlein's *I Sailed with Columbus* (HarperCollins, 1991).

Dorris, Michael. *Morning Girl.* Hyperion Books for Children, 1992. 74p. (4-6) Fic.

In this deceptively simple tale, which is well-suited for read-aloud, members of a family of Arawak Indians living in the West Indies pursue their daily lives. There is rich conversation among them, including Morning Girl and her brother, Star Boy. The alternating chapters, narrated by brother and sister, reveal a rich culture and warm family relationships. One day Morning Girl is swimming and sees a large clumsy canoe filled with strange people wearing unusual garments. She welcomes them and goes to find the village leaders. The book ends here, but is followed by an excerpt from Columbus's diary in which he concludes that the Native peoples would make good servants but "were a people poor in everything." This moving juxtaposition of the story and the diary must be followed up with additional information and discussion about the extermination of the Arawaks.

Dyson, John. *Westward with Columbus.* Photos. by Peter Christopher. Scholastic, 1991. 64p. (4-6) Fic.

The author presents a fictional account of the 1492 expedition, based on the premise that Columbus used a secret map to reach the "Indies." Along with the historical narrative, the author includes impressions and experiences from his own voyage across the Atlantic in 1990 aboard a replica of the caravel *Niña.* The story is full of drama and the book includes reproductions of period artwork and maps, along with many full-color photographs from the 1990 adventure that provide a brilliant visual picture of what the actual crossing might have been like. Includes a glossary and brief bibliography.

Faber, Harold. *The Discoverers of America.* Scribner's, 1992. 290p. (6-8) Non-fic.

Dispelling the myth that Christopher Columbus "discovered" America, Faber narrates the origins of the Native peoples, the coming of the Norsemen, Columbus's various voyages, and a host of other explorations, including those of Vespucci, Magellan, Balboa, Ponce de León, Cortés, Cartier, Pizarro, La Salle, Marquette, and Bering, just to name a few. Unlike many other "discovery" books, Faber's chapters deal with all of the Americas, from Alaska down to Cape Horn in South America. The well-researched text, often quoting from eyewitness accounts, presents a comprehensive picture of how the American continents were explored and settled. Includes an extensive bibliography, chronology, and index.

Fritz, Jean. *Where Do You Think You're Going, Christopher Columbus?* Ill. by Margot Tomes. Putnam, 1980. 80p. (4-6) Biog.

Hooks, William H. *The Legend of the White Doe.* Ill. by Dennis Nolan. Macmillan, 1988. 44p. (4-6) Fic.

In 1587, Sir Walter Raleigh established a colony of English families on the island of Roanoke, and soon after, one of the colonists gave birth to a child, Virginia Dare, allegedly the first white child born in English America. It was three years before Raleigh's ships returned to Roanoke and they found a deserted colony with only the word "CROATON" carved on a post. This is the imaginative story of what might have happened to those colonists, especially to young Virginia Dare, renamed Ulalee by her Native American family. Beautiful color, full-page paintings accompany this romantic tale. Another fictionalized account of the Roanoke colony is Sonia Levitin's *Roanoke: A Novel of the Lost Colony* (Atheneum, 1973).

Irwin, Constance. *Strange Footprints on the Land: Vikings in America.* Harper & Row, 1980. 182p. (6-8) Non-fic.

Jacobs, Francine. *The Tainos: The People Who Welcomed Columbus.* Putnam, 1992. 107p. (6-8) Non-fic.

This is a detailed, sad history of the destruction of the Tainos by the Spanish explorers whose search for gold led to the betrayal and enslavement of these peaceful island farmers. The author explains how archaeologists have traced the migration of the Tainos from South America to the islands of the Caribbean. Based on further documentation, readers will learn about the various attempts by some of the Tainos leaders to resist the Spanish, and the eventual work of some priests and a few Spanish planters to cease the cruel and inhuman treatment of these people. This is a well-written account of a series of grim events.

Jones, Jayne Clark. *The American Indian in America.* 2 Vols. Lerner, 1973. Vol. 1: 104p.; Vol. 2: 96p. (4-6) Non-fic.

This two-volume set traces the history of Native Americans, primarily in the United States, from pre-Columbian times to the present day. Indians are divided into six subsistence areas—Arctic, subarctic woodlands, northwest coast, American desert, eastern woodlands, and Great Plains. Some of the topics explored are food, clothing, housing, hunting habits, arts and crafts, and customs. The remainder of the series discusses, chronologically, the meeting of Native and white cultures, developing relationships between whites and Native Americans, the westward movement, and Native American living conditions in the twentieth century. The books are liberally illustrated with photographs, facsimiles, art objects, and maps. Includes a listing of tribes and language families and an index.

Katz, William Loren. *Black Indians: A Hidden Heritage.* Atheneum, 1986. 198p. (6-8) Non-fic.

Katz presents a study of the relationship between Native Americans and Africans on both American continents, a chapter largely unwritten in United States history. Beginning with documentation in the 1520s, the author explores the long and unique association these two minority groups have shared throughout America's growth. Among topics discussed are the close ties between blacks and the Seminole nation, and the theory that American Indians provided assistance and shelter to runaway slaves. Plentiful historical photographs and drawings accompany a fascinating and well-written text. Includes a bibliography and index.

Meltzer, Milton. *Columbus and the World Around Him.* Watts, 1990. 192p. (6-8) Non-fic.

O'Dell, Scott. *The King's Fifth.* Houghton Mifflin, 1966. 264p. (4-6) Fic.

As this story opens in 1541, 17-year-old Esteban de Sandoval is on trial in Vera Cruz, Mexico, charged with defrauding the King of Spain. While in prison, Esteban proceeds to write an account of his adventures as a mapmaker, leaving his homeland of Spain and then accompanying one of the expeditions led by Francisco de Coronado that traveled into the present-day American Southwest in search of the seven cities of gold. The greed for riches led to conflict among the Spaniards and to mistreatment of Native Americans. During the trip, a special friendship developed between Esteban, Father Francisco, and young Zia, their Indian guide. This adventure story about the Spanish exploration of North America is exciting, realistic, and well-told.

Pelta, Kathy. *Discovering Christopher Columbus: How History is Invented.* Lerner, 1991. 112p. (6-8) Non-fic.

The significant particulars of Columbus's life are narrated in the first several chapters of this book. The remainder of the work focuses on more controversial events in the explorer's life, and the author presents methods of historical research and existing theories regarding the exploration of the New World. The later chapters examine the primary sources from which information about Columbus is found. Numerous color and black-and-white illustrations and reproductions accompany the text of this well-researched volume that shows history to be an ever-changing discipline as scholars unearth new evidence.

Roop, Peter, and Connie Roop, eds. *I, Columbus: My Journal, 1492-3.* Ill. by Peter E. Hanson. Walker, 1990. 57p. (4-6) Non-fic.

Sattler, Helen Roney. *The Earliest Americans.* Ill. by Jean Day Zallinger. Clarion, 1993. 125p. (4-6) Non-fic.

This detailed book examines the archaeological and anthropological evidence regarding the origins of the Native peoples in America before the time of Columbus. Beginning with the Paleo-Indians who lived in the Americas 12,000 years ago, the author goes on to examine the human migration across the land bridge between Asia and North America, big game hunters during the time of the mammoths, and the development of the Mayan and Aztec civilizations. The author makes excellent use of archaeological artifacts to explain about life in the Americas during this time period, and the detailed, well-drawn illustrations enhance the fascinating text. Includes a time chart, extensive bibliography, and index.

Smith, Carter, ed. *The Explorers and Settlers: A Sourcebook on Colonial America.* Millbrook Press, 1991. 96p. (4-8) Non-fic.

Primarily a pictorial history, this book, part of the "American Albums from the Collections of the Library of Congress," presents a visually oriented account of the exploration and colonization of the continental United States from 1492 to 1775. Beginning with Columbus, the book continues with further Spanish and French explorations; English, French, and Dutch settlements in the 1600s; and the expansion of the early communities. Full captions accompany a wealth of black-and-white reproductions of archival paintings, prints, maps, and engravings, giving children a historical overview of the events, people, and land shown. In addition, three detailed time lines outline prominent events. Includes an index.

Spinka, Penina Keen. *White Hare's Horses.* Atheneum, 1991. 154p. (6-8) Fic.

Set in California close to 500 years ago, this is a fast-paced and fascinating story of the Chumash Indians when they first encounter Aztec Indians and horses. The peaceful Chumash accept the Aztecs as visitors and are awed by their horses which apparently were obtained from early Spanish explorers. They soon find that the Aztecs mean to convert them to their religion and enslave them. When the Aztecs threaten human sacrifice, teen-aged White Hare seeks the advice of her dead grandfather through the use of hallucinogen plants, usually reserved for use by the priests. White Hare rides the horses to freedom leaving the Aztecs with no power over her people. The use of the hallucinogen plants by White Hare and her tribe raises questions about the use of drugs.

Warren, Scott. *Cities in the Sand: The Ancient Civilizations of the Southwest.* Chronicle Books, 1992. 55p. (4-6) Non-fic.

The author begins his study of the American Southwest by explaining basic archaeological principles and how scientists date the artifacts they discover in the soil. After setting the stage for the prehistoric peoples of the Southwest, Warren focuses on three of the best known: the Anasazi, the Hohokam, and the Mogollon, dating back to 300 B.C. He writes about their dwellings, foods, pottery, jewelry, burial practices, hunting and agricultural habits, and the reasons why the civilizations waned. The author makes excellent use of his color photographs of the sites and rare artifacts, and includes a glossary, a list of national parks and monuments, and index.

Whitman, Sylvia. *Hernando de Soto and the Explorers of the American South.* Chelsea House, 1991. 111p. (6-8) Non-fic.

This book about the Spanish explorations in Florida and surrounding areas begins with Ponce de León's forays in the early 1500s and follows with such men as Alvar Nuñez Cabeza de Vaca, who journeyed throughout the American Southwest in the early 1530s. The different reasons for the explorations are discussed, along with the Spaniards' treatment of the Native peoples they encountered. The focus of the book, however, is on Hernando de Soto and his four-year expedition into the southern United States in 1539. The fascinating story of this daring venture is well-told, and the author includes many period illustrations, maps, a bibliography, chronology, and index. Two other books of related interest in the "World Explorers" Series published by Chelsea House are *From Coronado to Escalante: The Explorers of the American Southwest* by John Miller Morris (1992) and *LaSalle and the Explorers of the Mississippi* by Tony Coulter (1991).

Yue, Charlotte, and David Yue. *Christopher Columbus: How He Did It.* Houghton Mifflin, 1992. 136p. (4-8) Non-fic.

Through the well-written, informative text and detailed illustrations, readers will learn why Columbus was sure he could reach Asia by sailing west through uncharted waters and why his voyages were of great importance to European nations. The motives for the voyages, the means of support for the costly ventures, how ships of the time functioned, and Columbus's skills as a mariner are explained through the text and illustrations. This book presents the background information necessary for understanding how early voyages of discovery were carried out, as well as the impact of Columbus's discoveries.

* * * * * * * * *

UNIT
three
* * * * * * * * *

Colonial Period

OBJECTIVES

1. In small cooperative groups the students will select a colony for which they will become well-informed tour guides. After organizing their informational display, the students will present the information to the rest of the class.
2. After reading about people of the colonial period portrayed in novels and reference sources, students will be paired off to develop dialogues between colonists of different ethnic origins and the Native American peoples.
3. After identifying the kinds of workers needed in the various colonies, students will specify the ways in which children were part of the labor force in the colonial period. They will construct a Then and Now Chart comparing the lives of colonial children and children today.
4. After completing the Then and Now Charts, each student, writing as a colonist, will record in her or his History Journal some aspect of colonial life in which the student as colonist was self-reliant and able to solve problems.

LEARNING ACTIVITIES

1. Tour Guides for the Colonies

After an introduction to the 13 English colonies through reading textbooks or an expository lesson led by the teacher, the students will be divided into small cooperative-learning groups. Each group will select a colony to research. They will record the establishment of their colony on the time line and on the Outline Map. They will research and present an informational display telling about their colony. Help the students divide the research, construction, and presentation tasks among the members of the group by including the following information:

Name of colony: Date of settlement:

Location (include a map in the display)

Origin of the settlers

Reasons why this colony was established

Reasons why people want to live there

How people made their living

Important communities

Important people

Important events

Advantages of living there

Disadvantages of living there

Students may include library books about their colony, examples of products of the colony, pictures of the colony photocopied from various sources, maps, and other materials. Their information may be presented to the class as a travelogue to encourage new settlers to their colony, thereby informing the whole class about each colony.

2. Dialogues from the Past

After presenting the displays about the colonies and reading about the colonial period in novels, textbooks, and reference books, the students will work with a partner in writing dialogues set within or near the colonies they have researched. Encourage the students to use the dialogues as a way to tell about the colonists' everyday life, goals in life, and their hopes for the future of the colony. The dialogues may be read as a script to the class, or dramatized.

Students will record their dialogues in their History Journals selecting from among the following or other examples:

• a non-Puritan living in a Puritan settlement/a Puritan living in the same settlement

• a farmer/a craftsman living in a town

• farmer's wife/craftsman's wife

• a woman or girl who wants to learn to read and write/a person who thinks women and girls should not learn these skills

• a priest at a Spanish mission settlement/a Native American at the same settlement

- Native American who tries to continue his or her traditional ways of life/ colonist who moves onto the Native American's homeland
- Native American who tries to live peacefully near the colonists/colonist who respects the Native American
- Scotch-Irish frontiersman/German farmer
- an accused witch/the accuser
- indentured servant the age of the student/master or mistress of the servant
- African-American slave in North/a Quaker
- African-American slave in South/master or mistress of the slave

3. The Lives of Children, Then and Now

Have each group established in Activity 1 construct a Then and Now Chart to compare the lives of children living in their colony with children today. Compare the work, recreation, education, and homes of boys and girls in both time periods.

4. Self-Reliance, the Key to Survival and Advancement

After completing the Then and Now Charts, have the students, writing as colonists, record in their History Journals some aspect of colonial life in

THEN								
	Work		Recreation		Education		Homes	
	M	F	M	F	M	F	M	F
Colony: Date:								

NOW								
	Work		Recreation		Education		Homes	
	M	F	M	F	M	F	M	F
Place: Date:								

CHART 11 Colonial Children and Children of Today

which they were self-reliant and solved their own problems. Because colonial men, women, boys, and girls had different roles that sometimes overlapped, these accounts should be gender-specific. Take time to share these experiences within each group.

BOOK LIST

Note: Starred (*) books are reviewed in a previous section or unit of this book.

Altman, Susan. *Extraordinary Black Americans: From Colonial to Contemporary Times.* Childrens Press, 1989. 240p. (4-8) Biog.

This reference work provides brief biographies of over 80 African Americans who have played major roles in defining and shaping American beliefs, traditions, and customs. Most of these individuals, including a fair number of women, showed determination and courage as they struggled against racial and economic odds to advance in society. The biographies run two to four pages in length and include a portrait of the person along with highlights of their contributions. The book is arranged in chronological order and includes a brief bibliography and index.

Avi. *Night Journeys.* Pantheon Books, 1979. 143p. (4-6) Fic.

The year is 1767 and 12-year-old orphan Peter York is taken in by a stern Quaker justice of the peace named Mr. Shinn. Usually at odds with Mr. Shinn, Peter defies him when a local group of men seek Mr. Shinn's aid in catching two runaway bondsmen. Peter discovers one of the runaways—a girl not much older than himself—and he eventually helps in the successful escape of the girl and her 10-year-old companion. As Peter faces some difficult moral decisions, he comes to a better understanding of Mr. Shinn. The action-packed story takes place in a matter of days and would make an excellent read-aloud choice.

Bulla, Clyde Robert. *A Lion to Guard Us.* Ill. by Michele Chessare. Crowell, 1981. 117p. (4-6) Fic.

Ten-year-old Amanda Freebold and her younger brother and sister, who live in London in 1609, are at a loss when their mother dies. Their father left for Jamestown, Virginia, three years earlier, and with the help of a kindly doctor, the three children secure passage for America. After a difficult journey across the Atlantic, the travelers are shipwrecked on one of the Bermuda Islands where they remain for nine months. All the while, Amanda cares for her siblings. In the spring of 1610, the children are reunited with their ailing father. Based on the chronicles of the British ship, *Sea Adventure,* this story depicts the type of courage and determination that helped settle North America. This is a good read-aloud choice for younger children.

Clapp, Patricia. *Constance: A Story of Early Plymouth*. Puffin Books, 1986. 255p. (6-8) Fic.

Fifteen-year-old Constance Hopkins is very unhappy about her family's move to the New World in 1620 on the *Mayflower*. Told in journal format through Constance's eyes, this is the story of the Pilgrims' first six years at Plymouth—the devastation of the sickness during the first winter that killed half of the settlers, learning to interact with the Indians, the challenges of farming, and simply trying to survive against great odds. Based on extensive research, this novel is a realistic and interesting portrait of the early days of the Plymouth settlement in Massachusetts.

Dolan, Sean. *Junípero Serra*. Chelsea House, 1991. 111p. (6-8) Biog.

A Franciscan priest living in Majorca, Spain, Father Serra followed the missionary call and left his homeland in 1749 to serve in the New World. This well-researched biography tells of Serra's childhood, early priesthood, mission training in Mexico City, and how Serra chose to convert the Native peoples through persuasion and compassion rather than force. When the Jesuits were suddenly expelled from Spanish territory in 1767, Serra was assigned to take responsibility for their missions in the land known as California. It is here that Serra made his greatest contribution, founding nine missions in a 15-year-period, including San Diego and San Francisco, before dying in 1784. Many contemporary paintings and drawings accompany the text, and the author includes a chronology, bibliography, and index. This volume is part of the "Hispanics of Achievement" Series. For younger readers, a better choice is Florence Meiman White's *The Story of Junípero Serra: Brave Adventurer* (Dell Yearling, 1987).

Fleischman, Paul. *Saturnalia*. Harper & Row, 1990. 113p. (6-8) Fic.

William is a Narraganset Indian who was captured by whites in 1675. As the story opens in Boston in 1681, 14-year-old William serves as a printer's apprentice to Mr. Currie. Intelligent and well-read, William thinks that Jehovah is heartless and that Christians are brutal because they killed most of the members of his tribe. Quite by accident one night, William discovers his great-uncle and cousin who are apprenticed to a cruel master. Great-Uncle helps William recall his Narraganset heritage, and in the end, William must choose whether to stay in Boston with the Curries who love him or return to his tribe. The story contains some humor and would be a good read-aloud selection.

Fritz, Jean. *The Double Life of Pocahontas*. Ill. by Ed Young. Putnam, 1983. 96p. (4-8) Biog.

The myth of Pocahontas saving John Smith is put into the context of the historical setting and relationships between the English of Jamestown and the Native Americans. Pocahontas and her people were treated badly by the English who expected them to bring food, remain peaceful, and convert to Christianity. Pocahontas is kidnapped by the British and eventually marries John Smith, who is portrayed as an opportunist. During her marriage and subsequent travel to England, Pocahontas is caught between her heritage as an Indian and the English view that her people are barbarous savages who must live like Englishmen. Includes notes, bibliography, and index.

Green, Rayna. *Women in American Indian Society.* Chelsea House, 1992. 111p. (6-8) Non-fic.

Beginning with traditional roles prior to the arrival of the Europeans, the author, a Cherokee, presents an overview of women in Native American society through the present day. Interestingly, the economic, political, and social status of Native women declined significantly after the time of Columbus, since the white men refused to negotiate with Indian women and treated them with disrespect. Green then relates the heartbreak of the Removal Era, how reservation life changed family dynamics, and how women strove to preserve their cultural heritage. The book concludes with the reform movement from its beginnings through modern times, including the rise of Native American women's advocacy groups. Fascinating archival photographs, artwork, and writings by Indian women accompany the well-written text. Includes a bibliography, glossary, and index.

Hudson, Jan. *Dawn Rider.* Philomel, 1990. 158p. (6-8) Fic.

Set in the northern Great Plains in the 1730s, this story focuses on 16-year-old Kit Fox, a Blackfoot Indian girl, as she comes of age. Kit is an unusual girl; she longs to be a "manly hearted woman"—a woman with a man's power and skills as well as a woman's. A great horse lover, Kit rebels against her tribe's ban on women riders and, by so doing, manages to save her people during a time of crisis. This is a well-written story of a young woman's everyday life filled with plans for a great buffalo run, an older sister's wedding, and skirmishes with the Snake Tribe, the traditional enemy of Kit's people. Includes a bibliography.

Ilgenfritz, Elizabeth. *Anne Hutchinson.* Chelsea House, 1990. 111p. (6-8) Biog.

Part of the "American Women of Achievement" Series, this is the story of one of colonial America's most well-known and unusual women. Well-educated and quite outspoken, Anne Hutchinson, in one of the earliest tests of religious liberty, stood trial in Boston in 1637 and was subsequently excommunicated and banned from the Massachusetts Bay Colony. She eventually helped found the colony of Rhode Island and this well-written and thoroughly researched book narrates her struggles as a religious reformer. Includes numerous black-and-white illustrations, chronology, bibliography, and index.

Katz, William Loren. *Breaking the Chains: African-American Slave Resistance.* Atheneum, 1990. 194p. (6-8) Non-fic.

The myth of content and docile slaves is diligently demolished in this work which begins with the accounts of rebellion on slave ships, discusses slave life and the daily struggle for existence, follows the course of rebellion and flight, and concludes with African-American soldiers in the Civil War. The author quotes extensively from the writings of blacks, both slave and free, and historical photographs and other illustrations of the period enhance the moving text. The author brings many heroes to light, ordinary men and women, who strove to gain liberty, knowledge, and self-respect. Includes a bibliography and index.

Luhrmann, Winifred Bruce. *Only Brave Tomorrows.* Houghton Mifflin, 1989. 190p. (6-8) Fic.

In 1675, 15-year-old Faith Ralston's life is disrupted when her father decides to move from their native England to Springfield, Massachusetts. Before they even reach the small village, a band of Wampanoag Indians raid the settlement where the Ralstons are staying, killing some people and taking others prisoner. King Philip's War is raging in the colonies, and Faith, who survives the attack, must come to grips with a world turned upside down. Not only must she deal with guilt at having survived, but her life takes an unexpected turn when she is forced to marry Zachary Stedman, the local scout who brought her out of the wilderness. An author's note in this realistic and fast-paced story explains the background for King Philip's War.

McGovern, Ann. *If You Lived in Colonial Times.* Ill. by Brinton Turkle. Scholastic, 1964. 79p. (4-6) Non-fic.

McGovern, Ann. *If You Sailed on the Mayflower.* Ill. by J.B. Handelsman. Scholastic, 1969. 80p. (4-6) Non-fic.

Meltzer, Milton. *The Black Americans: A History in Their Own Words, 1619-1983.* Crowell, 1984. 306p. (6-8) Non-fic.

This book presents original accounts of the experiences of black people in the United States and how they came to shape the course of American history. The participants speak through diaries, letters, journals, speeches, resolutions, autobiographies, newspapers, pamphlets, and legal testimonies. An introductory note identifies each speaker and sets the historical stage for the individual's testimony. This excellent compilation of primary resources also includes photographs, facsimile reproductions, and an index.

Penner, Lucille Recht. *Eating the Plates: A Pilgrim Book of Food and Manners.* Macmillan, 1991. 117p. (4-6) Non-fic.

Rappaport, Doreen, ed. *American Women: Their Lives in Their Words: A Documentary History.* Crowell, 1990. 318p. (6-8) Non-fic.

This book presents firsthand accounts of the lives of American women, beginning with the settlers in the 1600s and Native American women, to women in the present day. The unique contributions of these women, including many minority women, to American society are detailed, along with the roles of women during the various periods in American history. Famous women, such as Abigail Adams and Sojourner Truth, along with unknown people, such as Mary Bailey and Helena Brylska, talk about their daily lives, responsibilities, and emotions. The author makes excellent use of primary documents, such as diaries, letters, newspaper articles, and other writings, and the archival photographs add richness to the text. Includes a bibliography and index.

Reische, Diana. *Founding the American Colonies.* Franklin Watts, 1989. 64p. (4-6) Non-fic.

Rinaldi, Ann. *A Break with Charity: A Story About the Salem Witch Trials.* Harcourt Brace Jovanovich, 1992. 257p. (6-8) Fic.

This superb story about the Salem witch hunts of 1692 is told from the viewpoint of 14-year-old Susanna English, the daughter of a rich merchant. A group of girls has begun meeting with Tituba, the slave of the Rev. Parris, and Susanna longs to be included in their circle. After speaking with Tituba, Susanna discovers what the girls are about and she watches in horror as the witch frenzy escalates. Susanna is scared to speak out, but when her own parents are arrested on suspicion of witchcraft, Susanna finds the courage. The author does an excellent job of presenting the sequence of events, showing how something that started out as mischief got out of control. An author's note explains the historical background of the book.

*Sewall, Marcia. *People of the Breaking Day.* Atheneum, 1990. (4-6) Non-fic. (Part 1, Unit 5)

*Sewall, Marcia. *The Pilgrims of Plimoth.* Atheneum, 1986. (4-6) Non-fic. (Part 1, Unit 5)

Speare, Elizabeth George. *The Sign of the Beaver.* Houghton Mifflin, 1983. 135p. (4-6) Fic.

In the spring of 1769, 14-year-old Matt Hallowell's father leaves Matt alone on their Maine homestead while he goes to Quincy, Massachusetts, to bring his wife and other children to their new home. Matt has his chores to keep him busy while Father is gone, and after a mishap with a beehive, Matt is rescued by an elderly Indian and his grandson, Attean. The two boys eventually become fast friends and Attean teaches Matt many hunting and survival techniques. With his father months overdue, Matt steals himself to winter alone, and the book presents a realistic portrayal of homesteading on the frontier. This is a good read-aloud choice.

Speare, Elizabeth George. *The Witch of Blackbird Pond.* Houghton Mifflin, 1958. 249p. (4-8) Fic.

Tunis, Edward. *Colonial Living.* World Pub. Co., 1957. 155p. (4-8) Non-fic.

Wisler, G. Clifton. *This New Land.* Walker, 1987. 124p. (4-6) Fic.

When the *Mayflower* sets sail in 1620, 12-year-old Richard Woodley and his family are aboard, searching for a better life in the New World. This is the story of the 100 or so Pilgrims who had planned to settle in Virginia, but who were blown off course and instead landed in Massachusetts. The difficulties and excitement of the crossing are related through the eyes of an adolescent, as are the hard times experienced by the colonists during their first year in America where one-half of their number died. The strength and perseverance of the settlers comes through strongly in this well-written novel.

UNIT
four

Revolution and the Constitutional Era

OBJECTIVES

1. Students will read or listen to novels about adolescents and others involved in the Revolutionary War after reviewing the examples of the colonists' self-reliance (see Unit 3, Activity 4) and their diminishing self-governance under British rule, such as the Sugar Act of 1764 and the Stamp Act of 1765.

2. After reading the novels and textbooks, and using references, such as *The American Revolutionaries: A History in Their Own Words, 1750-1800*, students will record the viewpoints and goals of the Patriots and Tories in their History Journals.

3. After reviewing the roles of African Americans and white women in the colonies, students will use reference books to identify and then record on the time line and a bulletin board display the involvement of women and African Americans in the Revolutionary War.

4. Based on the students' reading of textbooks, reference sources, and novels, the events of the Revolutionary War will be recorded on the Outline Map.

5. In cooperative-learning groups, students will research the leaders of the Revolutionary War who will then be portrayed through interviews. One student will assume the role of the leader, while the others in the group will be the panel of journalists interviewing the leader.

6. Students will construct "Wanted Posters" for the leaders of the Revolution, for the leaders of the Loyalists, and for the leaders of the British forces. The posters will summarize information about the leader's role or activities.

7. The problems of the new nation will be identified by the students based on their reading of *We the People: The Way We Were, 1783-1793* and other reference books.

8. In small cooperative-learning groups, the students will construct a classroom constitution using the organization of the U. S Constitution as a model.

9. After ratifying the classroom constitution, and discussing the U.S. Bill of Rights, students will write a classroom Bill of Rights using *The Bill of Rights: How We Got It and What It Means* as a reference and the recommendations of all of the students in the class.
10. Students will construct a display of newspaper and magazine articles that illustrate the application of the U.S. Constitution today.

LEARNING ACTIVITIES

1. Teen-aged Revolutionaries

Begin this unit by reading some of the excellent historical novels written for children in grades 4 through 8. If multiple copies of books can be arranged, *Johnny Tremain* and *War Comes to Willy Freeman* are especially recommended for reading by all the students, or as read alouds. While these and other books on the book list are rich in historical information, the students will need additional sources, such as history or social studies textbooks, in order to understand this era of American history. Have the students record in their History Journals a brief summary of the books they have read or listened to as part of this unit.

2. Patriot or Loyalist? Can Anyone Be Neutral in a Revolution?

Two novels, *My Brother Sam Is Dead* and *Sarah Bishop*, portray families split by their allegiances. These books may be read aloud or by students. The teacher or students who have read these books can summarize the plots emphasizing the viewpoints and goals of the Patriots and Tories. Writing as one of the book characters, students will write a paragraph about their reasons for being either a Patriot or a Tory. Some students may wish to write as a neutral and cite the problems they have because they are neutral.

3. Mapping the War

As the students read about events in the Revolutionary War, record places, dates, and encounters on the Outline Map. Mark the British victories in red to symbolize the Redcoats. What color would symbolize the Patriots?

4. Little-Known Stars of the Revolution: *Black Heroes* and *Patriots in Petticoats*

Divide the class into two groups in an arbitrary way, such as by counting off. Each group should consist of boys and girls, and, as much as possible, be racially diverse. All students in group one will research African Americans in the Revolutionary War, and students in group two will research the women in the war. Two excellent resources will aid this project: *Black Heroes of the American Revolution* and *Patriots in Petticoats*. Use these sources to obtain a list of black heroes and women in order to assign a specific person to each student. If these are the only references available, arrange to have the books circulate among the students.

Give each student a large paper star, about 8" by 8", on which they will write the person's name and a few sentences about their involvement in the war. Put all the stars on a bulletin board titled, "These People Helped to Make Our Nation." Also record these people on the time line.

5. Press Conferences with Leaders on Both Sides of the Revolution

Each small cooperative-learning group will select a leader from this period of history. After they have gathered information about the leader, they will present their information to the class in the form of an interview with one student assuming the role of the leader, and the others as journalists who ask questions. The questions asked in interview should be planned by members of the committee who work cooperatively to assemble the information so that the interviewee is not solely responsible for the information.

After the interview, members of the class could ask questions of the journalists or the leader. The teacher may wish to have the class take notes during the interviews.

6. "Wanted" Posters

Following the presentation of the interviews, each group will make a "wanted" poster about their leader. On the poster they will summarize the information about this leader's role and the activities that make the leader "wanted" by the other side.

7. Problems of the New Nation

The teacher will read aloud portions of *We the People: The Way We Were, 1783-1793*, and students will read the appropriate selections from their textbooks in order to identify the problems facing the new nation. As a class, list problems for the new nation under the headings of "Land," "Money," and "Trade." How could these problems be solved by one nation or by 13 individual colonies?

8. "In Order to Form a More Perfect Union. . . "

The book, *1787* by Joan Anderson, depicts the writing of the Constitution. It will help the students understand the remarkable task accomplished in that year, and will help them prepare for the task of writing their Classroom Constitution. Start with reading the U.S. Constitution and defining the purpose of each section:

Preamble: The introduction telling the purpose of the Constitution.

Article 1: Describes the legislative branch of government, telling what the Congress can and cannot do.

Article 2: Describes the executive branch of government telling what the president is expected to do.

Article 3: Describes the judicial branch and tells how the courts will be organized and what kinds of cases they will judge.

Article 4: Describes the rights and privileges of the states.

Articles 5, 6, and 7: Tell how the Constitution as the supreme law of the land can be changed, amended, and ratified.

Amendments: Changes and additions to the Constitution, including the first 10 amendments called the **Bill of Rights.**

Writing the Classroom Constitution: Divide the class into six groups: (1) Preamble; (2) Article 1, Legislative Branch; (3) Article 2, Executive Branch; (4) Article 3, Judicial Branch; (5) Article 4, diverging from the U.S. Constitution, will describe the rights and privileges of the classroom and the school, such as the school rules and regulations; (6) Articles 5, 6, and 7 will describe how the Classroom Constitution can be changed, amended, and ratified by the class. Each group will write its section of the Constitution, then present it to the class for constructive discussion and possible rewriting. The groups writing Article 3, Judicial, and Article 4, Rights of the School, will need the guidance of the teacher.

To implement the Classroom Constitution, elections will need to be held. Depending on the Articles of the Classroom Constitution, the various elected posts may be for terms of one month, or longer. The teacher may choose to complete the next activity, the Bill of Rights, before the election so that the teacher is the leader of the discussion of students' rights.

9. The Bill of Rights for Students

Following the ratification of the Classroom Constitution, and discussion of the U.S. Bill of Rights, each student will write down five rights that should be guaranteed to all students in the classroom. *The Bill of Rights: How We Got It and What It Means* will be a valuable resource. In their constitution-writing groups, have the students combine their individual lists of rights. Select five to ten of the most important rights from that composite list. Try to have the groups achieve a consensus of opinion, but accept voting as another means to select the rights that are most important to the students.

The teacher will collect these selected lists of rights, then duplicate the lists and give each student a copy. With the composite list in the hands of each student, and the teacher using the list as a transparency on the overhead projector, find and eliminate the duplications. Next find those statements that could be consolidated. Then begin the task of selecting the most important statements. This process of selection should be carefully pursued while also refining the statements. The final list may contain more than 10 rights in order to adequately represent the members of the class.

Make a poster of these rights to hang in the classroom. Have a copy for every student. Are these rights supported by the classroom rules? If not, in what ways does the Classroom Constitution provide for change?

10. The Constitution Today

While completing activities 8 and 9, ask students to bring in articles from newspapers and magazines in which they see the present-day application of the Constitution. In an election at any level of government, we see the application of Article 1. As we read about the president and his activities, we see Article 2 in action. Display the clippings under the headings from the Constitution. Have a special place for present-day illustrations of the Bill of Rights in action.

BOOK LIST

Note: Starred (*) books are reviewed in a previous section or unit of this book.

Anderson, Joan. *1787.* Ill. by Alexander Farquharson. Harcourt Brace Jovanovich, 1987. 200p. (6-8) Fic.

Jared Mifflin, a young Philadelphian college man, is given the opportunity of a lifetime during the summer of 1787 to serve as James Madison's aide during the Constitutional Convention. In this skillful blending of fact and fiction, readers will view the events of this fateful summer through the eyes of the participants. Men, such as Madison and Franklin, are portrayed as *real* people. Jared must contend with obnoxious delegates, irate merchants, and family concerns in this well-written story. Includes a text of the Constitution and a bibliography.

Avi. *The Fighting Ground.* Lippincott, 1984. 157p. (4-8) Fic.

This entire, fast-paced story takes place over a 24-hour period. Thirteen-year-old Jonathan is very patriotic and would love nothing better than to participate in a battle. On the morning of April 3, 1778, Jonathan's life changes forever. Following the alarm by the town bell, Jonathan, much against his father's wishes, becomes embroiled in a skirmish with the British, viewing first-hand the horror of war. Captured by three Hessian soldiers following the clash, Jonathan manages to escape and grapples with his conscience as the story closes.

Clyne, Patricia Edwards. *Patriots in Petticoats*. Ill. by Richard Leberson. Dodd, Mead, 1976. 144p. (4-8) Biog.

The author tells of 23 women—white, black, and Native American—who exhibited their bravery during the Revolutionary War and the War of 1812. The women fired cannons, carried gun powder to besieged forts, aided the wounded, and operated as spies. Each episode, well-suited for reading aloud, is interestingly written and exciting. Following each narrative is a detailed description of the places and artifacts related to the events that can be seen today.

Collier, James L., and Christopher Collier. *My Brother Sam Is Dead*. Four Winds Press, 1974. 216p. (6-8) Fic.

This is the story of 12-year-old Tim Meeker and how the American Revolution disrupted his family in Redding, Connecticut, and forever changed their lives. As the story opens in 1775, 16-year-old Sam Meeker has just joined the rebel army, despite the fact that his family is loyal to the king. Tim is confused by the murky facets of the Revolution, and even more so after his father is abducted by roving brigands and dies on a British prison ship. Both the patriot and rebel sides are presented in this story based on events that actually took place in Connecticut during the war. This powerful book represents historical fiction at its best.

Collier, James L., and Christopher Collier. *War Comes to Willy Freeman*. Delacorte, 1983. 178p. (4-8) Fic.

In this novel, which is part of a trilogy, a free, 13-year-old Connecticut black girl named Willy Freeman is caught up in the horror of the Revolution and the danger of being returned to slavery when her Patriot father is killed in battle and her mother disappears. Disguised as a boy, Willy makes her way to New York City in search of her mother. Willy ends up working at an inn owned by Sam Fraunces, a black man. Based on a true story, this book is a realistic depiction of how war can disrupt a family and the problems experienced by blacks, free or slave, during this era. The two other titles in the "Arabus Family Saga," published by Delacorte Press, are *Jump Ship to Freedom* (1981) and *Who Is Carrie?* (1984).

Davis, Burke. *Black Heroes of the American Revolution*. Harcourt Brace Jovanovich, 1976. 82p. (4-8) Biog.

DeFord, Deborah H., and Harry S. Stout. *An Enemy Among Them.* Houghton Mifflin, 1987. 203p. (6-8) Fic.

This story, which begins in 1776 with the arrival in America of a young Hessian soldier named Christian Molitor, is told from the viewpoint of Margaret Volpert, a young woman of German descent who lives with her family in Reading, Pennsylvania. Christian's life becomes interwoven with that of the Volpert family when he wounds John Volpert during the Battle of Brandywine Creek in 1777. Margaret encounters Christian as a prisoner of war in a hospital, and he eventually comes to live out his captivity with the Volperts, helping John regain his health. By the story's end, Christian is forced to make a momentous decision about this new country and the people he has grown to love. A similar novel, which takes place in the pacifist Moravian community of Bethlehem, Pennsylvania, is Ruth Nulton Moore's *Distant Thunder* (Herald Press, 1991).

DePauw, Linda Grant. *Founding Mothers: Women in America in the Revolutionary Era.* Ill. by Michael McCurdy. Houghton Mifflin, 1975. 228p. (6-8) Non-fic.

The author explores a topic often overlooked in the history books—the role of women during the American Revolution. Sex stereotyping and legal restrictions were not as restrictive in the eighteenth century as they later became in the nineteenth century, and women participated in the political, economic, social, and military activities of the day. The author includes chapters on women's work inside and outside of the home, women's rights, Native American and black women, and rebel and Tory women. The author quotes from primary sources in the narrative and includes a bibliography and index.

Faber, Doris, and Harold Faber. *We the People: The Story of the United States Constitution Since 1787.* Scribner's, 1987. 244p. (6-8) Non-fic.

Finlayson, Ann. *Rebecca's War.* Ill. by Sherry Streeter. Warne, 1972. 280p. (6-8) Fic.

In Philadelphia in 1778, Rebecca Ransome, at the age of 14, must shoulder some heavy responsibilities when she is left alone to run her family's household, including the care of two younger siblings. Life becomes very complicated when Rebecca is forced to billet an offensive English captain who delights in being ornery. Rebecca's worries increase when she is inadvertently embroiled in the war by having to hide gold bullion and some letters of great importance, and when she has to nurse a British captain who is convalescing from a near-mortal wound. This entertaining, well-written story about a strong-willed girl who must assume new obligations as a result of the war presents a different side of the Revolution—occupation by the enemy.

Forbes, Esther. *Johnny Tremain.* Houghton Mifflin, 1943. 256p. (4-8) Fic.

Fritz, Jean. *Early Thunder.* Ill. by Lynd Ward. Coward, McCann, 1967. 256p. (6-8) Fic.

A dedicated Tory living in Salem, Massachusetts, 14-year-old Daniel West is disturbed by the increasing tension between the Tories and patriots in his community in 1775. Drawn into local events, Daniel finds himself increasingly turning away from his Tory father, a recent widower who has just remarried, and turning more toward support of his native land. Daniel struggles long and hard with his beliefs in this well-told, coming-of-age novel about a boy with some difficult decisions to make. Includes illustrations and an author's note at the end of the novel.

Fritz, Jean. *The Great Little Madison.* Putnam, 1989. 159p. (4-8) Biog.

*Fritz, Jean. *Shhh! We're Writing the Constitution.* Putnam, 1987. (4-6) Nonfic. (Part 1, Unit 6)

Fritz, Jean. *What's the Big Idea, Ben Franklin?* Ill. by Margot Tomes. Scholastic, 1976. 48p. (4-6) Biog.

*Gauch, Patricia Lee. *This Time, Tempe Wick?* Ill. by Margot Tomes. Coward, McCann, 1974. (4-6) Fic.(Part 1, Unit 6)

Giblin, James C. *Fireworks, Picnics, and Flags: The Story of the Fourth of July Symbols.* Ill. by Ursula Arndt. Clarion, 1983. 90p. (4-6) Non-fic.

Graham-Barber, Lynda. *Doodle Dandy! The Complete Book of Independence Day Words.* Ill. by Betsy Lewin. Bradbury, 1992. 122p. (4-6) Non-fic.

Gross, Ruth Belov. *If You Grew Up with George Washington.* Ill. by Jack Kent. Scholastic, 1981. 63p. (4-6) Non-fic.

Hilton, Suzanne. *We the People: The Way We Were, 1783-1793.* Westminster Press, 1981. 203p. (4-8) Non-fic.

In this book, the author presents an interesting perspective on what it was like to be a young person during the Constitutional period. After America won its independence from Great Britain, the new nation had no capital city, no real borders, no money of its own, no navy, and only a meager volunteer army. Children will learn about how the new citizens were counted, how they obtained legal rights, and about the importance placed on schooling. Includes a bibliography and index.

McGovern, Ann. *The Secret Soldier: The Story of Deborah Sampson.* Ill. by Ann Grifalconi. Four Winds, 1975. 62p. (4-6) Biog.

In 1782, at the age of 21, Deborah Sampson disguised herself as a man and enlisted in the Continental Army as a foot soldier, where she remained for over a year until she was injured and her secret became known. Sampson's childhood is detailed as are her adventures in the army and what happened to her after the war. Based on real events, this exciting story will broaden children's thinking about Revolutionary heroes.

Meltzer, Milton, ed. *The American Revolutionaries: A History in Their Own Words, 1750-1800.* Crowell, 1987. 210p. (4-8) Non-fic.

In this nonfiction book, Meltzer attempts to help children understand the Revolution as a human experience—what did the new Americans feel, what did they hope for, what were their fears? By using excerpts from personal documents, such as diaries, letters, journals, memoirs, newspapers, songs, pamphlets, and speeches, Meltzer succeeds in bringing the events in the lives of ordinary Americans to life. Each chapter is prefaced by a brief statement that introduces the speaker and sets the stage for the writing. This excellent social history, illustrated with period pictures, includes a note on sources and an index.

Meltzer, Milton. *Benjamin Franklin: The New American.* Watts, 1988. 288p. (6-8) Biog.

Meltzer, Milton. *The Bill of Rights: How We Got It and What It Means.* Crowell, 1990. 179p. (6-8) Non-fic.

Meltzer, Milton. *Thomas Jefferson: The Revolutionary Aristocrat.* Watts, 1991. 255p. (6-8) Biog.

O'Dell, Scott. *Sarah Bishop.* Houghton Mifflin, 1980. 184p. (4-8) Fic.

Embittered by the deaths of her father and brother, who took opposite sides in the War for Independence, 15-year-old Sarah Bishop is accused of setting fire to the New York wharfs and so flees from the British. Through her solitary survival in the wilderness, she meets a few good people, an Indian couple, and a young Quaker man, who help restore her faith in humankind and her ability to trust others. This enthralling story of a strong, resourceful young woman would be a good read-aloud selection. An author's note explains the historical basis for the story.

Osborne, Mary Pope. *George Washington: Leader of a New Nation.* Dial, 1991. 117p. (4-6) Biog.

*Rappaport, Doreen, ed. *American Women: Their Lives in Their Words: A Documentary History.* Crowell, 1990. (6-8) Non-fic. (Part 2, Unit 3)

Reit, Seymour. *Guns for General Washington: A Story of the American Revolution.* Harcourt Brace Jovanovich, 1990. 98p. (4-8) Fic.

In the winter of 1775, fighting had ceased due to the weather, and young Will Knox was dissatisfied by the lack of action. However, his older brother, Colonel Henry Knox, was busily planning to move heavy cannons from Fort Ticonderoga to Boston to help General Washington. The suspense of this historical event is well-developed, as is the daily life of the Continental soldiers. The tactics of moving the guns will interest readers, as will Washington's strategy to prevent Howe's attack.

Rinaldi, Ann. *Time Enough for Drums.* Holiday, 1986. 249p. (6-8) Fic.

Nearly 16 years old, Jemima Emerson is the youngest child in a family of Patriots in Trenton, New Jersey, in 1775. Rather impulsive and unladylike, Jem is under the strict guidance of a young, but arrogant and demanding tutor named John Reid. As the story progresses over the years of the Revolutionary War, Jem comes to understand John's politics, which differ from her own. When her father is killed, she maturely assumes responsibility for the family store and home. An author's note gives additional background about the Revolution and a bibliography is appended.

Woodruff, Elvira. *George Washington's Socks.* Scholastic, 1991. 166p. (4-6) Fic.

Matt Carlton and several of his fifth-grade buddies, who are members of an adventure club, have just completed school reports on the American Revolution. When the four club members, along with Matt's seven-year-old sister, Katie, are suddenly transported back in time to December 1776, they find themselves crossing the Delaware River along with Washington and his troops. The children march with the barefoot army in the snowy weather, see new friends die, and encounter Hessian soldiers and Indians. The story is well done and readers will get a vivid sense of the reality of war and life during the Revolutionary era. This would be a good choice for reluctant readers.

Yates, Elizabeth. *Amos Fortune, Free Man.* Dutton, 1950. 181p. (4-8) Biog.

This story opens in 1725 in Africa when a group of At-mun-shi are attacked and taken as slaves. One of the abducted is 15-year-old At-mun, the prince, and he is taken to America where he is purchased by a Boston Quaker. The Quaker family welcomes At-mun, re-naming him Amos; it takes Amos 39 years to buy his freedom. This Newbery-award winning story presents the Revolutionary War years as seen through the life of a strong, intelligent man who is forced to forsake his African heritage, but who manages to retain his dignity, honor, and compassion.

THE NEW REPUBLIC

✻ ✻ ✻ ✻ ✻ ✻ ✻ ✻

INTRODUCTION TO UNITS 5 AND 6

Between 1800 and 1850, the nation's population tripled, and its territory expanded to the Pacific Ocean. The lives of Thomas Jefferson and James Madison connect the Revolution and Constitutional Era with the first three decades of the new Republic in the nineteenth century. Their lives encompassed the vision of the new nation and reflected its problems and dichotomies. Unit 5, "The New Republic," explores many factors that contributed to the growth of the nation. Concept webs, a major learning activity of this unit, outline and analyze the impact of the rise of industrialization, the changes in both modes and routes of transportation, the War of 1812, the expansion of territory, and the early Westward Movement. The expansion of the United States through purchases and wars can be shown through mapping activities. The History Journals will be used to record the exploration of the Louisiana Purchase and the students' understanding of Manifest Destiny. The use of the interlinking concept webs, time lines, and maps will be enhanced by the fiction and nonfiction books found in the Book List.

A sense of national identity and pride evolved and intensified during this period of rapid growth for the United States. Unit 6, "American Symbols, Literature, and Folk Tales," deals with aspects of this national identity.

Through comparisons of tales from diverse groups of Americans, students will become aware of the purposes of folk literature and the commonalities of human concerns. Students will read or listen to some of the authors and poets of this period, especially Henry Wadsworth Longfellow, John Greenleaf Whittier, and Washington Irving. For advanced students, Harriet Beecher Stowe's Uncle Tom's Cabin could be used to connect American literature to Unit 7: "Slavery, the Civil War, and Its Aftermath."

UNIT
five

The New Republic

OBJECTIVES

1. After reading about real people of this period, students will develop character folders in which they summarize the lives and accomplishments of these people.
2. In small cooperative-learning groups, students will develop large, detailed, interrelated concept webs showing the impact of the changes in the United States during the first half of the nineteenth century.
3. After identifying the Northwest Territory and its major rivers and natural features on the Outline Map, students will hypothesize about how settlers traveled to the Territory and how settling this area benefitted the United States.
4. After reading about the Louisiana Purchase, students will record the Purchase on the time line and on the Outline Map, including the major rivers, mountains, and other natural features included in the Purchase.
5. Students will write in their History Journals about a day as a member of the Lewis and Clark Expedition, as a mountain man, or as a Native American who encounters the white explorers or trappers and their groups.
6. After reading about the War of 1812, the students will complete a Cause-and-Effect Chart about that conflict, and record the war on the time line. Some students may wish to focus their Cause-and-Effect Chart on the influence of the technology of ship building on the War of 1812.
7. Cooperative-learning groups will construct annotated time lines showing how the United States acquired Texas, California, and Oregon.
8. After students identify the Native Americans and other people who occupied Texas, California, and Oregon, they will write in their History Journals either supporting or rejecting the idea of Manifest Destiny.

LEARNING ACTIVITIES

1. Character Folders

Students will construct character folders after reading or listening to books from the book list about illustrative people, such as Thomas Jefferson (*Thomas*

Jefferson: The Revolutionary Aristocrat), James Madison (*The Great Little Madison)*, Commodore Perry, Meriwether Lewis, William Clark, Sacagawea, Jim Bowie, Daniel Boone, Dolly Madison, the women mill workers, and others. Fold a piece of 9" x 12" construction paper in half to make a folder 4 1/2" by 6". On page one, students will record the person's name, birth date, home residence, death date, and a short phrase or description of the person, such as might be found on a monument dedicated to this individual. Students may also wish to include their own drawing of the person, or a photocopied picture. On page two, the students will list this man or woman's most important contributions to the new nation. Page three will include additional information about his or her life, and one or two questions the student would like to ask him or her. On page four, the students will try to answer the questions as they think this individual would have replied. Take time to share the questions and answers with the class.

2. Connections and Concept Webs

The period 1800 to 1850 includes many significant changes in the United States. Working in cooperative-learning groups, with the whole class, or as individuals, students will construct concept webs that show the impact of such changes as those listed below. Students will need information from their textbooks and from historical literature in order to construct concept webs. Encourage the students to brainstorm, use textbooks, books from the book list, and other sources of information so that accurate data will be presented in the concept webs. The book list indicates that these changes are well-supported by the selected children's literature.

Transportation Routes and Machines. See *Timmy O'Dowd and the Big Ditch: A Story of the Glory Days on the Erie Canal*; *Honey Girl* (on river travel; see Part 2, Unit 9); and *Commodore Perry in the Land of the Shogun* (improved ocean-going ships expand trade to Japan).

Northwest Territory. See *Brothers of the Heart: A Story of the Old Northwest, 1837-1838*; *Weasel*; *Daniel Boone*; *Next Spring, An Oriole*; and *Frontier Living*.

Louisiana Purchase. See *The Incredible Journey of Lewis and Clark*; *Bold Journey: West with Lewis and Clark*; *Hugh Glass: Mountain Man*; *Streams to the River, River to the Sea: A Novel of Sacagawea*; and *Thomas Jefferson: The Revolutionary Aristocrat*.

War of 1812. See *A Wish on Capitol Hill*; *The Great Little Madison*; and *1812: The War Nobody Won*.

American Contact with Spaniards and Mexicans. See *Last Stand at the Alamo; Carlota* (California, 1846); and *Piper's Ferry* (Texas war for independence, 1830s).

The Changes Produced by Industrialization. See *A Gathering of Days: A New England Girl's Journal, 1830-32* (everyday life in New England, 1830s); *A Spirit to Ride the Whirlwind; Lyddie;* and *Hannah's Fancy Notions,* (textile mills of Lowell, Massachusetts).

Concept webs can be drawn like spider webs with the main topic in the center, then branching out in all directions. See the concept web on flatboats shown below in Chart 12 for an example.

When the groups have completed the concept webs, each group will present their web to the class while the other groups search their own work for connections to the information being presented. Connect the interlinking concepts among the webs with bright-colored yarn. For example, the concept web about the Northwest Territory will be connected to the web about flatboats, as well as to webs featuring the Louisiana Purchase, the War of 1812, and other topics.

3. The Northwest Territory Becomes Part of the United States

Students will record the Northwest Territory on the Outline Map and include the major rivers and natural features. After completing the map,

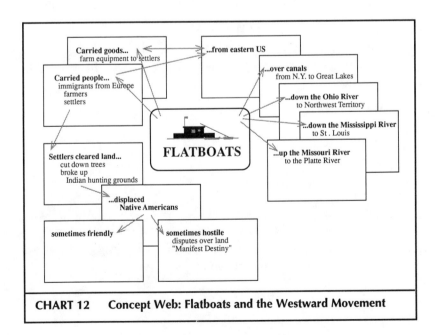

CHART 12   Concept Web: Flatboats and the Westward Movement

students will hypothesize how settlers traveled to the Territory. Refer to the concept webs from the previous activity for information about routes to the Northwest Territory.

4. Ads for the Northwest Territory

After determining the climate and natural features of the Northwest Territory from the maps and other sources, have students design advertisements that encourage people to become settlers in the Northwest Territory. Ads should include the benefits of the land to the settlers, and also tell how settling this territory would benefit the United States.

5. Exploring the Louisiana Purchase: A Day in the Life of. . .

Students will record the Louisiana Purchase on the Outline Map and the time line. After reading about the Louisiana Purchase and the explorers, trappers, and Indians in the area, students will write in their History Journals about a day as a member of the Lewis and Clark expedition, as a mountain man or trapper, or as a Native American who encounters the white explorers or trappers or their groups. Students should try to include descriptions of the terrain as well as the encounters between peoples. See Russell Freedman's *An Indian Winter* for a first-hand account of the Native Americans of the Plains in the 1830s.

6. The War of 1812

After reading about the events of the War 1812, students will record the War of 1812 on the time line. A Cause-and-Effect Chart for the war will be constructed as a whole class activity.

The War of 1812

Who:

When:

Problems:

Main Events:

Resolution of Problem:

When the chart is completed, challenge students to identify how this war helped to established national identity and pride.

Some students may wish to construct a Cause-and-Effect Chart showing the influence of developing ship building technology on the War of 1812, and on trade with other countries.

7. How the United States Acquired Texas, California, and Oregon

As a whole class activity based on reading history and social studies textbooks and selected books from the book list, students will construct annotated time lines about the acquisition of the territories of Texas, California, and Oregon. Annotated time lines will include illustrations, sentences, and phrases telling about each item or event listed on the time line. The illustrations may be photocopied or hand drawn, and the sentences and phrases may be quoted from various sources. The means of acquiring Texas and California will contrast sharply with that of Oregon, and will emphasize the United States as the aggressor in the southwest, and as a compromiser in the northwest. See Harold Faber's *From Sea to Sea: The Growth of the United States* for information on and anecdotal accounts of these acquisitions.

8. "Manifest Destiny"

Based on the annotated time lines developed in Activity 7, students will identify the Native Americans and other people living in Texas, California, and Oregon. Students will then write in their History Journals either supporting or rejecting the idea that the development of the United States in the West by American settlers justified removing Indians from their homes. In other words, they will be responding to the concept of Manifest Destiny.

In pairs, have the students review their journal entries on this topic, and together determine which of their statements are fact and which are opinion. Taking time to share the students' views of Manifest Destiny in this manner will encourage them to support their ideas and beliefs with evidence.

BOOK LIST

Note: Starred (*) books are reviewed in a previous section or unit of this book.

Bealer, Alex W. *Only the Names Remain: The Cherokees and the Trail of Tears.* Ill. by William Sauts Bock. Little, Brown, 1972. 88p. (4-6) Non-fic.

This is a poignant and well-told story of the Cherokee nation—a Native American tribe that lived in the mountains of northern Georgia for hundreds of years before the Spanish came in the 1540s, and the French and

English a hundred years later. The Cherokees fought the white men until after the American Revolution when they decided to adopt some of the white men's ways, including education, farming, and a Cherokee alphabet written down by Sequoyah. Despite a constitution and peace treaties with the American government, peace was denied, and in 1837, the Cherokee were betrayed under the leadership of Andrew Jackson. The story of the forced march to Arkansas on the "Trail of Tears" is sensitively told.

Berry, James. *Ajeemah and His Son.* Willa Perlman Books, 1991. 83p. (4-8) Fic.

In 1807, while Ajeemah and his son, Atu, are traveling to a neighboring village in their home country of Ghana to pay the bride-price for Atu's intended, they are ambushed and sold to white slavers. After a tortuous six-week sea voyage, the two men land in Jamaica, are sold to different masters, and never see each other again. The story, told from Ajeemah's viewpoint, is vivid in its representation of the anger, shame, pain, and horror of innocent people who were snatched from their families—people who felt they had done nothing wrong to deserve bondage. Although the setting is Jamaica, the story is universal for Africans who were brought as slaves to the Americas. This is a poignant, well-told tale.

Blos, Joan W. *Brothers of the Heart: A Story of the Old Northwest, 1837-1838.* Scribner's, 1985. 162p. (6-8) Fic.

Fourteen-year-old Shem Perkins, lame since birth, moves with his family from Ohio to the new town of Millfield, Michigan, in 1837. Following a misunderstanding with his father, Shem leaves his family, going to Detroit, where he finds work. Shem joins a trading party exploring the wilds of northern Michigan, becomes separated from his group, and spends the winter with an aged Indian healer woman named Mary Goodhue. Shem learns much from Mary and about himself during his six months in the wilderness in this well-written coming-of-age novel.

Blos, Joan W. *A Gathering of Days: A New England Girl's Journal, 1830-32.* Scribner's, 1979. 144p. (4-8) Fic.

Blumberg, Rhoda. *Commodore Perry in the Land of the Shogun.* Lothrop, 1985. 144p. (6-8) Non-fic.

Blumberg, Rhoda. *The Incredible Journey of Lewis and Clark.* Lothrop, 1987. 143p. (4-8) Non-fic.

Brady, Esther Wood. *A Wish on Capitol Hill.* Crown, 1989. 139p. (4-6) (Originally published in 1978 under title: *The Toad on Capitol Hill*) Fic.

Eleven-year-old Dorsy McCurdy learns to accept her new step-mother and step-brothers as they help take care of each other during the British attack on Washington, D.C., in 1814. While the burning of the capital is vividly portrayed, the courses and issues of the war are omitted. The response to the attack by the citizens of Washington is realistic and tense. This is a lively story of how a very independent girl learns to cope with some significant changes in her family situation.

Carter, Alden R. *Last Stand at the Alamo.* Watts, 1990. 64p. (4-6) Non-fic.

DeFelice, Cynthia. *Weasel.* Macmillan, 1990. 117p. (4-8) Fic.

Set in 1839 in Ohio, this story of the early white settlers and the U.S. government Indian fighters is primarily a contrast between good and evil. Eleven-year-old Nathan Fowler and his younger sister, Molly, are summoned one night by Ezra, a mute stranger, who takes them to their missing father. Nathan's Pa has been hurt by Weasel, an Indian fighter who has become a total degenerate. In this grim story, Nathan struggles with his feelings of anger, rage, and cowardice as he tries to deal with evil, personified by Weasel, in a manner to make his Pa proud. This powerful story should spur some interesting class discussion.

Faber, Harold. *From Sea to Sea: The Growth of the United States.* 2nd ed. Scribner's, 1992. 246p. (6-8) Non-fic.

The author uses lively anecdotes to describe the growth of the United States from the original 13 colonies to the Pacific coast. Chapters focusing on the Louisiana Purchase, Florida, Texas, Oregon, California, Alaska, and Hawaii show how the United States continued its growth through warfare, purchase, annexation, and treaties. The author examines the major players and events involved; this book is an interesting reference as to how these acquisitions took place. Includes many maps, historical illustrations and photographs, a bibliography, and index.

Freedman, Russell. *An Indian Winter.* Paintings by Karl Bodmer. Holiday House, 1992. 88p. (4-8) Non-fic.

Freedman uses the 1833 travel journal of the German Prince Alexander Philipp Maximillian and the paintings and drawings of his companion, Karl Bodmer, as the basis for this informative book about the Plains Indians of the middle 1830s. This eye-witness account of Native American lifestyles and the detailed paintings and drawings show the beginnings of the changes imposed on the Indians through the impact of the white explorers, trappers, and travelers. The illustrations are exceptionally beautiful color reproductions and portray individuals and village scenes. Includes a bibliography and list of museums to visit.

Fritz, Jean. *The Great Little Madison.* Putnam, 1989. 159p. (4-8) Biog.

*Green, Rayna. *Women in American Indian Society.* Chelsea House, 1992. (6-8) Non-fic. (Part 2, Unit 3)

Henry, Joanne Landers. *A Clearing in the Forest: A Story About a Real Settler Boy.* Ill. by Charles Robinson. Four Winds, 1992. 64p. (4-6) Fic.

Based on the diaries and reminiscences of a real frontier family, the Fletcher family of Indiana, this book tells the story of nine-year-old Elijah Fletcher who, in 1833, lives with his family in the small town of Indianapolis. Elijah is a normal boy who gets into trouble and who sometimes does not get along with his family. Through Elijah's eyes readers will experience living at a boarding school, the activity on the National Road, the fun of a county fair, traveling by stagecoach to Cincinnati, and an exciting escapade on a steamboat. Simple black-and-white drawings accompany the text, and an author's note at the end of the book provides additional information about the Fletcher family.

Hilts, Len. *Timmy O'Dowd and the Big Ditch: A Story of the Glory Days on the Erie Canal.* Harcourt Brace Jovanovich, 1988. 91p. (4-6) Fic.

Hughes, Dean. *Facing the Enemy.* Deseret Book Co., 1982. 143p. (4-8) Fic.

After fleeing their home in Jackson County, Missouri, in the late 1830s because of anti-Mormon sentiment, the Williams family relocates in the Mormon community of Far West. This story is told from the perspective of 16-year-old Joseph who is finding it very difficult to reconcile the hostilities taking place and who is sickened by the destruction, violence, and death. Hughes presents an unfortunate chapter in American history, as well as the tale of a young man's coming of age. Students might also want to read Hughes' *Under the Same Stars* (Deseret, 1979), which precedes this story.

Lawlor, Laurie. *Daniel Boone.* Ill. by Bert Dodson. Albert Whitman, 1989. 160p. (4-6) Biog.

Lord, Athena V. *A Spirit to Ride the Whirlwind.* Macmillan, 1981. 205p. (4-8) Fic.

Twelve-year-old Binnie helps her mother run a boarding house for the female textile millworkers in Lowell, Massachusetts, in 1836, and it is her great desire to get a job at one of the mills and earn money to help her family. The wretched working conditions of the women and girls are vividly portrayed through the boarders' and Binnie's experiences. Binnie becomes involved in the unionization effort, and the workers' courage and spirit of independence shines through. This is a fast-paced, moving story of the Industrial Revolution.

Macaulay, David. *Mill.* Houghton Mifflin, 1983. 128p. (4-6) Non-fic.

The author begins by explaining how mills and water power technology came into the forefront in the early 1800s in the United States. Starting in 1810, four cotton mills in Rhode Island are visually depicted in detailed drawings showing their inception, construction process, and ultimate operation. Macaulay includes excerpts from the diaries of the main participants, including mill owners and their workers. The shift to the use of steam is discussed, and an epilogue describes what happened to these mills in the twentieth century. Includes a glossary.

Marrin, Albert. *1812: The War Nobody Won.* Atheneum, 1985. 176p. (4-8) Non-fic.

McClung, Robert M. *Hugh Glass: Mountain Man.* Morrow, 1990. 166p. (4-8) Fic.

This exciting tale of courage and survival is based on the true experiences of mountain man Hugh Glass. Set in the far western frontier of 1836, Glass survives an attack by a grizzly bear, although he is left for dead by his companions. Drawing on his experiences of living with the Pawnees, Glass eats roots, berries, and animals killed by wolves as he literally crawls toward Fort Kiowa. As Glass discovered, Native American responses to the white fur trappers varied from hostility to friendship. This story is similar in time, place, and courage to that of Indian girl, *Naya Nuki: Girl Who Ran* by Kenneth Thomasma.

*Meltzer, Milton. *Thomas Jefferson: The Revolutionary Aristocrat.* Watts, 1991. (6–8) Biog. (Part 2, Unit 4)

O'Dell, Scott. *Carlota.* Houghton Mifflin, 1977. 153p. (4-8) Fic.

Sixteen-year-old Carlota de Zubarán is a self-assured, unconventional Spanish girl living in California in 1846; she has been raised by her father to be a *vaquero*, knowledgeable in the ways of horses and able to run their large ranch. The conflict in this story is the Battle of San Pascual, between the Americans and the Spanish; Carlota accompanies her father into the battle. Afterwards, while Carlota nurses her father and an injured American soldier, she struggles to understand what is right and wrong in the war. *Carlota* is patterned on the life of Luisa Montero, and it could be a starting point to examine the influence of Spanish culture in California and the American Southwest.

O'Dell, Scott. *Streams to the River, River to the Sea: A Novel of Sacagawea.* Houghton Mifflin, 1986. 191p. (4-8) Fic.

O'Dell, Scott. *Zia.* Houghton Mifflin, 1976. 170p. (4-6) Fic.

This sequel to the *Island of the Blue Dolphins* (Houghton Mifflin, 1960) takes place at the mission at Santa Barbara after the Mexican-American War. Fourteen-year-old Zia and her 12-year-old brother live at the mission where they are taught to be Christians, although both continue to honor their Indian gods. The interrelationships of the priests, Spanish soldiers, land owners, and Native Americans are part of the life of this brave Indian girl who strives to take care of her family members while trying to understand the vast changes in her way of life. This fast-paced, exciting story is good for reading aloud.

Paterson, Katherine. *Lyddie.* Dutton, 1991. 182p. (6-8) Fic.

In 1843, adolescent Lyddie Worthen's life is disrupted when her emotionally-disturbed mother disbands the family, hiring Lyddie out as a servant. Lyddie dreams of earning enough money to keep the family farm, so she becomes an operative at the textile mills in Lowell, Massachusetts. This is Lyddie's story as a mill girl, waking at 4:30 a.m. and putting in 13-hour days under deplorable working conditions. Fearing for her job, Lyddie resists becoming involved in the workers' reform movement, but is eventually dismissed on the grounds of "moral turpitude" when she tries to stop a case of sexual harassment in the mill. The characters are well-developed and readers will be drawn in by the poignant writing about a spirited young woman who made the most of limited opportunities during the middle 1800s. This is a superb historical novel.

Rinaldi, Ann. *Wolf by the Ears.* Scholastic, 1991. 252p. (6-8) Fic.

This is the story of Harriet Hemings, the light-skinned, red-haired daughter of Sally Hemings and, possibly, Thomas Jefferson. Although Harriet is a slave who works as a weaver during the day, she has also been well-educated and taught many refinements. Harriet will be set free at the age of 21 and she must make the difficult decision whether or not to leave her beloved Monticello and try to pass for white. The characters are deep and well-developed in this gripping and unusual novel. Includes a bibliography, glossary, and the family trees of Thomas Jefferson and Sally Hemings.

Ross, Pat. *Hannah's Fancy Notions.* Viking, 1988. 56p. (4-6) Fic.

After Mama's death and her older sister's departure to work in the textile mills at Lowell, Massachusetts, 10-year-old Hannah is left with responsibility for the care of her three younger sisters. Papa has not been himself since Mama died and Hannah longs for the carefree days of old. When Hannah makes a bandbox covered with beautiful wallpaper for her sister's birthday, she unknowingly embarks on a new livelihood for her family, for Hannah's boxes are soon in great demand. Black-and-white illustrations accompany this simply told story of life in the mid-1800s, which is based on the life of an actual person.

Thomasma, Kenneth. *Naya Nuki: Girl Who Ran.* Ill. by Eunice Hundley. Baker Book House, 1983. 131p. (4-6) Biog.

In 1801, Naya Nuki, a Shoshoni living in Montana, and her friend Sacajawea, are taken captive by enemy warriors and forced to walk with other captives to North Dakota. After hiding food and other necessities, Naya Nuki manages to escape. This book tells the story of her harrowing experiences with buffalo stampedes, hostile Indians, and other dangers. This book is based on a true story, and the author manages to maintain the tension of Naya Nuki's 1,000-mile run, presenting her as strong, capable, responsible, and believable. This story of high adventure conveys the lifestyles and survival skills of the northern Plains Indians of 1800.

Tunis, Edward. *Frontier Living.* World Pub. Co., 1961. 166p. (4-8) Non-fic.

Wallin, Luke. *In the Shadow of the Wind.* Bradbury, 1984. 203p. (6-8) Fic.

Set in Alabama in 1832, this harsh story centers on two adolescents, a white boy and a Creek girl, as they try to maintain their sense of love, loyalty, and honor despite brutal hostilities between the disillusioned Indians, who are being starved off their land, and the white settlers. Caleb McElroy joins the Creeks as he observes but cannot participate in the hostility and treachery of the whites against the Native peoples. Pine Basket, her brother, father, and great-uncle, who is a leader of the Creeks, accept Caleb as they try desperately to maintain their sense of honor in the face of loss and banishment to the Oklahoma Territory. This story, powerfully and realistically told from the viewpoint of Caleb and Pine Basket, finds both good and evil among the whites and Indians.

Whelan, Gloria. *Next Spring, An Oriole.* Random House, 1987. 60p. (4-6) Fic.

In 1837, land in the new state of Michigan is selling for $1.25 an acre. The Mitchell family leaves their home in Virginia and purchases 80 acres outside of Saginaw in northeast Michigan. The family is delighted with the natural beauty of Michigan, and they are soon busy building their homestead on the banks of a pretty pond. With the help of some Potawatomie Indians, the Mitchells are able to make it through their first winter. The story is based on a journal account of one of Michigan's early settlers and is seen through the eyes of 10-year-old Libby Mitchell. The hardships endured by the pioneers are realistically presented, as are the joys of starting over in a new state.

Wisler, G. Clifton. *Piper's Ferry.* Lodestar, 1990. 130p. (4-8) Fic.

Thirteen-year-old Tim Piper is the protagonist in this story set against the backdrop of Texas' struggle for independence. The tale begins in 1835 with Tim leaving his New Orleans home to work for his cousin who operates the Los Brazos ferry in Washington Town, Texas. Tim befriends a young Texan named Zack Merkins who discusses political matters at length with Tim and who subsequently dies at the Alamo. Tim is torn about the war, but eventually knows what course of action he must take. This exciting, fast-paced story reveals much about everyday life in Texas during the middle 1830s.

UNIT

six

American Symbols, Literature, and Folk Tales

OBJECTIVES

1. After examining the symbols of America and their meanings, students will design covers for their History Journals using several symbols, and include a section in the journal defining the meanings of the symbols.
2. Students will read selections by American poets and authors from the early nineteenth century, place these authors on the time line, and choose a selection to include in their History Journals.
3. After reading folk tales from several different groups of Americans, students will identify favorite characters, sources of stories, common themes, and unique characteristics of the stories using murals, puppet shows, and story telling.
4. The pre-Civil War African-American stories and songs will be examined as sources of strength and survival through a sense of community, religion, humor, and escape.
5. Students will read portions of Uncle Tom's Cabin by Harriet Beecher Stowe, identify why this book influenced many northern people to fight against slavery prior to the Civil War, and compare the fiction with the real lives of slaves cited in To Be a Slave.

LEARNING ACTIVITIES

1. American Symbols

"**E Pluribus Unum?**" Ask the students to imagine that they are unfamiliar with the United States and its money. Have students examine a U.S. dollar bill and several coins. List all the symbols that are observed, such as the mottos "In God We Trust" and "E Pluribus Unum" and the eagle, people, buildings, 13 stars, arrows, and an olive branch. What seems to be important to Americans as implied by the symbols on the money? The answers may include men with pony tails or beards, buildings, the number 13, God, and "one out of the many." What do these symbols tell about the United States? Use reference sources to find out more about the meanings.

"**Oh Say Can You See. . .** " Next, set the scene as Francis Scott Key wrote the words for the Star Spangled Banner during the War of 1812. After reading the words, ask the students whether they would revise the words. If so, how would they change the words and why would they change the words? Or, why would they keep the present words of the national anthem?

New and Old Symbols of America. Have each student select three recognized symbols of the United States to include in his or her History Journal along with the meaning of the symbols. Next, the students will use these symbols to create a cover for their History Journals. Some students will want to create new symbols of America to include in their cover designs along with explanations in their journals.

2. American Literature Is Born!

Among the American authors to be recognized during the first half of the nineteenth century were James Fenimore Cooper, Washington Irving, Nathaniel Hawthorne, Henry Wadsworth Longfellow, William Gilmore Simms, Ralph Waldo Emerson, Oliver Wendell Holmes, William Cullen Bryant, John Greenleaf Whittier, Edgar Allan Poe, James Russel Lowell, and others.

Select a stanza of a poem or a prose selection by one of these authors to share with the students. Then have the students determine what is uniquely American in the selection. For example, students will recall the beginning of the American Revolution in Emerson's "Concord Hymn:"

> By that rude bridge that arched the flood,
> Their flag to April's breeze unfurled,
> Here once the embattled farmers stood,
> And fired the shot heard around the world.

Have students locate poetry or prose by these American authors. Students will especially enjoy *Paul Revere's Ride*, illustrated by Ted Rand. Thomas

Locker's illustrations of Washington Irving's *Rip Van Winkle* bring to life this tale set in the Catskill Mountains. The eerie stories by Edgar Allan Poe will appeal to advanced readers. Check the schools' sources of films and videos for James Fenimore Cooper's *The Last of the Mohicans*.

The students will then select a stanza of a poem or a few paragraphs of prose to record in their History Journals along with their own interpretation of how this selection is *American* literature.

3. A Story! A Story! And What a Story It Is!

Introduce the folk literature by reading or telling several tales to the students, such as the Eskimo tale, "The Raven and the Marmot," in *The Boy Who Found the Light*, and a story from *The Adventures of High John the Conqueror*, the slave folk hero. In these stories from two diverse cultures, the "high and mighty" are outwitted by characters in the stories.

Story Map. Have each student select and read an American folk tale and complete a Story Map for the tale. Include the following in the Story Map:

Author or reteller, Title, Illustrator, Publisher, Date

Setting:
  Where
  When

Characters:
  list names and characteristics, including ethnic or cultural connections

Problem(s):
  Action 1
  Action 2
    and so on

Resolution:

Theme: (*pourquoi*, tricksters, outwitting the high and mighty, exaggerations, parables, creation, etc.)

Common Theme Character Collages. After completing the Story Maps, group students by the themes they identified: *pourquoi*, trickster, etc. In these theme groups, have the students identify their favorite characters. Working in their groups, the students will portray the characters on a collage showing their appearance and actions through drawings, photocopies, and words. For example, one group will construct a collage of tricksters, while another group's collage will feature legendary giants.

Mapping Folk Tales. Continuing to work in the same groups, the students will identify the origins of their folk tales, and, as much as possible, record the locations of the tales on the Outline Map.

Sharing Stories. Within the common theme groups, have the students select one story to share with others through a mural with captions that tell the story; a puppet show; creative dramatization; group story telling; or readers' theater. The time constraints of the class may determine which options may be practical. Give the students time to prepare the story they will share with their own class as an example of the folk tale theme, and then, time permitting, share the story with younger children.

4. African-American Stories and Songs

Read several stories to the students from *The People Could Fly* and *Black Folktales*, in which the longing for freedom is covertly portrayed. Discuss why seeking freedom had to be disguised in the story.

Examine the words of several African-American spirituals to find the double meanings and code words. For example, the drinking gourd meant the constellation, the Big Dipper, and implied traveling north. Wade in the water, crossing the river, and the glory train meant both crossing over to heaven and crossing the Ohio River or the Canadian border to freedom via the Underground Railroad. Discuss with the students how important the oral tradition was to the slaves, most of whom were forbidden to learn to read and write. Use this activity as a springboard to Unit 7, "Slavery, the Civil War, and Its Aftermath."

5. Uncle Tom's Cabin

Hundreds of thousands of copies of this book written by Harriet Beecher Stowe, an American woman, were published and read in both the North and the South before the Civil War. Published in 1852, the book was translated into 23 languages, and produced as a play. Read aloud portions of Stowe's book. Discuss and list the probable reactions from readers in the North and the South. Keep the list to use in the next unit.

Compare the lives of slaves depicted by Stowe with examples from Julius Lester's *To Be a Slave*.

BOOK LIST

Note: Many of the folk tales found in the book list for Part 1, Unit 3, may also be used with students in grades 4 through 8; please also refer to that section when choosing books for this folk tale unit.

Armer, Laura Adams. *Waterless Mountain.* Ill. by Sidney Armer and Laura Adams Armer. Longmans, Green & Co., 1931. 212p. (4-8) Fic.

Set on the Navajo reservation of northern Arizona in the late 1920s, this coming-of-age story is seen through the experiences of Younger Brother, a Navajo boy, as he learns the significance in his life of the traditional stories of his people. The tale is told with reverence for the Navajo way of life, but is also steeped in the reality of poverty, variable contacts with white traders, and the interpersonal relationships of a boy in late childhood and early adolescence. The integration of Navajo myths and stories into daily life is a strength of this Newbery-award-winning book.

Beamer, Winona Desha. *Talking Story With Nona Beamer: Stories of a Hawaiian Family.* Ill. by Marilyn Kahalewai. Bess Press, 1984. 76p. (4-8) Folk.

The art form of the Hawaiian "talking story" is a means of transmitting culture via the spoken word. In this book, professional story-teller Nona Beamer relates some of the folk tales and family stories that she grew up with. The book contains 12 stories—some of them about nature, and others about people important in Hawaiian culture and folklore. Black-and-white drawings accompany the text. Some of the stories are suitable for reading aloud.

Bierhorst, John, ed. *Lightning Inside You: And Other Native American Riddles.* Ill. by Louise Brierley. Morrow, 1992. 104p. (4-8) Folk.

Bierhorst begins this book of riddles with a lengthy explanation of the significance and use of riddles in Native American cultures, the art of riddling, hunters' riddles, riddle dances, and riddles in stories. The actual riddles are grouped along different topics, including the natural world, the human body, animals, things that grow, and things that are made to be used. The riddle is printed at the top of the page, with the answer(s) at the bottom of the page. Sometimes the same riddle has different answers from different tribes that range from Alaska to Brazil; Bierhorst lists the tribe associated with each answer and includes a brief definition of the major tribes associated with riddles. A bibliography is also included.

Bierhorst, John, ed. *The Naked Bear: Folktales of the Iroquois.* Ill. by Dirk Zimmer. Morrow, 1987. 123p. (4-6) Folk.

DeArmond, Dale, reteller. *The Boy Who Found the Light: Eskimo Folktales.* Sierra Club, 1990. [61]p. (4-8) Folk.

Three tales from the Eskimo tradition, illustrated with beautiful black-and-white woodcuts, tell of a world where magic and reality meet and explain the origins of natural phenomena, such as the sun, stars, and wind. Two of the tales, "The Boy Who Found the Light" and "The Doll," are *pourquoi* tales in which children are the principal conduits of good for their communities, succeeding where others have not. In "The Raven and the Marmot," a humble little marmot outwits a vain raven who thinks very highly of himself.

*Giblin, James C. *Fireworks, Picnics, and Flags: The Story of the Fourth of July Symbols.* Clarion, 1983. (4-6) Non-fic, (Part 1, Unit 6)

Hamilton, Virginia. *Drylongso.* Ill. by Jerry Pinkney. Harcourt Brace Jovanovich, 1992. 54p. (4-8) Folk.

Set in the Dust Bowl during the Great Depression, this story tells of the young, skinny African-American boy named Drylongso who suddenly appears one day in a dust storm. It has not rained in over three years and Drylongso helps Lindy and her family plant thistles and sunflowers to hold down the soil until the grasses grow again. He also helps by showing them how to find water to irrigate the crops. Drylongso is a folk hero with a mythical quality—a youth imbued with simple human kindness who comes to help families in time of need. The charming illustrations by Pinkney enhance the text.

Hamilton, Virginia. *The People Could Fly: American Folktales.* Ill. by Leo and Diane Dillon. Knopf, 1985. 180p. (4-8) Folk.

This collection of folk stories includes animal tales, extravagant and fanciful stories, the supernatural, and slave tales of freedom. The variety of these tales demonstrates the richness of the imaginative African-American folk tales.These tales should be read aloud in order to share the author's storytelling style. Hamilton's interpretive notes help readers and listeners understand the setting and power of each story.

Lester, Julius. *Black Folktales.* Ill. by Tom Feelings. Richard W. Baron, 1969. 159p. (4-8) Folk.

Lester, Julius. *How Many Spots Does a Leopard Have?: And Other Tales.* Ill. by David Shannon. Scholastic, 1989. 72p. (4-6) Folk.

This volume contains a collection of 12 witty and humorous African and Jewish folk tales of animals and people who outsmart tougher, bigger, and more powerful figures. Some of the stories are "Why Dogs Chase Cats," "Why Monkeys Live in Trees," "The Town Where Snoring Was Not Allowed," and "The Bird That Made Milk." In retelling the stories, Lester altered the language and images to make them more understandable to present-day American children. An author's note includes the origin of each story and how the stories have been transformed by Lester. Includes full-page color drawings and a bibliography.

Lester, Julius. *To Be a Slave.* Scholastic, in arrangement with Dial Books, 1968. 160p. (4-8) Non-fic.

Based on the preserved narratives of slaves in the nineteenth century and as part of the Federal Writers' Project of the 1930s, Lester uses these primary source materials to express the African Americans' own stories of their lives as slaves. The moving accounts of life, love, death, work, and faith are augmented by the author's interpretive explanations. Portions of the book would be appropriate for read-aloud or readers' theater.

Mayo, Gretchen Will, reteller. *Earthmaker's Tales: North American Indian Stories About Earth Happenings.* Walker, 1989. 89p. (4-6) Folk.

This is a charming collection of stories about the natural happenings of the earth, such as thunder, hot springs, high winds, floods, snow, daylight, and fog. Each story is prefaced by an explanation of the origins of the story, citing the ways the story was common to many Native American tribes. Humor is found in many of the 17 stories that are well-suited to story telling. The author provides a listing of the sources of each story, including the names of Indian story tellers, collectors of tales, and some published sources of the stories. Includes a glossary. A companion volume is Mayo's *Star Tales: North American Indian Stories About the Stars* (Walker, 1987).

McKissack, Patricia. *The Dark-Thirty: Southern Tales of the Supernatural.* Ill. by Brian Pinkney. Knopf, 1992. 122p. (4-8) Folk.

The 30 minutes before dark, known as the "dark-thirty" when the author was growing up in the South, was the time to get home safely before monsters came out. Many of these African-American stories, which range from the days of slavery to the civil rights era to the present day, were inspired by real events that the author shares with the reader. These historical settings and McKissack's delightful storytelling style make the stories of special value. Pinkney's haunting and dark scratchboard illustrations add much to the mood of these well-told tales. This book won the Coretta Scott King Award and is a 1992 Newbery Honor Book.

McLane, Gretel Blickhahn. *Kalia and the King's Horse.* Ill. by Tony Kenyon. Press Pacifica, 1982. 88p. (4-6) Folk.

This well-told tale is based on a true story about King Kamehameha in 1803, when American traders presented the king with a stallion and a mare—the first horses seen in the Hawaiian Islands. Kalia lived with her parents, grandmother, and younger brother in the traditional Hawaiian manner, as yet uninfluenced by European or American missionaries and traders. Kalia is fascinated by the horses and conceals herself in a tree so that she can watch the king train the horses, and through her bravery and quick thinking, she saves the king. This fast-moving story, rich in Hawaiian culture and folklore, is a good read-aloud choice.

Sanfield, Steve. *The Adventures of High John the Conqueror.* Ill. by John Ward. Orchard, 1989. 113p. (4-8) Folk.

The hero of this collection of 16 tales is High John, a slave folk hero who often managed to outsmart his master and triumph over oppressors. An author's note at the beginning of the book provides the background for the High John stories, explaining that humor is a big part of each story, even if the last laugh is on John himself. Interspersed between the stories are brief narrations about slavery, including living and working conditions, and how slaves showed their resistance as they tried to maintain their dignity in the face of adversity. Full-page, black-and-white drawings accompany the tales, and the author includes a bibliography.

Service, Robert W. *The Cremation of Sam McGee.* Ill. by Ted Harrison. Greenwillow, 1987. [32]p. (4-8) Poet.

Originally published around 1907, this poem relates the folklore of the Yukon Territory during the Gold Rush days of the late 1800s. Sam McGee comes north from Tennessee to search for gold, although he is always complaining of the cold. Sam dies while traveling across the Dawson Trail with a friend, and he elicits his friend's promise to cremate Sam upon his death. Sam's friend eventually finds a suitable "cre-ma-tor-eum"—the wreck of the ship *Alice May* and, when he sets fire to his friend's body, Sam is happy because he is warm for the first time since he left Tennessee. The brilliant illustrations will impress the readers. Includes a map.

Stevens, Reed. *Treasure of Taos: Tales of Northern New Mexico.* Ill. by Janice St. Marie. Mariposa Publishers, 1992. 119p. (4-8) Folk.

These well-written and intriguing tales are set in northern New Mexico at the time of settlement by Spanish families. While the stories may have originated in Spain, they carry the cultural history of the settlers near the mountains of New Mexico, telling of everyday life; their gardens of corn, beans, and chilis; herding sheep; religious and magical beliefs; work and bravery on behalf of others; humor; and the concepts of good and evil. In the romantic tales, including "Arcia and the Fallen Star," which centers on the "Cinderella" theme, goodness is rewarded and evil punished. While readers may need a Spanish-English dictionary, the stories are beautifully written and well-suited for reading aloud, story telling, and dramatization.

Tun-Ta-Ca-Tun: More Stories and Poems in English and Spanish for Children. Ed. by Sylvia Cavazos Peña. Ill. by Narciso Peña. Arte Público Press, 1986. 191p. (4-8) Folk.

This anthology of stories and poems exposes children to literature that reflects the customs, themes, and characters of Hispanic culture in the United States. Numerous well-known authors, including Nicholasa Mohr and Pat Mora, offer writings without stereotypes—tales that provide strong female and male role models in positive and creative situations. The entertaining stories will make children laugh, think, and use their imaginations, and most of the selections are in both English and Spanish.

Yee, Paul. *Tales from Gold Mountain: Stories of the Chinese in the New World.* Ill. by Simon Ng. Macmillan, 1990. 64p. (4-8) Folk.

Eight stories comprise this collection of the Chinese experience in the New World. Based on the rich folk traditions that these immigrants brought from China, the stories tell of the young men who worked on the railroads, of those who searched for gold, of gamblers who traveled the West, of destructive greed and gluttony, and of cannery workers. The stories demonstrate how the Chinese overcame great odds to carve a place in their new society where they prospered and contributed to their communities. Each tale is accompanied by a striking illustration.

Yep, Laurence. *The Rainbow People.* Ill. by David Wiesner. Harper & Row, 1989. 194p. (4-8) Folk.

The retellings of these Chinese and Chinese-American tales are divided into groups: Trickster, Fools, Virtues and Vices, In Chinese America, and Love. The mysterious and mystical tales of monsters, disappearing people, and ghosts are often scary and humorous. The stories tell of family loyalty, greed, and generosity, indeed, the whole range of human affairs, but in the distinctly Chinese style. Also recommended is Yep's *Tongues of Jade* (HarperCollins, 1991), a retelling of 17 Chinese-American folk tales.

CIVIL WAR AND WESTWARD EXPANSION

❋ ❋ ❋ ❋ ❋ ❋ ❋ ❋ ❋

INTRODUCTION TO UNITS 7 AND 8

This tumultuous period of American history is portrayed superbly through fiction and nonfiction representing the perspectives of the Union and the Confederacy. For many of the major campaigns and turning points of the Civil War, there are well-written novels and nonfiction books for intermediate and middle school students. The African-American stories and songs and *Uncle Tom's Cabin* from the previous unit introduce the topic of slavery, which is then further developed through such books as *Anthony Burns: The Defeat and Triumph of a Fugitive Slave*, *To Be a Slave*, and *Breaking the Chains: African-American Slave Resistance*. Additional books will help readers understand the history of the African Americans and the problems of slavery in the period directly preceding the Civil War.

As the students read about slavery, the Civil War, and the Reconstruction period, they will be constructing a series of newspapers or television newscasts from both Northern and Southern viewpoints. In this way they will be able to apply the information and the attitudes portrayed in the literature and in the historical accounts. The newspapers and newscasts will call for both cooperative-learning and independent projects involving reading, writing, mapping, and role playing.

Through the lives of the fictional and real people associated with the Civil War, students will see how the nation was ripped and torn when its people were unable to solve their differences peacefully. This destruction, which changed lives and lifestyles forever, emphasizes the need to maintain and uphold the democracy of this nation.

Although this period of history is supported exceptionally well by children's literature, students and teachers will need sources of factual, chronological information in order to understand the sequence, causes, and effects of events.

Throughout Unit 8, the multicultural composition of the peoples of the United States is emphasized through the students' independent and small group investigations. The Westward Movement in the mid-nineteenth to early twentieth centuries extended beyond the Mississippi River to the Pacific coast, bringing the new settlers into contacts with Native Americans, Mexicans, and other people living in the West.

In order for the students in grades 4 through 8 to examine the multicultural history of the United States, their reading and learning activities in these units will identify many different groups of American people. Students will work in cooperative-learning groups or independently to investigate various groups. The class could be divided so that half of the reports investigate the peoples of the American West, and half examine the waves of immigration in the late nineteenth and early twentieth centuries. By arranging the group and individual reports in chronological order, the students will see how the Westward Movement and the immigration of large numbers of Europeans and Asians coincided, resulting in the rapid and continuous growth of the nation.

Based on their research, the students will investigate their groups' migration or immigration to the West or other parts of the the United States, including their motivation to leave their old homes; the route and means of travel; their destination; the process of establishing a new home; and the changes in their lives. For the inquiries about Native Americans, the students will survey the traditional lifestyle of the people and the impact of the Euro-American settlers on them, citing the changes in the Indians' lives. The products of the investigations may be reports, displays, dramatizations, or murals, depending on the students' topics, skills, interests, and resources.

U N I T
seven

Slavery, the Civil War, and Its Aftermath

OBJECTIVES

1. After reading about slavery as it existed in the years prior to the Civil War, students will by lottery be designated as Northerners or Southerners. Then, in small groups or independently, students will write newspaper articles or scripts for newscasts that address the topic of slavery from various viewpoints.

2. Assuming roles and applying factual information, students will write newspapers or newscasts for the period after the Battle of Gettysburg, during the Reconstruction period, and for other major events of the Civil War.

3. Events of the Civil War will be recorded on the time line and on the Outline Map.

4. Each student will select a prominent American to record on the time line, such as Abraham Lincoln, Robert E. Lee, U.S. Grant, Clara Barton, Sojourner Truth, Anthony Burns, Harriet Tubman, Emma Edmonds, John Brown, Harriet Beecher Stowe, William Lloyd Garrison, or Dred Scott. The students will write brief biographical sketches to be included in a book, "Famous People of the Civil War."

5. Students will answer a real person's letter from *Voices from the Civil War*, *The Boys' War*, or another nonfiction source or write to another soldier or civilian involved in the war. The content of the letters should indicate that the writer understands the contributions of the person and the difficulties in the person's life.

6. After reading several fiction books about life in the North and in the South, students will compare the lives of the central characters and draw conclusions about the effects of the Civil War on children and families.

7. Students will construct charts showing the changes after the Civil War in the lives of former slaves, plantation owners, families in towns devastated by the war, Union and Confederate soldiers, and others.

LEARNING ACTIVITIES

1. News of the Civil War

After reading about slavery and the events that led to the Civil War, students can plan for a newspaper or newscast about those events in several ways. For the younger or inexperienced students, the teacher will need to help plan the topics to be included and aid the students in finding the references. One approach is to put the students into small cooperative-learning groups, then assign a topic to each group with half of the group taking the Northern viewpoint and half the Southern viewpoint. For example, on topics related to slavery, students could report on the efforts to maintain the Union through the various compromises aimed at balancing the number of free and slave states. Other topics to consider are *Uncle Tom's Cabin*; John Brown; the Dred Scott decision; Anthony Burns; the Underground Railroad; the question of slavery as viewed by the plantation owners and by the far more numerous, small independent farmers in the South; the slave trade, both legal and illegal, as viewed by ship owners; and slavery as viewed by the residents of Kansas and Nebraska in the 1850s.

In presenting the viewpoints as a newscast, try to prevent a debate by having the students focus on facts rather than opinions. The group newscasts could take the form of panel discussions with the teacher as moderator, if necessary.

In constructing a newspaper, groups and individuals will write their articles based on factual information. Some students could draw political cartoons about the topics; others may write editorials. Here is where students can again differentiate between fact and opinion.

The scope and duration of this project will depend on the research, writing, and speaking experience of the students, and on the available resources. The newscast or newspaper can be repeated several times throughout the study of the Civil War period. The period of the Battle of Gettysburg is especially recommended because the great losses on both sides serve to emphasize not only the devastation to the population but also the destruction of the ideal of "government of the people, by the people, and for the people," cited in Lincoln's Gettysburg Address.

The news at the close of the war and of the Reconstruction period would include the assassination of Lincoln, the carpetbaggers, the organization of the Ku Klux Klan, the emigration of some African Americans to the West, and the many changes in the South, especially in land use and the development of new ways to make a living.

Students may wish to include their articles, newspapers, and scripts for newscasts in their History Journals.

2. Recording Events of the Civil War

If the Outline Map of the United States is becoming over-crowded with information, this would be a good time to make a new map. Students will record the events of the Civil War on the Outline Map giving the date of each. The same information will be recorded on the time line.

3. Famous People of the Civil War

Each student will select a prominent American of this era to research, write a short biographical sketch about, and record on the time line. The biographical sketches can be included in a class book, "Famous People of the Civil War." Encourage students to include not only generals but many other people, such as Clara Barton, Anthony Burns, Dred Scott, Emma Edmonds, John Brown, Harriet Beecher Stow, William Lloyd Garrison, Abraham Lincoln, and Jefferson Davis. Students may wish to also include a copy of their biographical sketch in their History Journals.

Some students may have ancestors who were involved in the Civil War. If there is sufficient information, include these people in the class book.

In order to achieve appropriate depth of the biographies, have all the students include the following information:

- Name, home, birth and death dates
- How was this person involved in the Civil War?
- What changes did this person cause to take place? How did this person cause changes to take place?
- How did these changes help or hinder the preservation of the Union?

4. Letters to Our Brave Soldiers and Civilians

Using the nonfiction books in the Book List, the teacher will select published letters of soldiers and civilians, both famous and ordinary. As either an independent project or a class assignment, the students will answer the published letters or write to another soldier or civilian involved in the war. The letters should reflect the students' understanding of the contributions of this person and the hardships in this person's life.

Sources of letters and wartime experiences especially recommended are *A Separate Battle: Women and the Civil War; Undying Glory: The Story of the Massachusetts 54th Regiment; Clara Barton: Healing the Wounds; Lincoln: A Photobiography; Voices from the Civil War: A Documentary History of the Great American Conflict; The Boys' War: Confederate and Union Soldiers Talk About the Civil War; Behind the Blue and Gray: The Soldier's Life in the Civil War;*

Behind Rebel Lines: The Incredible Story of Emma Edmonds, Civil War Spy;
Gentle Annie: The True Story of a Civil War Nurse; and *Robert E. Lee.*

5. Comparing Lives

As a class, in groups, or individually, students will read several fiction books set during the Civil War. They will then construct Comparison Charts that show the similarities and differences among the books' characters from various regions. After completing the charts, the students will draw conclusions about the effects of the Civil War on families and children, and cite how the book characters' lives were changed.

Include the following areas of comparison in the chart by listing the book characters to be compared down the left side of the chart, and the book titles across the top of the chart.

COMPARISON	BOOK TITLE	BOOK TITLE	BOOK TITLE
Character name, age race, gender			
Setting time, date location home occupation(s)			
Loyalties North South neutral			
Involvement in war			
Changes in life causes effects decisions			

CHART 13 Comparison of Lives During the Civil War

BOOK LIST

Note: Starred (*) books are reviewed in a previous section or unit of this book.

*Altman, Susan. *Extraordinary Black Americans: From Colonial to Contemporary Times.* Childrens Press, 1989. (4-8) Biog. (Part 2, Unit 3)

Armstrong, Jennifer. *Steal Away.* Orchard, 1992. 206p. (4-8) Fic.

Orphaned as an adolescent, Susannah Emmons is taken by her uncle from her native Vermont to live with his family in Virginia in 1855. With an aversion to slavery, Susannah is horrified when she is given her very own slave, Bethlehem Reid. Unable to adapt to her new life, Susannah runs away, taking Bethlehem with her. Disguised as boys, the two girls make their way north alone by foot until they are helped by a Quaker family in Pennsylvania. The story shifts back and forth from 1855 to 1896, as Susannah shares her story with her granddaughter and Bethlehem shares hers with a very special pupil. This well-written, intense novel should spark some discussion.

Beatty, Patricia. *Charley Skedaddle.* Morrow, 1987. 186p. (4-8) Fic.

After 12-year-old Charlie Quinn's brother is killed at Gettysburg, the New York Bowery boy enlists as a drummer boy in the Union Army and is sent to Virginia. Charlie is sure he will be tough and brave; however, as his division enters the Battle of the Wilderness, Charlie is horrified and runs away, only to be captured by the Confederates. An officer lets him escape and he takes refuge in the Blue Ridge Mountains with Granny Bent, a part-Indian healer woman. The battle scenes are excellent in their detail and emotion, and, in the end, Charlie has a chance to prove his bravery.

Beatty, Patricia, and Phillip Robbins. *Eben Tyne: Powdermonkey.* Morrow, 1990. 227p. (4-8) Fic.

Eben Tyne, the 13-year-old son of a sea-faring family in Norfolk, Virginia, is thrilled when he is asked to join the crew of the ironclad *Merrimack* (C.S.S. *Virginia*) which is being renovated as a warship. Although not slaveowners, the Tynes are committed to states' rights and Eben is glad to have the chance to serve the Confederacy. He serves as a powderboy on the ship, helping to fire the guns, and readers will see the war from the perspective of an adolescent participant. An author's note at the end of this exciting story explains the role of children in the war and gives additional information about the clash between the *Merrimack* and the *Monitor*.

Beatty, Patricia. *Jayhawker.* Morrow, 1991. 214p. (4-8) Fic.

When Lije Tulley's father, a conductor on the Underground Railroad in Kansas and a follower of John Brown, is killed in a raid in Missouri, teenaged Lije decides to take up the cause. Agreeing to be a spy for the anti-slavery forces, Lije passes himself off as a Southerner and hires himself out on a Missouri farm. For several years Lije secretly carries out his duties, meeting such historical people as Frank and Jesse James, John Brown, and Wild Bill Hickok. An author's note explains further about the Civil War in the western border states and the role of children in the conflict. The realism and exciting action in this story make it suitable for reading aloud.

Beatty, Patricia. *Turn Homeward, Hannalee.* Morrow, 1984. 193p. (4-8) Fic.

In 1864, the Union forces arrived in Georgia where they burned the textile mills in Roswell and New Manchester, and shipped close to 2,000 millworkers, primarily women and children, up north. Among these work-ers was 12-year-old Hannalee Reed, her brother, Jem, and their older brother's girlfriend, Rosellen. Frightened and hungry, but determined to return home, Hannalee, disguised as a boy, and Jem make their way from Indiana back to Georgia through battlefields and considerable danger. This exciting story is based on true events and reveals the devastation of the South during the Civil War. A sequel, *Be Ever Hopeful, Hannalee* (Morrow, 1988), picks up in 1865 with Hannalee's family reunited and trying to rebuild their lives in Atlanta.

Beatty, Patricia. *Who Comes with Cannons?* Morrow, 1992. 186p. (4-8) Fic.

Recently orphaned, 12-year-old Truth Hopkins, a native of Indiana, has just come to live with her aunt and uncle on their North Carolina farm in 1861. As Quakers, Truth's family does not become involved in the fighting, but Truth discovers that her uncle's farm is a stop on the Underground Railroad. The harassment of the nonviolent Quakers begins with the war, and Truth's two male cousins are impressed into the Confederate Army. The story spans the four years of the war and shows Truth's coming-of-age and the discovery of an inner strength she did not know she possessed. An author's note provides additional information about Quakers during the Civil War and the Underground Railroad.

*Berry, James. *Ajeemah and His Son.* Willa Perman Books, 1991. (4-6) Fic. (Part 2, Unit 5)

Carter, Alden R. *The Battle of Gettysburg.* Watts, 1990. 64p. (4-6) Non-fic.

Chang, Ina. *A Separate Battle: Women and the Civil War.* Lodestar, 1991. 103p. (6-8) Non-fic.

This book explores the roles and contributions of women, northern and southern, during the Civil War. Ordinary women worked as spies, nurses, volunteers, and even disguised themselves as men in order to take part in battle. The author vividly describes the prejudice experienced by women who tried to take an active and public role in the war. Well-written, gripping vignettes describe the work and words of such women as Clara Barton, Sojourner Truth, Mary Chestnut, Harriet Tubman, Belle Boyd, Harriet Beecher Stowe, and Louisa May Alcott, as well as less well-known but equally courageous females. The author makes good use of primary sources, such as diaries and letters, and the text is interspersed with fascinating archival photographs and period illustrations. Includes a bibliography and index.

Clapp, Patricia. *The Tamarack Tree: A Novel of the Siege of Vicksburg.* Lothrop, 1986. 214p. (6-8) Fic.

In 1859, orphaned Rosemary Leigh leaves her London home to live with her brother, Derek, in Vicksburg, Mississippi. Rosemary is delighted with the beautiful city, finds a good friend in Mary Byrd Blair, and the Leighs quickly fall into the pattern of life in this southern city. The one thing Rosemary cannot reconcile is slavery and although their sentiments lie with the North, Rosemary and Derek remain in Vicksburg when war breaks out in 1861. By the close of the story in 1863, Rosemary has experienced hunger, constant shelling by northern gunboats, hospital work, and forced evacuation of her bombed house. The graphic description of a city under siege is realistic and helps make the psychological and physical horrors of war understandable.

Cosner, Shaaron. *The Underground Railroad.* Watts, 1991. 128p. (6-8) Non-fic.

Cox, Clinton. *Undying Glory: The Story of the Massachusetts 54th Regiment.* Scholastic, 1991. 167p. (6-8) Non-fic.

The history of the all-black Massachusetts 54th Regiment, which contained men from 22 states and which was made popular in the feature film *Glory*, is presented in a well-articulated and detailed narrative that includes many extensive quotes from primary and secondary sources. Children will read the words of editors, politicians, soldiers, and abolitionists regarding the discrimination experienced by this pioneer regiment whose valor during a thwarted campaign to capture Charleston paved the way for the 200,000 black troops who followed. This fascinating story about the important role of blacks during the Civil War focuses on the soldier's viewpoint. Includes many captivating archival photographs.

Dubowski, Cathy East. *Clara Barton: Healing the Wounds.* Silver Burdett, 1991. 122p. (4-6) Biog.

*Ferris, Jeri. *Go Free Or Die: A Story About Harriet Tubman.* Carolrhoda, 1988. (4-6) Biog. (Part 1, Unit 8)

*Ferris, Jeri. *Walking the Road to Freedom: A Story About Sojourner Truth.* Carolrhoda, 1988. (4-6) Biog. (Part 1, Unit 8)

Forman, James D. *Becca's Story.* Scribner's, 1992. 180p. (6-8) Fic.

Based on the diaries and letters of the author's ancestor, this novel tells of 16-year-old Rebecca Case who lives in the southern Michigan town of Jonesville at the beginning of the Civil War. She sends both of her beaus, Alex Forman and Charlie Gregory, off to war, and through their letters, readers will learn about life on both the home and military fronts. Alex's account of his experience in a field hospital is especially vivid, and children will learn more about life during this turbulent time in America's history. The events and characters ring true and Forman successfully creates a genuine sense of time and place.

Fox, Paula. *The Slave Dancer.* Ill. by Eros Keith. Bradbury, 1973. 176p. (4-8) Fic.

In 1840, 13-year-old Jessie Bollier is kidnapped off the streets of New Orleans to serve aboard an illegal slave ship bound for Africa. Jessie's job on the return voyage is to play his fife to force the slaves to "dance" in order to make them exercise. The grimness of the daily deaths, cruel punishment, and taunting of the Africans is hard to bear. When the ship is sunk during a violent storm near the American coast, Jessie and Ras, an African boy, are the only survivors. This Newbery-award winner is a moving account of the slave trade told through the experiences of a white boy who was an unwilling participant.

Freedman, Russell. *Lincoln: A Photobiography.* Clarion, 1987. 150p. (4-8) Biog.

Hamilton, Virginia. *Anthony Burns: The Defeat and Triumph of a Fugitive Slave.* Knopf, 1988. 193p. (6-8) Non-fic.

This is the true story of the slave Anthony Burns who escaped to Boston in 1854, where he was arrested and, in keeping with the Fugitive Slave Act, tried in court and then returned to his master. In flashbacks, Anthony's childhood and adolescence are revealed. These intense descriptions of life as a slave illustrate how African-American slaves were kept ignorant and dominated through "reason, gratitude, obedience and shame," and also through fear and humiliation. Burns' freedom is eventually bought by abolitionists, but it takes many years to recover from the degradation of his trial and re-enslavement. This is a powerful and moving account.

Hamilton, Virginia. *Many Thousand Gone: African Americans from Slavery to Freedom.* Ill. by Leo and Diane Dillon. Knopf, 1993. 151p. (4-8) Non-fic.

Through succinct vignettes, the African Americans' own stories describe the conditions of slavery, the experience of running away aided by the Underground Railroad, the lives of fugitives, and the "Jubilee" of emancipation. This collection of short biographical sketches, some of which are brutal, includes the role of the Quakers and other abolitionists, but truly documents the efforts of black people as they sought freedom. The illustrations are strong and somber, reflecting the moving and poignant content.

Hansen, Joyce. *Between Two Fires: Black Soldiers in the Civil War.* Watts, 1993. 160p. (4-8) Non-fic.

Hansen, Joyce. *Which Way Freedom?* Walker, 1986. 120p. (4-8) Fic.

Sixteen-year-old Obi has always been a slave. The only family he has ever known are 13-year-old Easter and seven-year-old Jason, and they are owned by John Jennings, who has a tobacco farm in South Carolina. When the Confederate Army plans to take Obi to work on the Charleston defenses in 1861, he runs away, taking Easter, who is disguised as a boy. In 1863, Obi joins the Union Army to avenge the death of his friend Daniel, and because he feels it is the right thing to do. The book closes as Obi survives the massacre at Fort Pillow, Tennessee, in 1864, having come of age as he discovers the direction his new life will take. Obi and Easter's story continues in *Out from This Place* (Walker, 1988).

*Hooks, William H. *The Ballad of Belle Dorcas.* Knopf, 1990. (4-6) Folk. (Part 1, Unit 3)

Hunt, Irene. *Across Five Aprils.* Follett, 1964. 224p. (6-8) Fic.

*Katz, William Loren. *Breaking the Chains: African-American Slave Resistance.* Atheneum, 1990. (6-8) Non-fic. (Part 2, Unit 3)

Keith, Harold. *Rifles for Watie.* Crowell, 1957. 332p. (6-8) Fic.

The central character in this Newbery award-winning book is Jeff Bussey, a Kansas farm boy who enlists in the Union Army in 1861. The story takes place in the far western theater of the war—Missouri, Kansas, Arkansas, and present-day Oklahoma. Jeff's romanticism about the conflict gradually erodes as he experiences first-hand the realism of war: its drudgery, poor rations and living conditions, stern discipline, looting, combat, injury, pain, and despair. When Jeff is accidentally captured by Confederate troops, he pretends to be one of them, and so glimpses the other side of the issue he thought was so clear-cut. The author relied on original sources, including diaries of Union veterans and interviews conducted with 22 Confederate veterans in the early 1940s.

*Lester, Julius. *To Be a Slave.* Scholastic, in arrangement with Dial Books, 1968. (4-8) Non-fic. (Part 2, Unit 6)

Levine, Ellen. *If You Traveled on the Underground Railroad.* Ill. by Richard Williams. Scholastic, 1988. 63p. (4-6) Non-fic.

Lunn, Janet. *The Root Cellar.* Scribner's, 1981. 229p. (4-8) Fic.

This time fantasy tells of 12-year-old orphan Rose Larkin who is sent to live with her aunt in Hawthorn Bay, Canada, just across from Oswego, New York, on Lake Ontario. When Rose is exploring her aunt's root cellar, she finds herself transported back to her aunt's house in 1862 where she befriends two people her own age, Susan and Will. The Civil War is raging across the lake, and on Rose's last visit in 1865, she and Susan travel to Washington, D.C., to search for Will who was believed to have been wounded in the Battle of Cold Harbor. Readers will not only learn about the Civil War, but also about life and traveling conditions in mid-nineteenth-century America and Canada. This is an excellent choice for reluctant readers.

Lyons, Mary E. *Letters From a Slave Girl: The Story of Harriet Jacobs.* Scribner's, 1992. 146p. (4-8) Fic.

Harriet Jacobs was born into slavery in 1813; this fictionalized account of her life is based on the autobiography she published in 1861. Harriet's story is told in a series of letters written to her relatives in which she reveals the everyday lives of a people in bondage. After bearing two children to a white man and no longer able to bear her enslavement, Harriet runs away, hiding for over seven years in a tiny garret in her grandmother's house. Harriet's story is filled with heartbreak and special joys, and the life of this ordinary woman comes alive through her writings. An author's note explains what happened to Harriet once she eventually escaped, and a bibliography is appended.

McClard, Megan. *Harriet Tubman: Slavery and the Underground Railroad.* Silver Burdett, 1991. 133p. (4-6) Biog.

McGovern, Ann. *If You Grew Up with Abraham Lincoln.* Ill. by Brinton Turkle. Scholastic, 1966. 72p. (4-6) Non-fic.

McKissack, Patricia, and Fredrick McKissack. *Sojourner Truth: "Ain't I a Woman?"* Scholastic, 1992. 186p. (4-8) Biog.

This well-written biography is the story of a brave, intelligent woman who was born into slavery but later became a leading abolitionist and advocate for women's rights and the dignity of all human beings. The authors use excerpts from Truth's autobiography and other sources, making this a very personal and well-documented story of a great woman as she sought freedom for her children and other African Americans. Truth used the existing laws to aid her children and other slaves, winning court cases against white men. In addition to Truth's moving story, the McKissacks include brief biographies of contemporaries of Truth's who were also pioneers in abolition and women's rights.

Meltzer, Milton. *Underground Man.* Harcourt Brace Jovanovich, 1990. 220p. (6-8) Fic.

This fast-paced novel is based on narratives of fugitive slaves, court records, and the reminiscences of abolitionists. Through his religious convictions, a 19-year-old farm boy named Josh Bowden finds his role in life as a conductor on the Underground Railroad, helping slaves escape the South. The intricate arrangements for buying and freeing slaves, escorting slaves into free territory, and violating the laws of the land prior to the Civil War are woven into this heart-breaking story of courage, success, and failure. This novel was inspired by Meltzer's research for a biography of a white abolitionist, and it graphically presents the abolitionist movement, prison abuse, and the inhumane treatment of slaves.

Meltzer, Milton, ed. *Voices from the Civil War: A Documentary History of the Great American Conflict.* Crowell, 1989. 203p. (6-8) Non-fic.

Meltzer does an admirable job of blending together the words of ordinary citizens with his own text to provide readers a clear understanding of the Civil War and the events leading up to it. Using diaries, letters, interviews, newspaper accounts, songs, memoirs, ballads, and speeches of the age, Meltzer brings the human element into this conflict—the observations of soldiers and civilians on both sides of the Mason-Dixon line and their feelings of patriotism, prejudice, and pain. The author's use of period illustrations enhances the book and the bibliography and index are helpful. This is a good read-aloud choice, especially for less-advanced students.

Murphy, Jim. *The Boys' War: Confederate and Union Soldiers Talk About the Civil War.* Clarion, 1990. 110p. (6-8) Non-fic.

Making extensive use of actual words obtained from the diaries, memoirs, and letters of boys who served in the Confederate and Union armies as fighting soldiers, as well as drummers, buglers, and telegraphers, the author describes the beginnings of the Civil War and goes further to explain the role of these young soldiers and their lives in the camps and in the field. The adventure they had longed for is soon replaced by the reality of war—its horror and drudgery—and this impressive book shows the effect of the war upon the lives of these juvenile participants. The archival photographs, some of them quite gruesome, will fascinate children. Includes a bibliography and index.

Murphy, Jim. *The Long Road to Gettysburg.* Clarion, 1992. 116p. (4-8) Non-fic.

Writing in an easy-to-understand but compelling style, the author details the events at Gettysburg from the preparations through the battle, concluding with the dedication of the national cemetery. The use of archival photographs coupled with the events make this an outstanding account of combat during the Civil War. Putting Lincoln's Gettysburg Address in the context of events following the devastating battle brings depth of understanding to his eloquent words.

Myers, Walter Dean. *Now Is Your Time!: The African-American Struggle for Freedom.* HarperCollins, 1991. 292p. (6-8) Non-fic.

This book tells the rich history of African Americans, beginning with the first slaves brought to America and continuing through their descendents, as well as the men and women of the Civil Rights Movement of the 1950s and 1960s, as personified by such people as Malcolm X and Martin Luther King, Jr. Interwoven with the narrative of historical events are brief biographical sketches of both powerful and ordinary people. The personal details make for a well-rounded portrayal of a people subjected to dehumanization, but who constantly struggled for freedom and dignity. There will be much to discuss after reading this well-documented book. Includes many photographs, illustrations, and a bibliography and index.

Paulsen, Gary. *Nightjohn.* Delacorte, 1993. 92p. (6-8) Fic.

This powerful portrayal of slavery features as its narrator a 12-year-old black girl named Sarny who does not speak much. She is quite curious about the new fieldhand, nicknamed Nightjohn, who is brought to the plantation one day. Treated harshly, Nightjohn is willing to trade something for tobacco, and Sarny discovers that what Nightjohn is offering is the chance to learn how to read and write. Nightjohn has made it his mission to teach others in captivity so that their stories will not be lost. Care needs to be taken with this book because it contains extreme violence and is graphic in its description of the cruel and inhuman treatment of slaves. However, what shines through is the indomitable human spirit and the quest for dignity and education.

Perez, Norah A. *The Slopes of War.* Houghton Mifflin, 1984. 202p. (6-8) Fic.

This story, which takes place in Gettysburg from July 1 to July 4, 1863, is told from several perspectives: Buck Summerhill, a teenaged Pennsylvania soldier; his cousin Custis Walker who is fighting in Lee's army; and 16-year-old Bekah Summerhill, Buck's sister, who lives with her family in Gettysburg. Buck is concerned about his friend Tully, who has totally withdrawn from reality; Custis hopes to see his cousins; and Bekah's life is changed forever when she witnesses the horror of battle in her hometown and when she nurses a captain from New York who collapses near her house. The tedium, poor living conditions, weariness, confusion, and fear of death and maiming of the soldiers is clearly depicted in this powerful, realistic story. Includes a map of the battle.

*Rappaport, Doreen. *American Women: Their Lives in Their Words: A Documentary History.* Crowell, 1990. (6-8) Non-fic. (Part 2, Unit 3)

Rappaport, Doreen. *Escape from Slavery: Five Journeys to Freedom.* Ill. by Charles Lilly. HarperCollins, 1991. 117p. (4-6) Non-fic.

This collection of five stirring stories of African-American slaves who find freedom before the Civil War is based both on written works and on the black oral tradition. The author's careful research and historical notes provide a good introduction to this time period. Children will learn about the social system of slavery, the Underground Railroad, and the emotional and physical sacrifices that people in bondage needed to make in order to obtain their freedom. The stories center on individual acts of bravery on the part of the escaping slaves, but also on the roles played by free blacks and abolitionists who risked their lives in order to help their fellow humans.

Ray, Delia. *A Nation Torn: The Story of How the Civil War Began.* Lodestar, 1990. 102p. (4-8) Non fic.

This well-researched book examines the events that led up to the firing on Fort Sumter that marked the beginning of the Civil War in 1861. The author describes social and economic differences between the North and South, and the work of such people as William Lloyd Garrison, Harriet Tubman, Henry Clay, John Brown, Stephen Douglas, and Harriet Beecher Stowe. Making excellent use of primary materials, such as diaries, newspaper articles, letters, and other eyewitness accounts, Ray presents a fascinating view of how the nation came to war. The book is liberally illustrated with archival photographs, paintings, maps, and other historical facsimiles. Includes a bibliography, glossary, and index. Ray's excellent history of the Civil War continues in *Behind the Blue and the Gray: The Soldier's Life in the Civil War* (Lodestar, 1991).

Reeder, Carolyn. *Shades of Grey.* Macmillan, 1989. 152p. (4-8) Fic.

In 1865, after having lost his entire immediate family, 12-year-old Will Page reluctantly leaves his city home to live with his aunt and uncle, Ella and Jed Jones, on their Piedmont farm. Uncle Jed did not fight in the Civil War, having been opposed to it in principle, and Will thinks him a coward and a traitor to the Confederacy. As Will comes to know Jed better, he sees him as one of the most decent men he has ever known, but still cannot seem to reconcile this with Jed's refusal to fight. This is a sensitively told story of a difficult year in a young boy's life that tells of personal growth and also shows the devastation of lives, land, and goods that resulted from the war.

Reit, Seymour. *Behind Rebel Lines: The Incredible Story of Emma Edmonds, Civil War Spy.* Harcourt Brace Jovanovich, 1988. 102p. (4-8) Biog.

Rinaldi, Ann. *In My Father's House.* Scholastic, 1993. 323p. (6-8) Fic.

Oscie Mason is seven years old when her widowed mother marries the gallant merchant, Will McLean, in 1852. Throughout the course of this novel, which is set in Virginia, Oscie and McLean cross swords as she grows into a well-educated, level-headed woman. The bulk of the story spans the years of the Civil War as the McLeans lose their plantation during the First Battle of Bull Run in 1861 and allow their home at Appomattox Court House to be used for the surrender in 1865. The characters are well-developed and readers will get a vivid sense of the longevity of the war and the daily toll it took on the people involved. A detailed author's note explains the factual basis for the story. Includes a bibliography and short chronology.

Rinaldi, Ann. *The Last Silk Dress.* Holiday, 1988. 350p. (6-8) Fic.

For 14-year-old Susan Chilmark of Richmond, Virginia, the outbreak of war in 1861 triggers some significant changes in her life. Her beloved father moves to Norfolk on navy business, leaving an anxious Susan to cope with an abusive mother. On the positive side, Susan becomes reconciled with her estranged older brother who helps her understand herself and the reasons for the war in this well-written, coming-of-age novel.

*Rinaldi, Ann. *Wolf by the Ears.* Scholastic, 1991. (6-8) Fic. (Part 2, Unit 5)

Robertson, James I. *Civil War!: America Becomes One Nation.* Knopf, 1992. 184p. (4-8) Non-fic.

*Sanfield, Steve. *The Adventures of High John the Conqueror.* Orchard, 1989. (4-8) Folk. (Part 2, Unit 6)

Shura, Mary Francis. *Gentle Annie: The True Story of a Civil War Nurse.* Scholastic, 1991. 184p. (4-8) Biog.

Anna Etheridge enlisted at the age 16 in 1861 in the Second Michigan Volunteer Regiment of the Union Army and served as a nurse for the duration of the war. The story begins when Annie is 10 years old and readers will be eager to follow her into the battlefield when the time comes. An author's afterword, "The Girl Behind the Story," explains some of the problems encountered in researching Etheridge's life, including some details that could not be verified. This is an exciting story about an American heroine.

Weidhorn, Manfred. *Robert E. Lee.* Atheneum, 1988. 150p. (4-8) Biog.

This is a humane portrait of the Confederate general whose loyalty to his native Virginia, sense of decency, and hard-driving determination enabled him to inspire an army that was significantly outnumbered. The author presents Lee's life from his cadet days at West Point and military service during the Mexican-American War to the personal crisis he faced when war broke out in 1861. The majority of the book focuses on Lee's career during the Civil War and shows a fascinating view of the conflict from the perspective of a key Southern participant. Includes maps, archival photographs, a bibliography, and index.

Wisler, G. Clifton. *Red Cap.* Lodestar, 1991. 160p. (6-8) Fic.

In 1862, 13-year-old Ransom Powell lies about his age in order to become a drummer boy in the 10th Regiment of Virginia Unionists. Quite small for his age, not even four feet tall, Ransom takes a lot of ribbing, but settles nicely into army life despite the bad food, sickness, hard work, cold weather, monotony, and, worst of all, loneliness. Ransom's nightmare begins when he is captured in January 1864 and sent to a new prison in Andersonville, Georgia. Earning the nickname "Red Cap," Ransom manages to survive the horror of Andersonville, which is described in graphic detail. Along the way, Ransom encounters good men on both sides of the Mason-Dixon Line in this well-researched and exciting survival story.

U N I T
eight

Multicultural Growth:
The Nation Looks Westward
and Immigration Increases

OBJECTIVES

1. Working independently or in cooperative-learning groups, students will choose for their research topic one group of people of the American West or one group of people who immigrated to the United States during the late nineteenth or early twentieth centuries, and optionally including recent immigrants.
2. The students will identify fiction and nonfiction resources for their topics.
3. After the topics are chosen, the students, with the help of the teacher and reference books, will list the topics in chronological order according to when the people being investigated first moved to or lived in the West or first immigrated to the United States.
4. Using a list of basic questions to be answered in all investigations, the small groups will develop a plan whereby each student in the group will have a specific responsibility in gathering and processing information. Students working independently will answer all the questions.
5. The individual student or group will design a means of presenting the research information to the rest of the class.
6. The individual and group reports, regardless of form, will be presented to the class in chronological order. Each individual and group will designate specific information the whole class will be responsible for learning.
7. All topics will be recorded on the time line and the Outline Map by the individuals or group members.
8. Writing from the viewpoint of a member of the group being investigated, each student will write a letter in his or her History Journal to friends or family "back

home." Those who investigated Native American groups will write what they would like to tell their descendants about their lives in the nineteenth century.

LEARNING ACTIVITIES

1. Who Are the Peoples of the Western United States?

Before reading about the Westward Movement, the students as a class will make a list of the people they think settled in the American West, such as Mexicans, Germans, and African Americans. Post this list, then as students read about other people who made their homes in the West, make a second list including peoples such as:

- Native Americans of the Plains, mountains, desert, Northwest, Southwest, or Pacific Coast
- Mountain men and early traders with the Native Americans
- Spanish settlers in the Southwest or California
- Mexican settlers in the Southwest or California
- Russians in California, the Northwest, or Alaska miners, including Japanese
- Miners, in California, Colorado, or other areas
- European immigrants from specific nations to farms
- European immigrants from specific nations to cities
- Early settlers of the local community
- United States soldiers including the "buffalo soldiers"
- Americans from the eastern United States who moved West:
    families of farmers or ranchers
    abolitionists settling in Kansas or Nebraska
    "exodusters," the freed slaves who went to the Plains
    black and white cowboys
    children of the orphan trains
    Asians who immigrated to the West Coast
    Japanese miners
    Chinese railroad workers
    Optional: recent immigrants

After the students have generated an extensive list, note which groups were predominantly men and which were composed of families.

2. Who Are the Peoples of the United States?

As a class, have the students list the national backgrounds of their own families and the predominant nationalities in their community. Then devise a simple questionnaire to gather immigration data about the students' ancestors. Add this information to the list generated in Activity 1. Using textbooks and reference books, check for omissions of other groups of immigrants. For example, if the students of Decorah, Iowa, where many families are of Norwegian descent, only investigated the experiences of the Norwegian immigrants, their multicultural perspectives of the peoples of the United States would be woefully curtailed.

From the expanded list of people in the West and immigrants to the United States, students will choose the groups they will investigate. Have individuals or small groups of three to five students select a group of people to investigate. The teacher may need to guide students so that the topics encompass both the Westward Movement and the nineteenth-century immigrants with a minimal duplication of the topics.

If recent immigrants are included in this unit or in Unit 13, The Middle Decades of the Twentieth Century, students will find that Activities 4–8 may be applied to immigrants in any time period.

3. What Sources of Information Are Available?

Prior to this unit, the teacher will need to assess the availability of sources of information for the students. The teacher and librarian may need to obtain books from the Book List for this unit by interlibrary loan, a process that may take two to three weeks. To make good use of scheduled library research time, give the librarian a list of the selected topics well before the class arrives in the library. During the scheduled classtime in the library, each student will identify a fiction source on his or her topic in addition to reference and other nonfiction sources. If students find there are few sources about their topic in the school library, the teacher may aid the students in selecting a different topic, or work out a way for the student(s) to use a public library or interlibrary borrowing.

At this point, the teacher or librarian should show the students how to list their sources in correct bibliographic form in keeping with the grade level guidelines of the school curriculum. A simple bibliographic form containing author, title, publisher and date can be found in the Book Lists throughout this volume.

4. When Did These People Arrive in the West or Other Parts of the United States?

After the topics are chosen, the students, with the help of the teacher and reference books, will list the topics in chronological order according to when the people being investigated moved to the United States or lived in the West. For example, the Native Americans lived in the West prior to the Spaniards, Mexicans, white Americans, and Asian and European immigrants.

5. Finding Out About the Peoples of the United States

Students who are working independently will answer the following questions based on their reading. Small groups will divide the questions among the members of the group, thus establishing individual accountability for the information. By answering these and other questions, a basic outline of information will be completed.

- Where did these people come from?
- Why did they move to the West or to the United States?
- When and how did they get to the West or to the United States?
- Where did they settle or live?
- Describe how these people lived and how they provided for their needs.
- What skills, problems, or information did they bring to the area where they settled?
- What evidence can be found today about where these people lived? In what ways can these people be identified today?

Following these research projects, students may investigate their own family's history. For students investigating their own family's history, see *Do People Grow on Family Trees?* or *My Backyard History Book* for guidelines on using family documents and conducting oral history interviews.

6. Presenting Research Information

The individual student or group will design a means of presenting their research information that includes answers for the questions in Activity 5, to the rest of the class. Encourage a variety of means of reporting the information to the class, such as simulated interviews with the people who moved west; a mural that shows the group and where and how they lived; a display or diorama; dramatization or readers' theater; or simulated newspaper accounts of their westward journey or of their voyage to the United States.

Regardless of the means of reporting, each group or individual report will include information, such as that cited in Activity 5. Using the list of questions, the presenters will designate the specific information that all members of the class will be responsible for learning.

7. When and Where Did These People Live?

As the reports are presented in chronological order, the presenters will place the people of their topic on the time line and the Outline Map.

8. Letters Home or to Descendants. . . and Replies from Today

Each student, writing as a member of the group investigated, will write a letter in their History Journal to friends or family "back home" telling about their new life in America or in the West. Those students who investigated Native Americans will write what they would like to tell their descendants about their lives in the nineteenth century.

After the letters are completed, ask students to answer their own letters telling what the nineteenth-century person's life and experiences mean in the life of the student today.

BOOK LIST

1. The Nation Looks Westward

Note: Starred (*) books are reviewed in a previous section or unit of this book.

*Alter, Judith. *Growing Up in the Old West.* Franklin Watts, 1989. (4-6) Non-fic. (Part 1, Unit 7)

*Altman, Susan. *Extraordinary Black Americans: From Colonial to Contemporary Times.* Childrens Press, 1989. (4-8) Biog. (Part 2, Unit 3)

Benchley, Nathaniel. *Only Earth and Sky Last Forever.* Harper & Row, 1972. 191p. (6-8) Fic.

Although born a Cheyenne, Dark Elk is adopted by the Oglala Sioux at the age of 12 and grows up on the Red Cloud Reservation. Not wanting to be an "agency Indian" waiting for government handouts, 18-year-old Dark Elk joins Crazy Horse in the mid-1870s, partly to demonstrate his pride, and partly to prove himself to the girl he loves. This is a vivid and realistic account of the changing way of life for Native Americans, the frustration of reservation living, and the Indians' valiant struggle to protect home and family. The book's climax comes with the Battle of the Little Bighorn.

Bloch, Louis M., Jr., compiler. *Overland to California in 1859: A Guide for Wagon Train Travelers.* Bloch & Co., 1983. 64p. (4-8) Non-fic.

The majority of this fascinating book consists of actual quotations taken from the *The Prairie Traveler,* a handbook for westward travelers written by Captain Randolph B. Marcy in 1859. This resource book is full of maps, illustrations, and advertisements from the period. The compiler includes information on routes, what to take and how to pack, the amount of provisions needed, clothing needs, how to take care of the animals, and what to expect from the Native peoples. Although the text is factual, it lends itself quite well for read-aloud.

Blumberg, Rhoda. *The Great American Gold Rush.* Bradbury, 1989. 135p. (4-8) Non-fic.

Conrad, Pam. *My Daniel.* Harper & Row, 1989. 137p. (4-8) Fic.

Most of this story is told by 80-year-old Julia Creath Summerwaite to her two grandchildren in a series of flashbacks. Julia has just flown into New York City to view, at the Museum of Natural History, the dinosaur her brother Daniel discovered in 1885. As Julia reminisces, the story of her parents' Nebraska farm unfolds—their sod house, Pa hitched to the plow like a horse, the death of the buffalo, and natural disasters, such as droughts and locust attacks. Sixteen-year-old Daniel fulfills his dream of finding a dinosaur fossil, but dies before he can see it unearthed. The cycle of life on the prairie is vividly and beautifully told in this moving story.

Conrad, Pam. *Prairie Songs.* Ill. by Darryl S. Zukeck. Harper & Row, 1985. 167p. (6-8) Fic.

Young Louisa Downing has always lived on the Nebraska prairie and she thinks it is beautiful, although she recognizes its loneliness. The Downing family is pleased when a doctor and his wife, William and Emmeline Berryman, move into the nearest sod house. Despite friendly support, Emmeline cannot seem to adjust, especially after the death of her baby, and she gradually loses the will to live.

Conrad, Pam. *Prairie Visions: The Life and Times of Solomon Butcher.* HarperCollins, 1991. 85p. (4-8) Biog.

Solomon Butcher spent many years fulfilling his dream of making a photographic documentary history of life on the prairie as it was happening in his time. His photographs and stories depict settlers in the late 1800s on their Nebraska homesteads. The author provides the historical background for Butcher's work, and much of the book relates accounts of the pioneers as told to Butcher during his photographic sojourns. Butcher's photographs are fascinating and the details of people and land will have children wanting to know more. Includes a bibliography.

Ferris, Jeri. *Native American Doctor: The Story of Susan LaFlesche Picotte.* Carolrhoda, 1991. 88p. (4-6) Biog.

This is the simply told story of Susan LaFlesche, an Omaha Indian born in 1865, who became the first Native American woman doctor in the United States. Her father, Iron Eyes, believed that the only way to survive the onslaught of the whites was to learn English, adopt some of the white ways of living, and maintain Indian beliefs and culture. Readers will see the problems LaFlesche encountered trying to live in both the Indian and white worlds. From the time of her graduation until her death in 1915, LaFlesche lived on the reservation, serving as physician, Indian rights advocate, and missionary. Black-and-white archival photographs enhance the well-researched text and bibliographical notes at the end of the book provide additional information.

Fisher, Leonard Everett. *The Oregon Trail.* Holiday, 1990. 64p. (4-6) Non-fic.

Fisher, Leonard Everett. *Tracks Across America: The Story of the American Railroad, 1825-1900.* Holiday, 1992. 192p. (4-8) Non-Fic.

Fleischman, Sid. *By the Great Horn Spoon!* Ill. by Eric von Schmidt. Little, Brown, 1963. 193p. (4-6) Fic.

In 1849, 12-year-old Jack Flagg and his family's butler, Praiseworthy, set sail for the gold fields of California. Aunt Arabella, who has custody of Jack and his two sisters, has lost her inheritance and Jack vows to find gold in order to save the family home in Boston. The five-month sea voyage is full of adventures, including some skirmishes with a dastardly character named Cut-Eye Higgins, but the two prospectors find mining gold an even bigger challenge. This humorous story, rather tongue-in-cheek at times, provides a look at the Gold Rush that swept through the United States in the late 1840s. This would be a good choice for reluctant readers.

Fleischman, Sid. *Jim Ugly.* Ill. by Jos. A. Smith. Greenwillow, 1992. 130p. (4-6) Fic.

Left orphaned in 1894 in Nevada, 12-year-old Jake Bannock suspects something is not quite right about the information he has been given about his father's death. With the help of his father's fearsome dog, Jim Ugly, Jake travels in search of the truth, discovering that a bounty hunter was trailing his father for having stolen some diamonds. Jake's adventures take him as far as San Francisco and even onto the stage in a play about William Tell. This exciting story would make a good read-aloud choice.

Folsom, Franklin. *Black Cowboy: The Life and Legend of George McJunkin.* Roberts Rinehart Pub., 1992. 162p. (6-8) Biog.

George McJunkin was born in 1851, a slave on a Texas ranch. It was here that he learned to ride and rope horses and cattle. At the age of 17, McJunkin, who had been inspired by the respect and acceptance afforded black cowboys, left home to become a full-fledged cowboy on the trail. His long career took him to different ranches in Texas and New Mexico where he became an outstanding horse trainer and ranch manager. McJunkin had a life-long interest in minerals and fossils, and his greatest discovery was that of a bone deposit containing the bone of an unusually large bison. This interesting book documents both an African American's life experiences following the Civil War and the realistic life of cowboys.

Freedman, Russell. *Buffalo Hunt.* Holiday, 1988. 52p. (4-8) Non-fic.

Based on the paintings of artist-adventurers Karl Bodmer and George Catlin and Native American picture-stories and other art forms portraying the buffalo hunts of the past, Freedman tells of the great importance of the buffalo herds in the lives of the Plains Indians. The scouting; the hunt; processing the meat, carcasses, and hides; and the thanksgiving and other rituals are clearly and respectfully described. The dependence of Native Americans on the buffalo is explained in detail.While the introduction of horses and fire arms aided the Indians, their lives were irreversibly altered by the wanton slaughter of the buffalo by the white men.

Freedman, Russell. *Children of the Wild West.* Houghton Mifflin, 1983. 104p. (4-8) Non-fic.

This is a photographic essay of the settlement of the American West during the second half of the nineteenth century. The photographs are authentic and supplemented by an informative and superbly written text. The book begins with a brief chapter on frontier photography, and continues by describing modes of travel, homesteading, different types of homes, frontier schools, building communities, what people did for entertainment, and Native Americans and their interaction with whites.

Freedman, Russell. *Cowboys of the Wild West.* Houghton Mifflin, 1985. 103p. (4-8) Non-fic.

Freedman, Russell. *Indian Chiefs.* Holiday, 1987. 151p. (4-8) Biog.

This book focuses on six Indian chiefs and the choice they faced once the white settlers began to pour into the West: Should they accept the dictates of Washington, D.C., and try to secure as much land as possible for their people, or should they resist and make war for what was rightfully theirs? The Indian leaders—Red Cloud of the Oglala Sioux; Satanata of the Kiowas; the Comanche Quanah Parker; Washakie of the Shoshoni; Chief Joseph of the Nez Percé; and the Hunkpapa Sioux Sitting Bull—handled this challenge in various ways. Freedman tells their stories with clarity, accuracy, and compassion, and the treasure-trove of archival photographs greatly enriches the text.

Giff, Patricia Reilly. *Laura Ingalls Wilder: Growing Up in the Little House.* Viking, 1987. 56p. (4-6) Biog.

*****Green, Rayna.** *Women in American Indian Society.* Chelsea House, 1992. (6-8) Non-fic. (Part 2, Unit 3)

Gunby, Lise. *Early Farm Life.* Crabtree Pub. Co., 1983. 80p. (4-6) Non-fic.

Highwater, Jamake. *Eyes of Darkness.* Lothrop, 1985. 191p. (6-8) Fic.

The clash of cultures is evident in this novel about Alexander East, a Native American medical doctor tormented by the slaughter he witnesses at the Battle of Wounded Knee in 1890. The bulk of the story takes place in the past and tells of the boy Yesa, who was raised by his grandmother to love his tribe, the Santee Sioux, and to respect tradition. The author paints a realistic picture of Native American life on the Great Plains in the late 1800s, and vividly describes the transformation of this young boy into a man who must put the past behind him as he adapts to formidable changes in his life. This is a well-written, deep, and moving account.

Highwater, Jamake. *Legend Days.* Harper & Row, 1984. 147p. (6-8) Fic.

Amana is orphaned at the age of 11 when small pox devastates her tribe. She is taken in by Grandfather Fox from whom she learns the courage to become a warrior and a hunter, while also learning the womanly tasks of cooking, sewing, caring for her invalid sister and her elderly husband. Through this poetically written tale, part narrative, part legend in style, the disintegration of the Plains Indians' lifestyle is evident as the white people decimate the buffalo, and bring the railroad and disease to the plains. Two other books published by Harper & Row follow in Highwater's "Ghost Horse Cycle": *Ceremony of Innocence* (1985) and *I Wear the Morning Star* (1986).

Holland, Isabelle. *The Journey Home.* Scholastic, 1990. 192p. (4-8) Fic.

In the late 1800s, Maggie and Annie are sent to Kansas by the Children's Aid Society after their mother dies in a New York slum. As Irish Catholics, the girls face religious ridicule and prejudice in the Protestant household where they are adopted, in the nearby Baptist Church, and in school. But their strength of character and that of their new family in the face of a difficult series of events eventually allows the girls to become true daughters of the family. This high-interest, low-vocabulary book would be a good read-aloud choice for younger children.

Hoobler, Dorothy, and Thomas Hoobler. *Treasure in the Stream: The Story of a Gold Rush Girl.* Ill. by Nancy Carpenter. Silver Burdett, 1991. 55p. (4-6) Fic.

Hotze, Sollace. *A Circle Unbroken.* Clarion, 1988. 202p. (6-8) Fic.

In 1845, 17-year-old Burning Sun has been living happily with the Oglala Sioux for seven years since her abduction from a white people's fort by a group of renegade Indians. One morning, a group of white men come to Burning Sun's camp to reclaim her. She is taken to her family in Missouri where she must become Rachel Porter and resume life as a white girl. Rachel longs to return to her Sioux people and, in the end, her beloved aunt's death forces Rachel to resolve her own conflicting feelings about living her life as a white or a Sioux woman. This sensitive, superbly written story provides a viewpoint not often seen in children's literature.

Hudson, Jan. *Sweetgrass*. Philomel, 1989. 159p. (6-8) Fic.

Set in the Montana prairies in the 1830s, this is the story of 15-year-old Sweetgrass, the only daughter of an honored warrior. Sweetgrass is determined to direct her own life, including choosing her own husband as her warrior grandmother had done. When the camp is attacked, Grandmother organizes the family for flight, putting Sweetgrass at the head of the procession carrying the ceremonial lance. When small pox strikes the family over the winter, Sweetgrass nurses and cares for her family, thus demonstrating her maturity and responsible nature. The characters and their family relationships are well-developed and ring true.

*Kalman, Bobbie. *Early Pleasures and Pastimes*. Crabtree Pub. Co., 1983. (4-6) Non-fic. (Part 1, Unit 7)

*Katz, William Loren. *Black Indians: A Hidden Heritage*. Atheneum, 1986. (6-8) Non-fic.(Part 2, Unit 2)

Katz, William Loren. *Black People Who Made the Old West*. Crowell, 1977. 181p. (4-8) Non-fic.

Lasky, Kathryn. *Beyond the Divide*. Macmillan, 1983. 254p. (4-8) Fic.

Feeling stifled in her strict Amish community, 14-year-old Meribah Simon decides to accompany her father out West in 1849; this book is the story of their trek across America, from Missouri to California. Meribah's character is well developed and the author skillfully handles her maturation and reconciliation of her Amish ways with those of the rest of the world. Lasky presents a lifelike portrait of a wagon train journey and her imagery is remarkably vivid—readers will easily picture the changing prairie landscape and feel the heat and dust of the trail.

Lawlor, Laurie. *Addie Across the Prairie*. Ill. by Gail Owens. Albert Whitman, 1986. 128p. (4-6) Fic.

The year is 1883 and Addie's family has just left their comfortable home in Iowa to homestead in the Dakotas. As the oldest of five children, nine-year-old Addie now has the responsibility of helping her mother care for the children. Addie finds their sod house a poor comparison to their old two-story frame house, and she does not like the isolation of the prairie. Addie does not see herself as the "sodbusting pioneer type," but by the end of the book she proves this to be the case through a series of exciting adventures.

Addie's story continues in two other books published by Albert Whitman: *Addie's Dakota Winter* (1989) and *Addie's Long Summer* (1992).

Levine, Ellen. *If You Traveled West in a Covered Wagon.* Ill. by Charles Shaw. Scholastic, 1986. 80p. (4-6) Non-fic.

MacLachlan, Patricia. *Sarah, Plain and Tall.* Harper & Row, 1985. 58p. (4-6) Fic.

Mazzio, Joann. *Leaving Eldorado.* Houghton Mifflin, 1993. 170p. (6-8) Fic.
Set in Eldorado, New Mexico Territory, this story opens in 1896 when 14-year-old Maude Brannigan's mother dies. When her gold-hunting father decides to leave Eldorado for the Yukon gold fields, Maude puts her foot down and says she will not accompany him. Maude hires herself out to work for nasty Mrs. Steckler at her boardinghouse and she befriends Annie, an Apache girl who does not speak, and Yee, the Chinese cook. Fending for herself is difficult in this rough town, but Maude has the dream of becoming a real artist, although everyone tells her that a woman cannot become an artist. Maude is a strong, unconventional girl who has to make some serious decisions about the direction her life will take. The novel is fast-paced, realistic, and well-written.

McClain, Margaret S. *Bellboy: A Mule Train Journey.* Ill. by Sara Brown Stuart. New Mexico Publishing Co., 1990. 152p. (4-6) Fic.
Twelve-year-old Jake, as the oldest son in the family, tries to take his dead father's place, but misses having someone to guide him. He takes a summer job as a bellboy, the boy who rides the lead mare of a mule train. Although the work is difficult, Jake finds the men helpful and enjoys the masculine company and role models. This is an interesting look at the transportation of goods to and from mining areas in the late 1870s in California. Although the story is realistic, the characters seem too good at times.

McGraw, Eloise Jarvis. *Moccasin Trail.* Coward-McCann, 1952. 247p. (4-8) Fic.
When 12-year-old Jim Keath is left for dead after a bear attacks his fur trapper camp, Jim is nursed by a tribe of Crow Indians. Jim remains with his adopted tribe for six years, earning both an Indian name and the right to wear the signs of Indian manhood. When a letter arrives from his younger brother asking Jim to come claim the family's homestead in Oregon, Jim is in a quandary, feeling more Indian than white. He eventually goes to help his family and, after several adventures, he is able to resolve his conflicting feelings. This exciting, well-told tale would make a good read-aloud selection.

Meyer, Carolyn. *Where the Broken Heart Still Beats: The Story of Cynthia Ann Parker.* Harcourt Brace Jovanovich, 1992. 197p. (6-8) Fic.

This is a fictionalized biography of Cynthia Ann Parker, a white woman who was captured from her Texas home at the age of nine in 1836 and lived with the Comanche Indians until she was "rescued" by whites 25 years later. This touching story is told from the dual perspective of Parker and her 12-year-old cousin, Lucy, who befriends Parker and writes of her experience in her diary. Parker's relatives mourn because she has "gone Indian" and readers will see both sides of the issue—Parker's resistance towards white ways and her longing to return to her husband and people, and how her family tried to get her to renounce her Comanche ways. Parker's reminiscences reveal the cadence of Comanche tribal life and readers cannot help but feel the heartache endured by this woman. Includes a bibliography.

Miller, Robert H. *Reflections of a Black Cowboy: Book Two: The Buffalo Soldiers.* Ill. by Richard Leonard. Silver Burdett, 1991. 89p. (6-8) Non-fic.

The narrator, Old Cowboy, tells stories to his faithful dog, Sundown, that relate the contributions of African Americans to the settlement of the West. Miller narrates the experiences of a few of the 8,000 African Americans who were recruited as Indian-fighting soldiers in all-black regiments. Readers will learn about such notable blacks as Emanuel Stance, the first black soldier to receive the Medal of Honor, and the men of the 9th and 10th Cavalries who fought at the Battle of San Juan Hill in the Spanish-American War. Book 1 in the two-volume set of *Reflections of a Black Cowboy: Cowboys* (Silver Burdett, 1991) discusses the 5,000 blacks who worked as cowboys following the Civil War. Includes a bibliography.

Morrow, Honoré. *Seven Alone.* Scholastic, 1954. (Orig. pub. under title: *On to Oregon!*) 234p. (6-8) Fic.

In 1844, the Sager family is traveling by wagon train from Missouri to a new home in Oregon. When disease takes both his parents, 13-year-old John Sager is determined to continue the journey with his six younger brothers and sisters. Despite hunger, sore feet, chilblains, threadbare clothing, and countless dangers, the Sager children travel 1,000 miles alone until they reach the Whitman Mission in Oregon. Based on a true story, this remarkable adventure will appeal to children of all ages, and would be an excellent read-aloud choice. This book was produced as a motion picture by Doty-Dayton Productions, and is also available as a video recording and filmstrip.

Murrow, Liza Ketchum. *West Against the Wind.* Holiday, 1987. 232p. (6-8) Fic.

This is the story of the Parker family—14-year-old Abby, her mother, her older brother, Uncle Joseph and Aunt Emma—who are traveling to California in 1850 in search of Mr. Parker who succumbed to "gold fever" and left the year before. Abby keeps a diary of her experiences, forming the narrative of the story. The hardships, disillusionments, discomforts, dangers, and good times are all recorded as this family, facing starvation, finally accomplishes its goal. This story will appeal especially to girls.

Myers, Walter Dean. *The Righteous Revenge of Artemis Bonner.* HarperCollins, 1992. 140p. (6-8)

Children will enjoy this tongue-in-cheek Western that features as its hero 15-year-old Artemis Bonner, an African-American boy from New York City who travels out West in 1880 to avenge the murder of his uncle, Ugly Ned Bonner. Artemis's foes are the ever-crafty Catfish Grimes and his female companion, Lucy Featherdip. Armed with a copy of his uncle's treasure map, Artemis travels throughout the West, as far south as Mexico and all the way north to Alaska. Along the way, Artemis teams up with a half-Indian youth named Frolic Brown and the boys have a number of adventures as they attempt to complete their mission. Although the story contains considerable violence, it is very humorous and would be a good choice for reluctant readers.

Nixon, Joan Lowery. *A Family Apart.* Bantam, 1987. 162p. (4-8) Fic.

As this first book in the "Orphan Train Quartet" opens, Grandmother is telling her bored grandchildren the story of her great-grandmother's life, who is 13-year-old Frances Mary in the story. The family history begins in New York City in 1860 when widowed Mrs. Kelly, facing poverty and starvation, decides to send her six children out West on the "orphan trains" in order to secure a better life for them. Once they reach St. Joseph, Missouri, the six children are parceled out to four different families. A *Family Apart* is primarily Frances Mary's story, as she disguises herself as a boy, "Frankie," in order to remain with her youngest sibling, six-year-old Petey. The couple who take in the youngest and oldest Kelly children are good people, but Frances Mary must come to terms with her mother's "betrayal" before she can be at peace with herself and begin to create a new life in the West. The other books in the series, all published by Bantam, are *Caught in the Act* (1988), *In the Face of Danger* (1988), and *A Place to Belong* (1989). These exciting, historically accurate novels are popular read-alouds with children.

O'Dell, Scott. *Sing Down the Moon.* Houghton Mifflin, 1970. 137p. (4-8) Fic.

Set in the 1860s in Arizona and New Mexico, this is the story of 14-year-old

Bright Morning, a Navajo Indian who is captured by Spaniards and sold into slavery. Eventually Bright Morning escapes and makes her way back to her home, with the help of some young braves. However, when white soldiers tell Bright Morning's tribe that they must vacate their canyon, the Indians must trek over 300 miles to their new home, a reservation in present-day New Mexico. Told from the Native American perspective, this is a story about the relations between whites and Indians as the West became more and more settled by white people.

O'Dell, Scott, and Elizabeth Hall. *Thunder Rolling in the Mountains.* Houghton Mifflin, 1992. 128p. (6-8) Fic.

The poignant story of Chief Joseph of the Nez Percé and his people's flight from the United States Army is told from the perspective of Sound of Running Water, Joseph's 14-year-old daughter. In 1877, the Nez Percé are mandated to leave their home in Wallowa Valley in Oregon, and subsequent disharmony among the People leads to bloodshed with the white soldiers, triggering a war and a dangerous and desperate flight north to safety. Sound of Running Water feels her father is too pacifist and she sides with the young warriors who want to stand and fight. The authors did considerable research, including studying eyewitness accounts by both Nez Percé and army personnel, and this heart-breaking story is told with accuracy and sensitivity.

Pellowski, Anne. *First Farm in the Valley.* Ill. by Wendy Watson. Philomel, 1982. 189p. (4-8) Fic.

The year is 1876 and Anna's family and their Polish neighbors farm land in Latsch Valley, Wisconsin, welcome new immigrants, celebrate holidays with the traditional foods and customs of Poland, and experience the conflicts of being Polish and becoming American. The appeal of this story lies in the ethnicity of the everyday events of this immigrant family who, with well-established customs, values, and good humor, become at home in their new country. Three other books published by Philomel trace the lives of this Polish-American family: *Stairstep Farm* (1981), *Willow Wind Farm* (1981), and *Winding Valley Farm* (1982).

*Rappaport, Doreen, ed. *American Women: Their Lives in Their Words: A Documentary History.* Crowell, 1990. (6-8) Non-fic. (Part 2, Unit 3)

Robison, Nancy. *Buffalo Bill.* Watts, 1991. 64p. (4-8) Biog.

Smith, Carter, ed. *Native Americans of the West: A Sourcebook on the American West.* Millbrook Press, 1992. 96p. (4-8) Non-fic.

*Stein, R. Conrad. *The Story of the Golden Spike.* Childrens Press, 1978. (4-6) Non-fic. (Part 1, Unit 7)

Stein, R. Conrad. *The Story of the Homestead Act.* Ill. by Cathy Koenig. Childrens Press, 1978. 31p. (4-6) Non-fic.

Stewart, George Rippey. *To California by Covered Wagon.* Ill. by William Moyers. Random House, 1954. 182p. (4-8) Non-fic.

Set in 1844, this is a true story based on the diary of 17-year-old Moses Schallenberger who was in the "Stevens Party," the first wagon train to cross all the way to California. The trip is seen through his eyes and this informative and well-written nonfiction book reads like a great adventure story, especially when Moses, separated from his party, is forced to spend the winter alone in an abandoned cabin. This exciting, well-researched book lends itself well to reading aloud.

Talbot, Charlene Joy. *An Orphan for Nebraska.* Atheneum, 1979. 208p. (6-8) Fic.

Orphaned on the journey from Ireland to America in 1872, 11-year-old Kevin O'Rourke becomes a newsboy to try and support himself. When winter comes, Kevin is sent out West by the Children's Aid Society on one of the "orphan trains." Kevin is selected by the editor of the *Cottonwood Clarion*, the local newspaper in Cottonwood City, Nebraska. The book contains detailed accounts of how newspapers were published at the time, and depicts the lifestyle and habits of a nineteenth-century western bachelor.

Tunis, Edward. *Frontier Living.* World Pub. Co., 1961. 166p. (4-8) Non-fic.

Turner, Ann W. *Grasshopper Summer.* Macmillan, 1989. 144p. (4-8) Fic.

In 1874, a Kentucky family moves to South Dakota, and their story is told by 11-year-old Sam who does not want to move, disliking the open spaces of the prairies. The character development of this southern family is well-crafted, especially through the viewpoints, fears, and pleasures of Sam and his 10-year-old brother, Billy, and through the loneliness of parents and children. The work of building their sod house and planting their fields is back-breaking, and the description of the grasshopper attack is particularly graphic. This is a vivid portrayal of homesteading, family relationships, and the courage to persevere.

Van Steenwyk, Elizabeth. *The California Gold Rush: West With the Forty-Niners.* Watts, 1991. 63p. (4-6) Non-fic.

Waheenee, as told to Gilbert L. Wilson. *Waheenee: An Indian Girl's Story.* University of Nebraska Press, 1981. (Orig. pub.: Webb Pub. Co., 1921) 189p. (4-8) Biog.

Set in North Dakota in the second half of the nineteenth century, this book is an account by Waheenee, a Hidatsa Indian, of everyday life from childhood through old age. The chapters on childhood games and home life will be of special interest to children, and the descriptions of the work of men, women, and children will help young readers understand the old way of life of the Northern Plains Indians. Includes explanatory notes, a glossary, and a final chapter entitled "After Fifty Years," which must be read with children.

Wallace, Bill. *Buffalo Gal.* Holiday, 1992. 185p. (6-8) Fic.

In 1904, 15-year-old San Franciscan Amanda Guthridge tries to cope with her crusading mother. Mrs. Guthridge, a member of the Save the Bison Society, drags Amanda with her to Oklahoma to meet with Major Gordon Lillie in the hopes of saving a herd of buffalo. Led by a half-Comanche youth named David Talltree—who irritates Amanda as much as he fascinates her—the Guthridges ride the trail into the hill country of Texas where the herd was last sighted. Life on the trail is difficult for two city women and Amanda has numerous adventures in this fast-paced story about the West in the early 1900s.

Wallace, Bill. *Red Dog.* Holiday, 1987. 185p. (4-8) Fic.

It has been a difficult year for 12-year-old Adam—his mother remarried a man named Sam and the family has moved from their native Tennessee to the rugged Wyoming Territory. Resenting his new stepfather, Adam is struggling to find his niche, and feels his only friend is the wild young pup named Ruff that has become his companion. When Sam leaves the family on a short trip, Adam is left in charge and finds his courage and fortitude tested when a dangerous group of gold miners take his family hostage. This very exciting, well-written story about homesteading in the 1860s and a boy's coming of age would be a good read-aloud choice.

Weidt, Maryann N. *Mr. Blue Jeans: A Story About Levi Strauss.* Ill. by Lydia M. Anderson. Carolrhoda, 1990. 64p. (4-6) Biog.

In 1847, German-born Levi Strauss left his homeland for America where he hoped to find a better life. A peddler by trade, Strauss eventually travels by sea to San Francisco in the early 1850s to go into business with his brother-in-law. Back to peddling, Strauss hits on the idea of making trousers from tent material for miners and cowboys, and so was born the patented, riveted blue pants that became the original 501 jeans. The author explains where the name "jeans" comes from and how "501" was the lot number of Strauss's blue fabric. A hard-working entrepreneur, Strauss opened the Levi Strauss & Company dry goods store and became a rich man. Blue jeans can probably be found in every American household and children will find this brief biography very interesting.

Wilder, Laura Ingalls. *Little House in the Big Woods.* Ill. by Garth Williams. Harper & Row, 1953. 237p. (4-6) Fic.

This first of the "Little House" books focuses on two young girls growing up in frontier Wisconsin in the late 1800s who help their mother with the day-to-day chores, enjoy listening to their father's stories and music, and share special celebrations with family, friends, and neighbors. Numerous other books follow this one, including *By the Shores of Silver Lake, Little House on the Prairie, Little Town on the Prairie,* and *On the Banks of Plum Creek.*

Wood, Ted, with Wanbli Numpa Afraid of Hawk. *A Boy Becomes a Man at Wounded Knee.* Walker, 1992. 42p. (4-6) Non-fic.

In 1990, eight-year-old Wanbli Numpa Afraid of Hawk, an Oglala Lakota living on the Cheyenne River Reservation in South Dakota, was given permission to accompany his male relatives on a 150-mile ride to Wounded Knee to commemorate the 100th anniversary of the massacre there. Wood sets the stage by providing a brief description of the events leading to the slaughter of over 350 Lakota men, women, and children at Wounded Knee on December 28, 1890. Then, readers accompany young Wanbli Numpa as he rides his horse during the rigorous, six-day journey in sub-zero weather. This moving account explains how the events of 100 years ago grievously wounded the heart and soul of the Lakota People and how, a century later, a special march retracing the steps of their ancestors would begin to heal the wounds.

Yates, Diana. *Chief Joseph: Thunder Rolling Down from the Mountains.* Ward Hill Press, 1992. 141p. (4-8) Biog.

This biography of Chief Joseph of the Nez Percé tells the story of this quiet, dignified, and gentle Indian leader who made war against the white men and lost. Born in 1840, Joseph became Chief at the age of 31 and soon found that the American government was dishonest in their dealings with the Indians. Joseph resisted the use of force as long as possible, but after unsettled disputes and many insults suffered by his people, he participated in the Nez Percé War in 1877. The author based this story on Joseph's own account of his life, and the use of quotations and eyewitness accounts is excellent. This well-written book tells a heart-breaking story in America's settlement of the West. Includes archival photographs, maps, chronology, bibliography, and index.

Yue, David, and Charlotte Yue. *The Tipi: A Center of Native American Life.* Knopf, 1984. 77p. (6-8) Non-fic.

The role of the tipi as the center of family and tribal life is explained through descriptions of the Great Plains Indians of the nineteenth century.

Tipis were comfortable and portable, lending themselves well as shelter for a people that camped in different locations. The use of special tipis, such as burial or medicine lodges, is explained, and the authors use clear line drawings to illustrate the text. The simple language of the book will help children understand the ordinary utility, as well as the spiritual significance of the tipi. Another excellent book by the Yues is *The Pueblo* (Houghton Mifflin, 1986).

2. The Rise of Immigration

Note: Starred (*) books are reviewed in a previous section or unit of this book.

Ada, Alma Flor. *My Name Is María Isabel.* Ill. by K. Dyble Thompson. Trans. from Spanish by Ana M. Cerro. Atheneum, 1993. 57p. (4-6) Fic.

This short novel tells the story of young María Isabel Salazar López whose new teacher changes her name to Mary Lopez because there are already two Marias in the class. María Isabel feels her Puerto Rican identity is being taken away and she is unresponsive to her new name. Misinterpreting her silence, the teacher penalizes María Isabel by not permitting her to act in the Winter Pageant play. Eventually, María Isabel is able to communicate with her teacher. María Isabel's experiences are universal to immigrant children. Black-and-white illustrations accompany the well-written text.

Ashabranner, Brent. *An Ancient Heritage: The Arab-American Minority.* Photos. by Paul S. Conklin. HarperCollins, 1991. 148p. (4-8) Non-fic.

This book begins with a brief history of Arab Americans, including their influx to the United States in the late nineteenth century and the reasons for recent immigration. A series of interviews with Arab-American men and women from different parts of the country and different social strata follows. Readers will learn about dealing with adversity, strong bonds of kinship, the value placed on education, and how young people handle growing up in two cultures. The personal stories of *real* people are the book's greatest strength. Many black-and-white photographs accompany the text. Includes a bibliography and index.

Beatty, Patricia. *Lupita Mañana.* Morrow, 1981. 192p. (6-8) Fic.

Thirteen-year-old Lupita Torres lives in a poor but happy home in Baja California. Her life changes dramatically when her father dies, and her mother decides to send her two oldest children, 15-year-old Salvador and Lupita, to live with her "rich" sister in California. Not speaking English and having no idea how they will cross the border, Lupita and Salvador make their way north, eventually entering the United States hidden in food crates. Upon reaching their aunt, the Torres children discover that she is very poor, and they become pickers in order to send money back to their mother. This touching story, full of realistic adventures and fears, presents the plight of the poor in Mexico and their dreams of a better life in the United States.

Bode, Janet. *New Kids on the Block: Oral Histories of Immigrant Teens.* Franklin Watts, 1989. 126p. (6-8) Non-fic.

This book contains the stories of 11 adolescent immigrants who recently made the United States their home. Young people from India, Cuba, the Philippines, Afghanistan, China, South Korea, El Salvador, Vietnam, Greece, the Dominican Republic, and Mexico answer questions about their home countries, why they left, and what they hope for in their new lives. Although each experience is unique, all the teenagers faced the stress of new schools, communicating in a language they often did not know, and encountering feelings of hate and prejudice on the part of Americans. The stories are touching and will make non-immigrants appreciate the merit of diversity in this nation. Includes a bibliography.

Brownstone, David M. *The Chinese-American Heritage.* Facts on File, 1988. 132p. (4-8) Non-fic.

This fascinating history of the Chinese in America begins with a brief history of China and the social and economic events that led to the immigration of the Chinese people beginning in the middle of the nineteenth century. The author carefully explains the origins of the prejudicial myths against the Chinese immigrants by comparing the stereotypes with the reality of their lives. Close family and ethnic ties developed among the Chinese as an effort to overcome the difficulties of immigration, obtaining work, and finding a place to live. Despite the hard times experienced by the Chinese in the United States, Chinese Americans have become valued citizens whose history is well-told in this volume.

Buss, Fran Leeper, with Daisy Cubias. *Journey of the Sparrows.* Lodestar, 1991. 155p. (6-8) Fic.

In this poignant story, 15-year-old María Acosta and her older sister and younger brother have just been smuggled into the United States in vegetable crates, leaving their mother and younger sister in Mexico. Fleeing political terror in their homeland of El Salvador, the Acosta children end up in Chicago, barely managing to subsist. The girls find occasional work, but they are all going hungry and María begins to question her faith in God. When Mrs. Acosta is deported back to El Salvador, María makes the perilous trip to Mexico to bring her young sister to Chicago. This is a well-written, bittersweet story of the courage and tenacity of political refugees trying to make a new life in the "land of plenty."

Bylinsky, Tatyana. *Before the Wildflowers Bloom.* Crown, 1989. 70p. (4-6) Fic.

This story, based on events in the life of the author's grandmother and seen through the eyes of eight-year-old Carmela, tells of an Italian family whose father works as a coal miner in Colorado in 1916. The five brothers and sisters lead typical lives—fighting with each other, attending school, and doing chores around the house. This all changes the day that the mine explodes and their father is killed, leaving a broken family whose members must somehow cope. Includes a map and a simple black-and-white drawing at the beginning of each chapter.

Conlan-McKenna, Marita. *Wildflower Girl.* Ill. by Donald Teskey. Holiday, 1992. 173p. (6-8) Fic.

In the middle 1850s, a spirited 13-year-old girl named Peggy O'Driscoll leaves her brother and sister in Ireland to travel to find a new life in America. The six-week journey on board a ship in steerage is graphically recounted and readers will get a vivid sense of the difficulties immigrants faced. Upon arrival in Boston, Peggy works as a maid for an abusive woman in a boarding house before finding more permanent employment as a kitchen maid in a wealthy home. Peggy does not allow her loneliness to get the better of her, but she experiences many hardships as she tries to adjust to her new life. This novel, written by an Irish author, is a fine tribute to the memory of the many immigrants who dared to come to the New World in the hopes of a better life.

Fisher, Leonard Everett. *Ellis Island: Gateway to the New World.* Holiday, 1986. 64p. (4-6) Non-fic.

Freedman, Russell. *Immigrant Kids.* Dutton, 1980. 72p. (4-6) Non-fic.

The everyday life of the immigrants of the late 1800s and early 1900s who came to the cities and towns of America are portrayed through archival photographs and a fine text. The simply written and sensitive narrative describes the trip across the Atlantic, home life, school activities, work, and play for immigrant children. The importance of the family is the central theme along with the cooperation among family members in their quest to find a better life in the United States. The crowded and unsafe conditions of the city tenements, child employment, and poverty are part of the immigrants' story.

Garver, Susan, and Paula McGuire. *Coming to North America: From Mexico, Cuba, and Puerto Rico.* Delacorte, 1981. 161p. (6-8) Non-fic.

This is a factual account of three major groups of Hispanic immigrants into the United States—Mexicans, Cubans, and Puerto Ricans. The authors explore the history of each country, the different reasons for immigration, how the different groups have fared in their new home, and how, despite a shared language and heritage, all three groups have had a different set of experiences. The authors make good use of original sources, including books, poems, interviews, reports, and newspaper accounts.Reading the immigrants' own words gives the book great authenticity. Includes photographs, detailed bibliographical references, a brief history of U.S. immigration laws, and an index.

Graff, Nancy Price. *Where the River Runs: A Portrait of a Refugee Family.* Photos. by Richard Howard. Little, Brown, 1993. 70p. (4-6) Non-fic.

Cambodian refugees Sohka Prek and her three sons are modern pilgrims living near Boston, trying to adjust to their new way of life while maintaining the religion and customs of their homeland. The boys, who speak fluent English and Khmer, attend public school where they meet many new immigrant children. Their grandmother, Sok Eng, watches the boys so that Sohka can attend college and aspire to a better job. While there are special people, such as the teachers who are helping the Prek family, there are also others who insult the new immigrants through ignorance and prejudice. The book is illustrated with numerous photographs.

Gross, Virginia T. *It's Only Goodbye: An Immigrant Story.* Ill. by Larry Raymond. Viking, 1990. 54p. (4-6) Fic.

The author bases this story on the experiences of her Italian father and grandfather—a young boy, Umberto Ameliori, and his father, Pietro, who travel in 1892 by ship from France to New York City. They travel in steerage and readers will learn of the many hardships suffered by immigrants as they crossed the Atlantic Ocean. In an unfortunate turn, Pietro is arrested for assaulting a passenger who insulted him, and he is thrown into the brig. Umberto must then work off the payment for their trip by helping the captain. This is a simple introduction to the topic of immigration.

Hesse, Karen. *Letters from Rifka.* Henry Holt, 1992. 148p. (4-8) Fic.

In 1919, 12-year-old Rifka Nebrot and her family flee their Ukranian home to escape the army. The family is headed for America where Rifka's three older brothers have been for the past 14 years. The book takes the form of a series of letters that Rifka writes to her cousin, detailing their experiences. When Rifka contracts ringworm, she must remain alone in Belgium for six months of treatment while her family goes on to America. Rifka's letters reveal a scared but spirited girl who never loses sight of her goal. This excellent, touching story would make a good read-aloud. Rifka's tale is based on the experiences of the author's great-aunt.

Howard, Ellen. *Her Own Song.* Atheneum, 1988. (4-6) Fic.

The story of Mellie, an adopted child who seeks to discover her heritage, is set in Portland, Oregon, in 1908. When her father is injured in an accident, she is befriended by Gemm-Wah, the Chinese laundry man. While searching her memory to try and understand why the Chinese home, food, and language is so familiar, Mellie learns that she was adopted by a Chinese couple, who loved and cared for her during her first four years of life. Because of prejudice, she was taken from them by white authorities. This story highlights the unreasonable discrimination against Chinese during this period and the universality of family love.

Lee, Marie G. *Finding My Voice.* Houghton Mifflin, 1992. 165p. (6-8) Fic.

Ellen Sung is a high school senior living in the small town of Arkin, Minnesota. Ellen is American, although her parents are Korean by birth, and she struggles to maintain a balance between the old and new ways. There is parental pressure to do as well in school as her older sister who is now studying at Harvard. Ellen is motivated academically, but she also wants time to try out for a gymnastics letter and to date. Throughout this difficult year, Ellen must also learn to deal with the racism that results from her being the only Asian student in a small high school. This well-written story presents the perspective of a modern Korean-American girl.

Lehmann, Linda. *Better Than a Princess.* Thomas Nelson, Inc., 1978. (6-8) Fic.

This story of seven-year-old Tilli, who leaves her native Germany in the late 1800s to join her parents in the United States, is based on the life of the author's grandmother. Tilli makes the difficult crossing with two siblings she did not even know she had. Upon reaching America, the three young children are helped by officials through the various checkpoints, and are placed on a train bound for Missouri. This story continues in *Tilli's New World* (Elsevier/Nelson, 1981) with Tilli and her family adjusting to their new life, experiencing prejudice and language barriers as they try to preserve their heritage.

*Levine, Ellen. *...If Your Name Was Changed at Ellis Island.* Ill. by Wayne Parmenter. Scholastic, 1993. (4-6) Non-fic. (Part 1, Unit 7)

Levitin, Sonia. *Journey to America.* Atheneum, 1970. 150p. (6-8) Fic.

In 1938, conditions for Jews in Germany are deteriorating and the Platt family decides they cannot remain in Berlin. Mr. Platt departs first, leaving his wife and three daughters to follow him to America. The story is told from the perspective of 12-year-old Lisa and readers will share the uncomfortable train trip to Zurich, the humiliation suffered at the hands of the Nazi soldiers, and the dreadful conditions at the refugee camp that Lisa and her older sister must go to. Their journey to America is delayed when Mrs. Platt becomes ill, but at the end of a year's separation, the Platt women are finally sailing for the United States. The story of the Platt family in the United States continues in Levitin's *Silver Days* (Atheneum, 1989).

Lord, Bette Bao. *In the Year of the Boar and Jackie Robinson.* Ill. by Marc Simont. Harper & Row, 1984. 169p. (4-6) Fic.

In 1947, a 10-year-old Chinese child, who renames herself Shirley Temple Wong, comes to live in Brooklyn with her parents. The Wongs find life in New York very different from China, but Shirley is most eager to embrace everything American. She has a difficult time blending into the fifth grade at Public School No. 8, but after months of intense loneliness, one of Shirley's classmates introduces Shirley to the joys of baseball. In no time at all, Shirley is a staunch Brooklyn Dodgers and Jackie Robinson fan. Despite the wonders of her new life, Shirley does not forget her Chinese heritage and vows she will always remember the land of her ancestors. Much of this well-told story is based on the author's own experiences as a newcomer to America.

Meltzer, Milton. *The Hispanic Americans.* Photos. by Morris Camhi and Catherine Noren. Crowell, 1982. 149p. (6-8) Non-fic.

Mohr, Nicholasa. *Felita.* Ill. by Ray Cruz. Dial, 1979. 112p. (4-8) Fic.

The Puerto Rican family of eight-year-old Felita Maldonado lives in a declining area of New York City where they are surrounded by other Puerto Ricans and recent immigrant families. The close-knit family works hard to save the money to move to a better neighborhood, but after the children are threatened, insulted, and attacked, the family reluctantly leaves the new apartment and moves back to their old block. The story strongly makes the point that although Puerto Ricans are Americans, they are subjected to prejudicial actions on the part of some of their fellow Americans. The Hispanic culture is accurately portrayed in this story of life in a modern, close-knit urban community.

Morey, Janet Nomura, and Wendy Dunn. *Famous Asian Americans.* Cobblehill, 1992. 170p. (4-8) Biog.

Myerson, Evelyn Wilde. *The Cat Who Escaped from Steerage: A Bubbemeiser.* Scribner's, 1990. 66p. (4-6) Fic.

In the opening years of the twentieth century, nine-year-old Chanah is moving with her family from Poland to America. Traveling by steamship in steerage class, packed together with 900 other people on the lower decks, the family undergoes many hardships during the two-week voyage. A lively girl, Chanah smuggles a scrawny cat aboard who escapes, leading Chanah and her deaf-mute cousin, Yaacov, into several misadventures. Upon reaching Ellis Island, it appears that Yaacov's handicaps will prevent him from being admitted, but Chanah's quick thinking saves the day. This is a good introduction to the immigrant experience in America.

Namioka, Lensey. *Yang the Youngest and His Terrible Ear.* Ill. by Kees de Kiefte. Litte, Brown, 1992. 134p. (4-6) Fic.

Nine-year-old Yingtao Yang is the youngest of four children in a very musical family. When the family moves from China to Seattle, Mr. Yang becomes a music teacher, but he fails to understand why his youngest son cannot make proper music on his violin. Poor Yang tries, but he is tone deaf. As Yang struggles to blend into his new environment, he becomes friends with another violinist, a red-haired boy named Matthew Conner, who teaches Yang about the joys of baseball. This humorous, well-written book recounts the present-day immigrant experience along with children's efforts to assert their individuality and be accepted for who they are.

Perera, Hilda. *Kiki: A Cuban Boy's Adventures in America.* Pickering Press, 1992. 108p. (4-6) Fic.

This is the story of eight-year-old Jesús Lendian Gómez, otherwise known as Kiki, who in the early 1960s leaves his homeland of Cuba with his brother, Tony, and their cousins. The children are supposed to go live with their grandfather, but he is an old man who cannot take care of them. The children are eventually placed in foster homes, and Kiki ends up living with a doctor's family where he is loved and where he begins to forget his Cuban ways. He is shocked, at the age of 12, to learn that his parents have arrived in the United States and he has a difficult time adjusting to living with his family again. This story shows the common experience of immigrant children who sometimes do not know if they belong to the old world or the new. The story is based on a real-life event named "Operation Peter Pan," which brought 14,000 unaccompanied children from Cuba to the United States in 1961 and 1962.

Perkins, Mitali. *The Sunita Experiment.* Little, Brown, 1993. 176p. (4-8) Fic.

When eighth-grader Sunita's grandparents come from India for an extended visit, she has difficulty accepting their customs, clothing, and traditional Indian ways. Her mother tries to make them feel at home by rejecting the family's established American customs. It takes time for everyone in Sunita's family to relax, enjoy the older couple's contributions to the family, and appreciate that they are a blend of two cultures. The story of this young teenager, her friends, and her family is spiced with humor and insights about early adolescence and about the lives of twentieth-century immigrants.

Perrin, Linda. *Coming to America: Immigrants from the Far East.* Delacorte, 1980. 182p. (6-8) Non-fic.

Immigrants from China, Japan, the Philippines, and Vietnam are the focus of this well-documented work. The author examines different reasons for immigration—economic, political, and social—but a common thread is the hope of all immigrants for a better life in America. Many of these immigrants, whether they came in the nineteenth or twentieth centuries, have experienced discrimination and harassment, and most have faced the challenge of trying to mesh their native cultures with that of America's. The author makes extensive use of original sources, including newspaper, personal, and eye-witness accounts. Includes a bibliography, index, and brief history of U.S. immigration laws.

Pinchot, Jane. *The Mexicans in America.* Lerner Publications, 1989. 94p. (6-8) Non-fic.

Beginning with a definition of "Mexican Americans," this book explores the contact of Mexicans with the Spanish, the intermingling of these peoples, and the early Mexican settlements. After 1848, much of the American Southwest and many Mexicans came under American rule. The author chronicles the struggles of Mexican Americans to obtain fair employment, enjoy full rights in this country, and maintain a sense of community and pride in their Mexican heritage. The closing chapter highlights the contributions of Mexican Americans in the areas of government, business, literature, the arts, community service, and sports. Includes many black-and-white photographs, maps, and an index.

*Rappaport, Doreen, ed. *American Women: Their Lives in Their Words: A Documentary History.* Crowell, 1990. (6-8) Non-fic. (Part 2, Unit 3)

Sachs, Marilyn. *Call Me Ruth.* Doubleday, 1982. 134p. (4-6) Fic.

In 1908, eight-year-old Rifka and her mother leave Russia to join Papa in Manhattan. Eager to adopt anything American, Rifka gladly changes her name to Ruth, but her mother has a more difficult time adjusting. After Papa dies, Mama is forced to work in a "sweatshop," and Ruth has conflicting feelings about her mother's growing involvement in the union movement and participation in a strike. In the end, following some mother-daughter conflict, Ruth realizes that her mother has succeeded in becoming an American. This book is a realistic depiction of immigrant life in turn-of-the-century New York and presents the Shirtwaist Makers' Strike of 1909 and the conditions that prompted the rise of unions.

Sherman, Eileen Bluestone. *Independence Avenue.* Jewish Publication Society, 1990. 145p. (4-8) Fic.

In 1907, 14-year-old Elias Cherevnosky leaves his Russian homeland to accompany his elderly, ailing uncle to the United States as part of the Galveston Movement which promised jobs for Jewish immigrants. When his uncle is deported back to Russia, Elias remains, finding a job as a tailor in a department store in Kansas City. The lives of the immigrants are clearly portrayed as they seek to learn English, maintain their religious practices, deal with prejudice, and improve their lives. The characters are well-developed and believable in the early 1900s setting, and the story will help explain why Russian Jews fled the *pogroms* to seek freedom and independence.

Sinnott, Susan. *Extraordinary Hispanic Americans.* Childrens Press, 1991. 277p. (6-8) Biog.

Beginning with the age of exploration, the author presents biographical sketches of the Spanish-speaking peoples of the United States. In addition to such well-known people as Francisco Vásquez de Coronado, Hernando De Soto, and Father Junípero Serra, the first chapters contain minor explorers and colonists not commonly known. The book progresses chronologically into the twentieth century and is illustrated with photographs and historical drawings. People from all walks of life are included—sports, science, the arts, and government—and together they present a composite picture of the different contributions made by Americans of Hispanic descent. Includes a bibliography and index.

Soto, Gary. *Local News.* Harcourt Brace Jovanovich, 1993. 148p. (6-8) Fic.

In this collection of 13 short stories, the author presents vignettes of growing up in a Mexican-American neighborhood in Fresno, California. In "Blackmail," Angel's mean older brother, Weasel, snaps a picture of him in the shower and threatens to show it to everyone at school. On December 31, 10-year-old Blanca Mendoza longs to stay up until midnight and encounters some adventures on this special night in "New Year's Eve." Sixth-grader Robert Suarez bungles his one and only line in "The School Play," incurring the wrath of his tough classmate, Belinda Lopez. The stories are full of humor and Soto's characters and situations ring true. Pair this with Soto's first book of short stories, *Baseball in April* (Harcourt Brace Jovanovich, 1990).

Soto, Gary. *Neighborhood Odes.* Ill. by David Diaz. Harcourt Brace Jovanovich, 1992. 68p. (4-6) Poet.

In a poetical celebration of everyday life, the author writes about daily life in his Mexican-American neighborhood. He writes odes about such things as ice cream trucks and sprinklers on hot summer days, his pet dog and cat, foods such as tortillas and fried pork rinds, playing in the park, the joy of visiting the library, fireworks on the Fourth of July, and family celebrations, including a birthday and a wedding. The crisp text clearly evokes the mood of growing up in an ethnic neighborhood and black-and-white woodcuts accompany the poems. Readers will enjoy composing their own poems after reading this book. Includes a glossary of Spanish words.

*Talbot, Charlene Joy. *An Orphan for Nebraska*. Atheneum, 1979. (6-8) Fic. (Part 2, Unit 8, Sect. 1)

Uchida, Yoshiko. *The Invisible Thread*. Julian Messner, 1991. 136p. (4-8) Biog.

In this frank and well-written account, children's author Yoshiko Uchida talks about growing up Asian in Berkeley, California, in the 1930s. She discusses having to reconcile how she and her sister viewed themselves as Americans, but how others primarily saw them as Japanese. Uchida experienced discrimination in retail establishments and in school and learned how to deal with it. She relates the feelings of incredulity when Executive Order 9066 was issued, which led to the internment of 120,000 Japanese Americans, two-thirds of whom had been born in the United States. Uchida's recollections of her family's internment in the Topaz camp in Utah are excellent and would tie in nicely with a unit on World War II. For a fictional account, see Uchida's *Journey to Topaz: A Story of Japanese-American Evacuation*, Part 2, Unit 12.

Uchida, Yoshiko. *A Jar of Dreams*. Atheneum, 1981. 131p. (4-6) Fic.

Rinko Tsujimura lives in Berkeley, California, during the mid-1930s and she considers herself an average, 12-year-old American girl. However, her obvious Japanese heritage makes her ostracized at school, and the family experiences trouble with their laundry business. Despite the strains, Rinko learns from Papa and Uncle Kanda that pride and belief in one's self can conquer many conflicts. When Aunt Wada arrives from Japan to spend the summer, she helps her troubled family to put matters into perspective and to take pride in being Japanese. This is a moving story about how Japanese Americans fought for acceptance in the 1930s.

Uchida, Yoshiko. *Samurai of Gold Hill*. Ill. by Ati Forberg. Scribner's, 1972. (6-8) Fic.

Following the death of their family in 1869, nine-year-old Koichi and his father leave Japan and journey to California where they hope to raise silkworms. They experience severe discrimination upon their arrival and have a run of bad luck, but, despite their adversities, they find friends in their neighborhood, including a Native American. Although they fail in their farming efforts, these stalwart immigrants carry on as they struggle with the conflict of homeland traditions and adjustments to their new country.

Westridge Young Writers Workshop. *Kids Explore America's African-American Heritage.* John Muir Publications, 1993. 115p. (4-6) Non-fic.

Written by 86 children in grades 3 through 8, this book will help teach others about taking pride in an African-American heritage. The book begins with a history of African Americans, including the Civil Rights era, and follows with chapters on famous black Americans; contributions to art, music, and dance; foods and celebrations; and African-American stories and literary writings. The book closes with a chapter on real African Americans whom the children interviewed. The book is illustrated with photographs and drawings made by the children themselves. This inexpensive resource for teachers will prove invaluable. Includes an index.

Westridge Young Writers Workshop. *Kids Explore America's Hispanic Heritage.* John Muir Publications, 1992. 100p. (4-6) Non-fic.

This book *for* children, written *by* children, presents many aspects of Hispanic culture in the United States. Eighty-two students in the Westridge Young Writers Workshop in suburban Denver, Colorado, write about the history of the early Spanish explorers in America, the missions in the Southwest, and Hispanic foods, festivals, dances, crafts, art, words, and folk tales.They also present short biographies of real Hispanic Americans. The book is liberally illustrated with photographs, historical reproductions, and pictures drawn by the students themselves. This is a unique and useful book for beginning the study of Spanish culture in American life. Includes an index.

Yep, Laurence. *Dragonwings.* Harper & Row, 1975. (6-8) Fic.

Life in San Francisco's Chinatown in the early 1900s is seen through the eyes of a young boy named Moon Shadow who, after arriving in America, learns to ignore the taunts and insults of the *demons*, the Chinese term for white people. After Windrider, Moon Shadow's father, kills a man in self-defense, he and his son move into a stable owned by Miss Whitlaw, an advocate of Chinese rights. Moon Shadow, in his friendship with Miss Whitlaw and her young niece, learns to overcome his own prejudices. The strong, realistic characterizations are non-stereotypic portrayals of Chinese and white people, and the account of the San Francisco earthquake is memorable.

Yep, Laurence. *The Lost Garden.* Julian Messner, 1991. 117p. (6-8) Biog.

This memoir by a Chinese-American author tells of his childhood years growing up in the Pearl Apartments in San Francisco in the 1950s and 1960s, including the corner grocery store run by his parents, neighborhood friends, and forays into Chinatown. Yep recalls not feeling "Chinese" and wishing no association with his family's ethnic heritage and how his grandmother gradually changed his attitude. Yep candidly talks about his days as an altar boy; life at the all-boy's, predominantly white high school, St. Ignatius; and the culture shock of his college career at Marquette University. This is a fascinating personal account by a beloved children's author.

Yep, Laurence. *The Star Fisher.* Morrow, 1991. 150p. (6-8) Fic.

The year is 1927 and 15-year-old Joan Lee and her family have just moved from Ohio to Clarksburg, West Virginia, where Mr. Lee opens a laundry. Because of their Chinese origin, the Lees are quite conspicuous in town and experience prejudice in their everyday dealings. American-born Joan, who must interpret for parents who speak little English, is caught between two cultures as she strives to fit into an unwelcoming community. This humorous, well-written story is based on family stories about Yep's own grandparents, who opened a laundry in a converted schoolhouse in West Virginia.

AMERICA IN THE LATE NINETEENTH AND EARLY TWENTIETH CENTURIES

❀ ❀ ❀ ❀ ❀ ❀ ❀ ❀

INTRODUCTION TO UNITS 9 AND 10

During the late nineteenth and early twentieth centuries, the United States grew increasingly stronger as a recognized world power and industrial nation. This expansion of world recognition and power is the central theme of Units 9 and 10, along with the inventions and technology that accelerated industrial production, expanded agriculture, and made transportation, trade, and communication easier and more effective.

These interrelated changes will be examined by the students through the development of flow charts, time lines, maps, and informative posters showing the changes brought about by war, technology, annexation, and the work of the reformers.

UNIT
nine

America in the Late Nineteenth Century through the Great War

OBJECTIVES

1. As a whole class activity, the students will develop a time line or flow chart showing the events during the late nineteenth and early twentieth centuries that contributed to the United States' rise as a world power.
2. Using maps from a variety of sources, the students will identify the changes brought about by the Spanish-American War and World War I.
3. Through reading fiction and biography, students will identify the changes in the lives of ordinary people during this period, how they coped with change, and how those coping strategies could be applied today.

LEARNING ACTIVITIES

1. The United States Becomes a World Power

As students read about events in the rise of the United States as a world power in their history and social studies textbooks and the books on the Book List, they will write brief descriptions of the events, including important dates on 5" by 8" cards. Designate a large bulletin board as the time line or flow chart titled "The United States Becomes a World Power." The students will then place the descriptions in appropriate chronological order for a time line, or suitably connected within the flow chart. This visual representation of the themes of this period of history will continue to grow and develop throughout the study of Units 9 and 10. As this project develops and extends into Units 11 through 13, challenge the students to point out those events that impacted *only* the United States.

To aid in the organization of the flow chart/time line, the bulletin board may be divided into vertical sections: war, annexation, the work of the reformers, changes in technology, environmental concerns, agriculture, industry, life in the cities, rise in labor unions, women's movement, transportation, communication, and other topics. Horizontally, the bulletin board will be divided into 10-year segments. This will provide a visual, dated representation of how the events are interrelated throughout Units 9 and 10, such as the development of flight and World War I; the development of factories and industries and the work of reformers that resulted in the rise of unions and the child labor laws. The connections between events may be shown by pieces of yarn that link the appropriate 5" by 8" cards.

The Book Lists for Units 9 and 10 will provide sources of information for this project.

2. Mapping Changes in the World

Using books from the Book List and other sources, the students will locate maps showing the changes resulting from the Spanish-American War and World War I. As a class, list the changes found. Next, determine if any of these areas of change are in the news currently. If so, what clues for unrest can be found in the maps?

3. Changes for Ordinary People

While Activities 1 and 2 deal with the world picture, this activity will again focus the students' attention on how world events impact individuals. Each student will choose a book from the Book Lists for Units 9 or 10 that deals with a major topic from the flow chart/time line in Activity 1, but from the viewpoint of ordinary people, both real and fictional. See such books as: Eight Mules from Monterey; No Hero for the Kaiser; Native American Doctor; Words by Heart; After the Dancing Days; Mother, Aunt Susan and Me; and The Long Hard Journey.

In their History Journals, the students will write how a book character's life was changed by events and how this person coped with the changes. After this writing assignment is completed, group the students according to their book choices: those dealing with the labor movement would constitute one group; those set in and after World War I another group, and so on. In the groups, the students will share their writing and develop a composite list of how national and world events changed people's lives and how people coped with these changes. The groups will then present their lists to the class. After each group has shared their findings, have the class develop a list of the ways

1990-2000	1980-1990	1970-1980	1960-1970	1950-1960	1940-1950	1930-1940	1920-1930	1910-1920	1900-1910	1890-1900	YEAR
									etc.	Spanish-American War	War
										Guam Philippines Cuba	Annexation
										etc.	Reformers
											Technology
											Environment
											Agriculture

CHART 14　The United States Becomes a World Power

in which people cope with change. For example, people work together toward a common goal, use existing laws and try to change laws, educate themselves so that they are better able to help others, etc.

Students will record in their Journals how they could apply one or more of these coping strategies in their lives today.

BOOK LIST

Note: Starred (*) books are reviewed in a previous section or unit of this book.

Archer, Jules. *Breaking Barriers: The Feminist Revolution from Susan B. Anthony to Margaret Sanger to Betty Friedan.* Viking, 1991. 207p. (6-8) Biog.

The author proposes that the three women whose biographies are in this book did the most to advance the women's movement for sexual equality in America. Each defied convention, sometimes at great personal risk, in their

1990-2000	1980-1990	1970-1980	1960-1970	1950-1960	1940-1950	1930-1940	1920-1930	1910-1920	1900-1910	1890-1900	YEAR
											Industry
											City Life
											Labor Unions
											Women's Rights
											Transportation
											Communication

CHART 14 The United States Becomes a World Power *(continued)*

struggle to liberate women from the restrictions of a world dominated by men. Each of these women made a significant contribution to the women's movement—Susan B. Anthony was primarily responsible for securing the vote for women, Margaret Sanger was the pioneer in obtaining for women the right to family planning, and Betty Friedan was responsible for the modern movement commonly known as women's liberation. The biographies are well-written and Archer makes excellent use of primary source materials. Includes photographs, bibliography, and index.

Beatty, Patricia. *Eight Mules from Monterey.* Morrow, 1982. (6-8) Fic.

This novel, based on the journals of an actual librarian, tells the story of Lettie Ashmore, a widow and a recent library trainee who volunteers to go into the California mountains in 1916 to establish library outposts in the many isolated communities located there. Lettie and her two children meet many different kinds of mountain people and have numerous adventures with the difficult mules. The characterizations are well done and an author's note helps to differentiate between fact and fiction.

Bosco, Peter. *World War I.* Facts on File, 1991. 124p. (6-8) Non-fic.

*Bylinsky, Tatyana. *Before the Wildflowers Bloom.* Crown, 1989. (4-6) Fic. (Part 2, Unit 8, Sect. 2)

Cheney, Cora. *Alaska: Indians, Eskimos, Russians, and the Rest.* Dodd, Mead, 1980. 143p. (4-8) Non-fic.

This is a well-written book about the history of Alaska from the Ice Age to the present day. More than one-half of the book is devoted to the Russian exploration and settlement of Alaska and many of the chapters read like exciting adventure stories. The author explains how Alaska was purchased by the United States in 1867, precipitating running jokes about "America's icebox," and polar bears being given the right to vote. The Gold Rush of the late 1800s is examined as is Alaska's road to statehood. The book is liberally illustrated with historical photographs, maps, and portraits, and includes an index.

Cullen-DuPont, Kathryn. *Elizabeth Cady Stanton and Women's Liberty.* Facts on File, 1992. 133p. (6-8) Biog.

*Ferris, Jeri. *Native American Doctor: The Story of Susan LaFlesche Picotte.* Carolrhoda, 1991. (4–6) Biog. (Part 2, Unit 8, Sect. 1)

Frank, Rudolf. *No Hero for the Kaiser.* Ill. by Klaus Steffens. Trans. from German by Patricia Crampton. Lothrop, 1986. (Orig. pub. in 1931) 222p. (6-8) Fic.

Fourteen-year-old Jan and his dog, Fox, survive the bombardment of their village in Poland. Afterwards, Jan joins the German battalion, more out of desperation than any feelings of loyalty. They welcome him because he knows the territory and speaks Polish and German. As they move from battle to battle, each described in horrifying detail, Jan and his dog seem to bring them good luck, although Jan cannot pledge ultimate loyalty to Germany. Most chapters begin with strong anti-war statements concerning weapons, *cannon fodder*, different treatment of officers and foot soldiers, and the futility of the deaths in this war. Although the book is a little difficult to read, the teacher might want to read aloud some of the spine-chilling descriptions of the fighting on the front in World War I. This powerful book was banned in Germany when Hitler came into power.

Fritz, Jean. *Bully for You, Teddy Roosevelt!* Ill. by Mike Wimmer. Putnam, 1991. 127p. (4-6) Biog.

Roosevelt the man, as well as the leader and president, comes alive in this zestful biography. Beginning with a childhood plagued with asthma but bursting with interests in the natural world, Roosevelt was ever the energetic crusader for personal and national causes. The author presents a multi-faceted view of this fascinating man who was the champion of the National Park System, of participatory democracy, and of peace. The setting of Roosevelt's life makes this biography an especially important book about the late 1800s and early 1900s. This is a good read-aloud selection. For older readers, a good biography of Roosevelt is Nancy Whitelaw's *Theodore Roosevelt Takes Charge* (Albert Whitman, 1992).

Gardner, Robert, and Dennis Shortelle. *The Forgotten Players: The Story of Black Baseball in America.* Walker, 1993. 120p. (4-8) Non-fic.

This is a well-written tribute to the role of the black baseball leagues in African-American culture and to the talented men who were barred from major league baseball because of the color of their skin. Beginning around the time of the Civil War, the authors trace the history of black baseball, and feature such men as Rube Foster, who began the Negro National League in the 1920s, and Gus Greenlee, who reorganized the League a decade later. Readers will learn about the versatility and rigorous life of African-American baseball players, and the discrimination they experienced as they traveled around the country. The final chapter discusses the integration of professional baseball. The book includes many photographs, a bibliography, and an index.

Giblin, James Cross. *Edith Wilson: The Woman Who Ran the United States.* Ill. by Michele Laporte. Viking, 52p. (4-6) Biog.

This is a simple biography of Edith Bolling Wilson, the 42-year-old widow who married President Woodrow Wilson in 1915. The president took his wife into his confidence and she was a constant source of support and advice for him during the troubled years of World War I. Following the war, when President Wilson suffered a stroke in 1919, Mrs. Wilson helped to run the country so that her husband would not have to resign before the League of Nations became a reality. Includes black-and-white illustrations.

Gregory, Kristiana. *Earthquake at Dawn.* Harcourt Brace Jovanovich, 1992. 192p. (4-8) Fic.

The horror of the San Francisco earthquake of 1906 is viewed from the perspectives of two women: 22-year-old Edith Irvine, a schoolteacher and photographer, and her 15-year-old maid, Daisy Valentine. Traveling through San Francisco, the women arrive the morning of the quake and remain a number of days before making their way back home. They experience fires, collapsing buildings, looting and lawlessness, crude sanitary facilities, and a lack of food, clothing, shelter, and water. Edith Irvine was a real person, who, against police orders, took 60 photographs of the devastated city which remained hidden for 80 years. The book is well researched and the vivid writing style makes for a realistic portrayal of the event. Includes a bibliography.

Harrah, Madge. *Honey Girl.* Avon, 1990. 120p. (4-6) Fic.

Set in 1908 and based on the true experiences of the Stahmann family, *Honey Girl* is the story of the family's move from Wisconsin to Arkansas along with their hundreds of beehives. Dorothy, the Honey Girl, was her father's helper with the bee-keeping business, and aided her ailing mother by taking care of her younger siblings. The family is moving south on account of Mother's health and the trip down the Mississippi River on a barge is full of dangers and challenges. Dorothy makes many new friends and learns that she can indeed be a responsible, ingenious, and courageous member of the family. This is a realistic look at travel on the Mississippi and lifestyles of the early 1900s.

Hoobler, Dorothy, and Thomas Hoobler. *An Album of World War I.* Watts, 1976. 96p. (4-6) Non-fic.

This pictorial study of the First World War narrates the origins of the war, followed by short essays on the major military engagements, new weapons, the war on the seas, the Russian Revolution, America's entry in the war, life on all of the home fronts, the Versailles treaty, and the effects of the war. The clear text is accompanied by countless historical photographs that poignantly depict the devastation, hardships, and emotions of war. This excellent introduction for middle readers could be paired with Dorothy and Thomas Hoobler's *The Trenches.* Includes an index.

Hoobler, Dorothy, and Thomas Hoobler. *The Trenches: Fighting on the Western Front in World War I.* Putnam, 1978. 191p. (6-8) Non-fic.

Houston, Gloria. *Littlejim.* Ill. by Thomas B. Allen. Philomel, 1990. 176p. (4-6) Fic.

The Blue Ridge Mountains of North Carolina during World War I are the setting for this story of 12-year-old Littlejim Houston and his relationship with his stern father. Against the wishes of his father, who thinks that book-learning is "tomfoolery," Littlejim enters an essay-writing contest on "What it means to be an American," in the hopes that he will win and make his father proud. The well-told story is based, in part, on the childhood of the author's father and contains a wealth of regional and historical detail.

Jacobs, William Jay. *Mother, Aunt Susan and Me: The First Fight for Women's Rights.* Coward, McCann, 1979. 61p. (4-6) Non-Fic.

Sixteen-year-old Harriot Stanton narrates the activities of her mother, Elizabeth Cady Stanton, and her mother's colleague, Susan B. Anthony, in their efforts to win equal rights for women in the second half of the nineteenth century. These remarkable women began their fight for women's rights in 1848 at the women's meeting in Seneca Falls, New York, and they continued as a team throughout their lives, fighting not only for the rights of women, but also for the abolition of slavery, an eight-hour work day, the end of child labor, and other social issues. The well-written text is accompanied by fascinating archival photographs and illustrations. Includes a list of sources.

Karr, Kathleen. *It Ain't Always Easy.* Farrar Straus Giroux, 1990. 228p. (6-8) Fic.

Two homeless children, ten-year-old Jack McConnell and eight-year-old Mandy Kerrigan, are the central characters in this story set in 1882. After trying to survive outdoors during a hard winter, the children take themselves to the Children's Aid Society for shelter. They miss the orphan train going West, and so they walk from New York City to New Hope, Pennsylvania, hoping to find a family to take them in. They are split up and Jack is so desperate to rescue Mandy from an abusive family that he eventually returns to New York to seek help. This is an exciting, well-written story about the difficult lot of orphan children during the late 1800s.

Kinsey-Warnock, Natalie. *The Night the Bells Rang.* Ill. by Leslie W. Bowman. Cobblehill, 1991. 79p. (4-6) Fic.

Mason, a boy of 11 or 12, lives with his family on their Vermont farm. The year 1918 is an important one in Mason's life as he struggles with the local bully, Aden Cutler, helps his father in the birth of a colt, and assists with farm chores, sugaring, and making cider. Mason is astounded when he hears that Aden has run off to war, and must grapple with conflicting feelings when he learns that Aden died in the Argonne Forest. This timeless story portrays life in the United States in the early twentieth century.

*Kudlinski, Kathleen V. *Hero Over Here.* Viking, 1990. (4-6) Fic. (Part 1, Unit 10)

Lenski, Lois. *Strawberry Girl.* Lippincott, 1945. 193p. (4-8) Fic.

This story, set in southern Florida in the early 1900s, centers on two very distinct families—a Christian and loving family, the Boyers, and their very antithesis, the Slater family, ruled by an alcoholic, abusive father. The story is told from the perspective of 12-year-old Birdie Boyer, who earned the nickname "Strawberry Girl" by marketing the family's crop. The animosity between the two families escalates into violence and a series of dramatic incidents, including a fire. The author's attention to detail and realism is admirable and this winner of the 1946 Newbery Award is a timeless and classic case of good versus evil, with the eventual triumph of dignity over adversity.

Marrin, Albert. *The Spanish-American War.* Atheneum, 1991. 182p. (6-8) Non-fic.

Miller, Luree, and Scott Miller. *Alaska: Pioneer Stories of a Twentieth-Century Frontier.* Cobblehill, 1991. 116p. (6-8) Biog.

This compilation of biographical stories about twentieth-century pioneers in Alaska, begins with the authors' own relatives, Frank and Mary Miller, who came to Alaska in 1906 in search of gold, and Millie and Jim Dodson, who ran an air service in the "bush" in the 1930s. Other people include the daughter of early Valdez settlers, a Native Inuit leader, wilderness people who earned their living during the oil boom, and a fishing family. The authors intertwine factual articles about the purchase of Alaska; its culture, climate, and geography; its involvement in World War II; and its renewed cultural ties with the former Soviet Union. The book is illustrated with photographs and maps, and includes a glossary, bibliography, and index.

Ray, Delia. *Gold! The Klondike Adventure.* Lodestar, 1989. 90p. (4-8) Non-fic.

When prospectors Skookum Jim, George Carmack, and Tagish Charley spread the news of their gold findings in the Klondike River Valley in Canada's Yukon in 1897, they triggered a massive gold rush. This book tells of the thousands of people who headed north to escape a depressed American economy, not knowing what was in store for them. Although the rush lasted only several years, it had significant effects upon settlement in Alaska and the desolate corner of Canada known as the Klondike. The more than 50 historical photographs are fascinating and show many women participating in the rush. Includes a glossary and index.

Robinet, Harriette Gillem. *Children of the Fire.* Atheneum, 1991. 134p. (4-6) Fic.

Eleven-year-old Hallelujah, a black child living in Chicago in 1871, is fascinated with the fires that have occurred during the summer and fall. The fire that begins in Chicago on October 8 burns over four miles of the city and leaves one-third of the population homeless. Hallelujah's adventures during the fire, which forever change her, will transport readers back to this devastating occurrence. Rich and poor, black and white—all were affected by the fire, and Chicago children played important roles during the blaze and its aftermath. The author explains the historical basis for the story, and includes a map and bibliography.

Rostowski, Margaret. *After the Dancing Days.* Harper & Row, 1986. 217p. (6-8) Fic.

It is the summer of 1919, and 13-year-old Annie Metcalf's doctor father has just returned to Kansas City to work at a special hospital for returning veterans. Haunted by the sight of the sick, disabled soldiers, Annie begins to visit the hospital, eventually befriending a horribly disfigured soldier named Andrew Clayton. Although bitter and cynical, Andrew begins to change after weeks of Annie's company and the two come to be special friends. Annie is devastated when Andrew leaves at the end of the summer to take a job as a physical therapist, but she finds the strength in herself to be happy for him. This beautiful story tells of a girl's coming-of-age, how she comes to the grips with the aftermath of war, and how she redefines the meaning of patriotism.

St. George, Judith. *Panama Canal: Gateway to the World.* Putnam, 1989. 159p. (6-8) Non-fic.

This fascinating, well-researched account tells of the 10-year effort, begun in 1904, to build the famous waterway linking the Atlantic and Pacific Oceans. The story is filled with political intrigue, arrogant and egotistical leaders, hard-working men, torrential rains and mud-slides, life-threatening diseases, such as yellow fever and malaria, and incredible technical, medical, and engineering accomplishments. The author quotes extensively from original sources, making the story of the building of the Panama Canal read like an exciting adventure novel. The book is filled with enthralling archival photographs and maps that help readers visualize what was taking place. Includes a bibliography and index.

Sebestyen, Ouida. *Words by Heart.* Little, Brown, 1968. (6-8) Fic.

This powerful story tells of 11-year-old Lena Sills, a black girl whose family sharecrops on a farm in an almost all-white town in the American Southwest in the early 1900s. After Lena wins a local Bible-verse memorization contest, she is shunned by many of the townspeople and Lena struggles, with the help of her wise and kind father, to understand why she is different. When her father dies as a result of a vicious attack, Lena must reconcile her feelings of hate and revenge with the peaceful way her father has taught her to deal with adversity.

Skurzynski, Gloria. *Good-bye, Billy Radish.* Bradbury, 1992. 138p. (4-8) Fic.

The steel town of Caanan, Pennsylvania, in 1917 is the setting for this story of friendship and life on the home front during World War I. Small for his age, 11-year-old Hank Kerner has become fast friends with Bazyli Radichevych (known as Billy Radish), a big, 13-year-old immigrant from the Ukraine. The two boys celebrate the 4th of July and Billy's new citizenship, see older boys go off to war and be killed, celebrate a wedding and a Ukranian name day party, and experience changes in their relationship when Billy goes to work full time at the steel mill on his fourteenth birthday. The author evokes a strong sense of time and place in this well-crafted coming-of-age novel.

Stanley, Fay. *The Last Princess: The Story of Princess Ka'iulani of Hawai'i.* Ill. by Diane Stanley. Four Winds, 1991. 40p. (4-6) Biog.

This lavishly illustrated book tells the story of Princess Ka'iulani, the last royal princess of the Kingdom of Hawaii. From her fairy-tale childhood to boarding school in England, Ka'iulani was reared to rule. But on the Hawaiian Islands, the white Americans were determined to annex Hawaii against its will. At the age of 17, Ka'iulani made a personal appeal to President Grover Cleveland, who was able to stop the annexation until he left office in 1897. This is a sensitive biography of a princess who never governed.

Stewart, Gail B. *World War I.* Lucent Books, 1991. 112p. (4-8) Non-fic.

Van Raven, Pieter. *Harpoon Island.* Scribner's, 1989. 150p. (6-8) Fic.

Schoolteacher Frank Barnes is at the end of his rope when he accepts a teaching job in a one-room school on Harpoon Island, off the coast near Portland, Maine. His 10-year-old son, Brady, is very small and slow for his age, and people often show intolerance of father and son. Mr. Barnes manages to succeed in his new position, but things go awry when the United States declares war on Germany in 1917 and the islanders discover Mr. Barnes' German heritage. This is a excellent vehicle for examining both prejudice and ignorance about handicaps.

White, Florence Meiman. *First Woman in Congress: Jeannette Rankin.* Julian Messner, 1980. 95p. (4-6) Biog.

Whitney, Sharon, and Tom Raynor. *Women in Politics.* Watts, 1986. 143p. (6-8) Non-fic.

This book focuses on the political process—how women gained political recognition and appointment, what motivates women to run for office, what women in government have achieved and where they get their support, and what inequities in representation still remain. The authors give the historical background of women's suffrage and provide information about pioneer female political leaders, such as Jeannette Rankin and Shirley Chisholm. Also discussed are the careers of many individual women in the twentieth century, including women in the legislative, judicial, and executive branches of municipal, state, and national governments. Includes photographs, a bibliography, and an index.

Wyman, Andrea. *Red Sky at Morning.* Holiday, 1991. 230p. (6-8) Fic.

Life for 12-year-old Callie Common changes dramatically in 1909 when, with her father away in Oregon looking for new land, her mother dies in childbirth. In order to make ends meet, Callie's 15-year-old sister, Katherine, must leave home to work in a deplorable boarding house. Callie is left to care for their aged grandfather, Opa, a gruff German immigrant, and to help run the family's Indiana farm. Readers will see a vivid portrayal of rural farm life in the early 1900s and the of the strength of two sisters who took on obligations beyond their years. Includes a glossary of German words.

❈ ❈ ❈ ❈ ❈ ❈ ❈ ❈

UNIT

ten

❈ ❈ ❈ ❈ ❈ ❈ ❈ ❈

Technology, the Twentieth-Century Industrial Revolution, and the Rise of Unions

OBJECTIVES

1. Students will continue working on the charts and History Journal activities from Unit 9.
2. Working in small groups or individually, the students will make posters advertising new products, outstanding people, and social concerns.
3. Through discussion of the posters completed in Activity 2, students will determine the connections of the new products, outstanding people, and social concerns to the time line/flow chart completed in Unit 9, Activity 1, showing the rise of the United States to the status of world power.

LEARNING ACTIVITIES

1. New Products, Services, and Concerns

In small groups or individually, students will choose an invention, individual, or social concern of this era. They will then make posters advertising the invention, the services or accomplishments of the individual, or elicit support for a social concern.

2. Connections

After the small group and individual posters are completed, the class will examine each chart and determine how it connects with the large chart completed by the class in Unit 9, Activity 1, The United States Becomes a World Power. The process of identifying the connections will serve to summarize and pull the events of this period together.

BOOK LIST

Note: Starred (*) books are reviewed in a previous section or unit of this book.

Alter, Judith. *Eli Whitney*. Watts, 1990. 63p. (4-6) Biog.

Although best known for his invention of the cotton gin, Eli Whitney's greatest achievement was probably his contribution of the concept and use of standardized parts in manufacturing. When the cotton gin did not bring Whitney the wealth he had hoped for, he then turned his creative energies to the systematic manufacturing of rifles and muskets. Alter relates some of the facts of Whitney's life, including his late start in college, his unsuccessful dealings with the newly established Patent Office, and his late marriage. The book's many illustrations and period reproductions enhance the readable text. Includes a glossary, bibliography, and index.

*Altman, Susan. *Extraordinary Black Americans: From Colonial to Contemporary Times*. Childrens Press, 1989. (4-8) Biog. (Part 2, Unit 3)

Boyne, Walter J. *The Smithsonian Book of Flight for Young People*. Atheneum, 1988. 127p. (4-8) Non-fic.

This outstanding history of flight is illustrated with nearly 100 photographs of various flying machines, their inventors, and pilots, from pioneers, such as Otto Lilienthal and Wilbur and Orville Wright, to the present day. The text is clearly and concisely written by the former director of the National Air and Space Museum in Washington, D.C. The book is an excellent source for the chronology of flight and for information on specific planes. The closing chapter touches on the future of manned flight into space.

Briggs, Carole S. *At the Controls: Women in Aviation*. Lerner, 1991. 72p. (4-8) Biog.

Among the aviation pioneers of the early 1900s were such women as African American Bessie Coleman, Amelia Earhart, and Katherine Stinson.

They led the way for the Women Airforce Service Pilots of World War II, the International Association of Female Pilots, and the female pilots of recent decades who have set flight records. The author tells the stories of the pioneer pilots, along with the more recent accomplishments of Sheila Scott, a polar flyer; astronaut Jerrie Cobb; Bonnie Tiburzi, a major airline pilot; and Jacqueline Cochran, the first female flyer to break the sound barrier. Their combined stories tell not only of the progress of women pilots, but also the history of flight. Many color and black-and-white illustrations and photographs accompany the succinct text.

Collins, David R. *Pioneer Plowmaker: The Story of John Deere.* Ill. by Steve Michaels. Carolrhoda, 1990. 63p. (4-6) Biog.

Dunn, Andrew. *Alexander Graham Bell.* Bookwright Press, 1991. 48p. (4-6) Biog.

Fisher, Leonard Everett. *Tracks Across America: The Story of the American Railroad, 1825-1900.* Holiday, 1992. 92p. (4-8) Non-fic.

Fleming, Thomas. *Behind the Headlines: The Story of American Newspapers.* Walker, 1989. 154p. (4-8) Non-fic.

Goldin, Barbara Diamond. *Fire! The Beginnings of the Labor Movement.* Ill. by James Watling. Viking, 1992. 54p. (4-6) Fic.

The narrator of this short book is 11-year-old Rosie, the younger daughter in a Russian-Jewish immigrant family living in New York in 1911. Rosie longs to work in the shirtwaist factory like her older sister, Freyda, in order to help the family financially, but her parents insist she remain in school. When fire breaks out at the Triangle Shirtwaist Company on March 25, the place where Freyda works, Rosie rushes down to the scene and is horrified by what she sees. An author's note explains the circumstances surrounding the fire and how it led to reforms and the rise of labor unions. Includes black-and-white drawings.

Greene, Katherine, and Richard Greene. *The Man Behind the Magic: The Story of Walt Disney.* Viking, 1991. 183p. (4-8) Biog.

Haber, Louis. *Black Pioneers of Science and Invention.* Harcourt Brace Jovanovich, 1970. 264p. (4-8) Biog.

Landau, Elaine. *Robert Fulton.* Watts, 1991. 62p. (4-6) Biog.

*Macaulay, David. *Mill.* Houghton Mifflin, 1983. (4-6) Non-fic. (Part 2, Unit 5)

McKissack, Patricia, and Fredrick McKissack. *A Long Hard Journey: The Story of the Pullman Porter.* Walker, 1989. 144p. (4-8) Non-fic.

This fascinating account of the black men who were porters on the Pullman coaches begins with the ex-slaves who were polished household servants and proceeds to the unionization of the porters. The strength of this history is the context it gives for the events in the long struggle for fair labor practices for black porters. The portrayal of the role of the porters' wives' in establishing the union gives ample credit to women. The authors provide an excellent vehicle for helping children understand why African Americans felt ostracized by white labor management and worked so hard for so many years to establish a union. The archival photographs add reality to this informative work.

Mitchell, Barbara. *A Pocketful of Goobers: A Story About George Washington Carver*. Ill. by Peter E. Hanson. Carolrhoda, 1986. 64p. (4-6) Biog.

The black man who invented over 300 uses for the peanut is the focus of this well-written, brief biography. Born as a slave in Missouri around the time of the Emancipation Proclamation, Carver struggled to get an education, and eventually entered Simpson College in Iowa at the age of 27. After earning his master's degree at the Iowa Agricultural College in Ames, Carver became a professor at the Tuskegee Institute in Alabama. There, he devoted his entire life to education and research, eventually convincing local farmers to raise goobers (the African word for peanuts). This gentle, dedicated teacher is an excellent role model for today's youth. Includes black-and-white drawings.

O'Connor, Karen. *Sally Ride and the New Astronauts: Scientists in Space*. Watts, 1983. 88p. (4-6) Non-fic.

Perez, Norah A. *Breaker*. Houghton Mifflin, 1988. 206p. (6-8) Fic.

A coal-mining community in northeast Pennsylvania in 1902 is the setting for this story about 14-year-old Pat McFarlane and his family. After losing his father in a mining accident, Pat is forced to leave school and become a breaker boy to support his family. The noise and working conditions are horrendous and Pat has never been so tired in his life. There are many tensions in town between the Irish and the other immigrants—Poles, Germans, and Hungarians—and the story portrays prejudice and discrimination. When the recently organized miners strike, life becomes very difficult for the mining families in this rich and well-written story of early labor organizing, fear, support, and family love.

*Rappaport, Doreen, ed. *American Women: Their Lives in Their Words: A Documentary History*. Crowell, 1990. (6-8) Non-fic. (Part 2, Unit 3)

Rappaport, Doreen. *Trouble at the Mines*. Ill. by Joan Sandin. Crowell, 1987. 85p. (4-6) Fic.

Rosie Wilson's father, two brothers, and uncle are all coal miners in the town of Arnot, Pennsylvania. Following an accident that claims the life of a miner, Mr. Wilson helps lead a miners' strike. Thinking the strike will not last long, the families are dismayed when it continues month after month. At a low point, Mary Harris "Mother" Jones arrives on the scene, providing encouragement and organizing the women to help in the effort. The story of this challenging time is told from young Rosie's perspective and readers will learn about the hardships, anxieties, hunger, and divided families that resulted from the eight-month strike. Includes a brief bibliography.

*Sachs, Marilyn. *Call Me Ruth.* Doubleday, 1982. (4-6) Fic. (Part 2, Unit 8, Sect. 2)

St. George, Judith. *The Mount Rushmore Story.* Putnam, 1985. 128p. (4-8) Non-fic.

*St. George, Judith. *Panama Canal: Gateway to the World.* Putnam, 1989. (6-8) Non-fic. (Part 2, Unit 9)

Shapiro, Mary J. *How They Built the Statue of Liberty.* Ill. by Huck Scarry. Random House, 1985. 61p. (4-8) Non-fic.

This fascinating account of the Statue of Liberty takes readers from the birth of the idea for the famous statue, through the fund-raising, to the actual building of the sculpture in France and its final erection on Bedloe's Island in New York Harbor in 1886. The detailed black-and-white drawings, cross sections, and diagrams are integral to the story and are nothing short of captivating as readers get an idea of the monumental size of this famous landmark and the impressive feat of engineering involved in building "Liberty Enlightening the World."

Veglahn, Nancy T. *Women Scientists.* Facts on File, 1991. 134p. (4-8) Biog.

Part of the "American Profiles" series, this book presents brief biographies of 11 American women scientists, including Alice Eastwood, Edith Quimby, Margaret Mead, Barbara McClintock, Gerty Cori, and Rachel Carson. The biographies, which focus on the individual's professional accomplishments, will instruct young readers about the advances these women made in botany, chromosome research, radiation physics, industrial medicine, solid state physics, anthropology, genetics, and the environment. Each biography concludes with a bibliography and a chronology of the scientist's life. Includes an index.

*Weidt, Maryann N. *Mr. Blue Jeans: A Story About Levi Strauss.* Carolrhoda, 1990. (4-6) Biog. (Part 2, Unit 8, Sect. 1)

Yount, Lisa. *Black Scientists.* Facts on File, 1991. 97p. (4-8) Biog.

In this volume of the "American Profile" series, the author presents concise biographies of eight African-American scientists, including one woman, whose fields range from cell and blood plasma research to computer engineering to heart surgery. The author successfully makes the accomplishments of these individuals understandable to children and places their achievements in the proper historical perspective. Most of the biographies focus on the individual's professional achievements, although Yount does include some human interest stories. Each biography concludes with a bibliography and a chronology of the major events in the scientist's life. Includes an index.

AMERICA IN THE TWENTIETH CENTURY

❋ ❋ ❋ ❋ ❋

INTRODUCTION TO UNITS 11, 12, AND 13

Unit 11, "The Roaring Twenties and the Great Depression," examines how Americans in the 1920s, hoped for continued prosperity and growth of industry and business. Prosperity seemed to be the central concern as agriculture, industry, and business grew, supported by the ever-expanding stock market in which many Americans had invested their money. When the value of stocks dropped an average of 40 percent on "Black Thursday," October 24, 1929, Americans despaired and many wondered what had happened.

Slowly but surely, the United States recovered from the disastrous results of the Great Depression, but every family felt its devastation. Students will examine the multiple causes and effects of the Depression through newspapers, interviews, and reading.

As students read about World War II and the Holocaust in Unit 12, aspects of the various theaters of war will capture immediate attention, while the larger questions of the effects of totalitarianism and persecution, of loyalty, moral conscience, and courage will also be addressed. In this unit, the students will use newspapers, interviews, and reading to examine the factual accounts of the war and the stories of the people, both real and fictional, whose lives were affected by this global conflict. They will respond to the Second World War and its events by writing in their History Journals about the lives of various people before, during, and after the war.

In Unit 13, "The Middle Decades of the Twentieth Century," students will survey the problems of human rights, environmental concerns, and international conflicts in the twentieth century by continuing the time line/flow chart begun in Units 9 and 10. Students will pursue several summarizing activities that assess recent events and their historical antecedents. Students will construct a memorial wall showing names, dates, and accomplishments of the people throughout U.S. history who have been involved in the quest for civil and human rights. They will close the unit by reviewing the Bill of Rights and selecting the 10 most significant events in the history of the United States.

The Roaring Twenties and the Great Depression

OBJECTIVES

1. Using newspapers from the period of the Depression, supplemented by textbooks and other reference sources, the students will list multiple causes of the Depression.
2. Students will design a questionnaire to use when interviewing people who remember the Depression years.
3. Based on Objectives 1 and 2 and selected fictional accounts of the Depression, students will write in their History Journal about how families coped with the Depression.

LEARNING ACTIVITIES

1. Events Leading to the Stock Market Crash

Read portions of Russell Freedman's *Franklin Delano Roosevelt* to the class. Freedman's description of the events leading to the Depression are clearly stated and easily understood. Using photocopied newspapers from the period prior to October 1929, have students search for accounts of the causes of the Depression. From the newspaper accounts, Freedman and other sources, including the social studies and history textbooks, students will cite causes of the Depression and list these events on a chart.

2. How Did the Depression Affect the Lives of Ordinary People?

In small groups, students will examine newspapers from the Depression years for accounts of the effects of the Depression on ordinary people. Be sure to look at the comics, the homemaking section, advertisements, and human interest stories. Each group will report their findings to the class.

Following these reports, the class will compile a list of questions to ask people who remember the Depression years. The teacher or librarian may arrange to have several people come to the class. Seek to help students understand the differences in family life then and now. For example, fewer women worked outside of the home during the Depression than now; Social Security and other social services payments had not been established; some children worked in factories; people living in rural areas were able to raise food if they could stay on the land; and there were different jobs then as compared to now. Be sure to include questions about how the people's lives changed as the New Deal was implemented.

3. If I Had Lived During the Depression. . .

After completing Activities 1 and 2, students will write in their History Journals about their lives as children of the 1930s during the Depression. Divide the class so that their accounts represent the various regions of the United States and include both rural and urban settings. Use the fictional accounts in the book list to supplement the information in Activities 1 and 2.

BOOK LIST

Note: **Starred (*) books are reviewed in a previous section or unit of this book.**

*Armer, Laura Adams. *Waterless Mountain.* Longman's, Green, 1931. (4-8) Fic. (Part 2, Unit 6)

Cleary, Beverly. *A Girl from Yamhill: A Memoir.* Morrow, 1988. 279p. (6-8) Biog.

Well-known and beloved children's writer Beverly Cleary, born in 1916, recounts her childhood in this memoir that tells of growing up on the family farm in Yamhill, Oregon. Cleary describes small town activities, such as May Day pageants, 4th of July parades, and dances at the Masonic Hall. At the age of six, the family moved to Portland where Cleary was caught up in school, ballet lessons, and big city life. Readers will suffer with the family during the days of the Great Depression and during difficult times in Cleary's adolescence. This is a fascinating portrait of a young girl's coming of age in the not-too-distant past.

Freedman, Russell. *Franklin Delano Roosevelt.* Clarion, 1990. 200p. (4-8) Biog.

This biography, richly illustrated with photographs, documents the life of Franklin D. Roosevelt, who served as president during the Great Depression and the Second World War. While FDR was well-loved by the majority of Americans, he also had his weaknesses and enemies. Freedman deals candidly with Roosevelt's powerful leadership style, his relationship with wife Eleanor, and his personal foibles. The chapters about the Depression have lucid explanations of the complex causes, effects, and solutions to this difficult challenge. Freedman helps readers know Roosevelt as a courageous man and a dynamic president who succeeded despite his crippling bout with polio. See also Freedman's *Eleanor Roosevelt: A Life of Discovery* (Clarion, 1993).

Glassman, Bruce. *The Crash of '29 and the New Deal.* Silver Burdett, 1986. 63p. (4-6) Non-fic.

Green, Connie Jordan. *Emmy.* Margaret K. McElderry. 1992. 152p. (4-6) Fic.

For 11-year-old Emmy Mourfield, life in the summer of 1924 is hard in her eastern Kentucky mining home. After losing his arm, Pa is permanently disabled and has turned into an invalid. Because Emmy has to serve meals to the company's employees and help take care of her brothers and sisters, she has no time for herself. Tensions in the Mourfield home escalate when 14-year-old Gene, Emmy's oldest brother, is forced to work in the coal mines in order for the family to maintain their company home. Despite its problems and grim existence, the family is rich in a love that permeates their lives. This wonderful story evokes an intense feeling of time and place.

Hamilton, Virginia. *Willie Bea and the Time the Martians Landed.* Greenwillow, 1983. 208p. (6-8) Fic.

It is nearly Halloween in the year 1938 and 12-year-old Willie Bea Mills is looking forward to "begging for treats." The large extended African-American Mills family has gathered in rural southern Ohio for their customary Sunday dinner. Things are normal as the children play and bicker and the adults cook and talk. But this is the day when Orson Welles made his famous nighttime broadcast about Martians landing in New Jersey, and Willie Bea has a harrowing experience when she encounters a huge alien being in the cornfield. This well-written story describes a black family's existence during the 1930s in a rural Ohio community.

Hooks, William H. *Circle of Fire.* Atheneum, 1982. 147p. (4-6) Fic.

Harrison Hawkins, an 11-year-old white boy, and his best friends, a black boy and his younger sister, live in the Tidewater country of North Carolina in 1936. During the Christmas season, the children discover a group of Irish tinkers camped nearby. They also overhear a local white landowner plotting with other members of the Ku Klux Klan to attack the Irish people on Christmas Day. The children courageously warn the tinkers and find that others have come to their aid. The bigotry and illegal actions of the Klan are vividly portrayed, along with Harrison's personal dilemma, since he suspects his father is a member of the Klan.

Howard, Ellen. *Circle of Giving.* Atheneum, 1984. 99p. (4-6) Fic.

A brand-new Los Angeles neighborhood in the late 1920s is the setting for this story of Jeannie, and her older sister, 12-year-old Marguerite, who have relocated from Oregon. Marguerite is unhappy in her new home and finds the street dull until the Hanisians move in. Mrs. Hanisian is glamorous and Marguerite is fascinated by the youngest daughter, Francie, who is afflicted with cerebral palsy. The story spans a number of months as Marguerite befriends Francie and succeeds in opening the minds of the other residents towards Francie. This is a heart-warming story of life in an urban neighborhood during the 1920s.

Meltzer, Milton. *Brother, Can You Spare a Dime? The Great Depression, 1929-1933.* Knopf, 1969. 181p. (6-8) Non-fic.

Myers, Anna. *Red-Dirt Jessie.* Walker, 1992. 107p. (4-6) Fic.

During the years of the Great Depression, nine-year-old Jessie Harper is living with her farm family in Oklahoma. When her younger sister dies of pneumonia, Jessie's father goes into a deep depression and just sits in a rocking chair all day. Although Jessie does her best to help her mother keep the family going, everyone is affected when Aunt Maybell and Uncle Delbert decide to move to California. They leave a half-wild dog named Ring in Jessie's care and she believes that in taming and caring for Ring, she will induce her father's recovery from his illness. The everyday life of poor farmers is realistically told in this short novel.

Olsen, Violet. *View from the Pighouse Roof.* Atheneum, 1987. 176p. (6-8) Fic.

Rural Iowa in 1934 is the setting for this coming-of-age story about 13-year-old Marie Carlsen. The impact of the Depression is seen in the lives of the Carlsens and their neighbors. Marie's older brother and two sisters have left home in search of employment, while the younger children and their mother continue farming. Although the economic difficulties affect everyone, life goes on as Marie starts high school in town and begins wondering about boys, growing up, menstruation, and her future. The closeness of the family and their neighbors, through both good times and tragedy, is portrayed with sensitivity and humor within the setting of the Depression. This book is the sequel to *The Growing Season* (Atheneum, 1982).

Pearson, Gayle. *The Coming Home Cafe.* Atheneum, 1988. 200p. (6-8) Fic.

In the summer of 1933, the Great Depression is in full swing and 15-year-old Elizabeth Turnquist finds it increasingly difficult to live with the tensions in her home caused by her father's unemployment and her mother's illness. Elizabeth runs away from her Chicago home looking for work to help her family make ends meet, and she teams up with a teenaged boy and a black woman. As Elizabeth rides the rails throughout the Midwest and the South, she experiences firsthand the hunger and despair of the Depression, meets both kind and nasty people, and comes to a greater self-awareness as she faces life on her own. This is a good, high-interest, low-vocabulary choice for reluctant readers.

Peck, Robert Newton. *Arly.* Walker, 1989. 153p. (6-8) Fic.

The arduous and poverty-stricken life of farm produce pickers in Florida's Shack Row in 1927 is seen through the eyes of an 11-year-old illiterate boy named Arly Poole. Arly waits for the day when he turns 12 so that he can pick in the fields with his father. This all changes with the arrival of an indomitable schoolteacher named Miss Hoe, who brings Arly hope and a chance to break out of the picker life. Arly blossoms under the tutelage of this special teacher; and when his father suddenly dies, Arly must make a difficult and courageous choice. The story of Arly's ill-fated life continues in *Arly's Run* (Walker, 1991).

Pendergraft, Patricia. *As Far as Mill Springs.* Philomel, 1991. 151p. (4-6) Fic.

Set during the early 1930s, this story centers on 12-year-old Robert, a boy who has lived his entire life in foster homes. Currently living with an abusive couple, Robert runs away, taking his good friend, 11-year-old Abiah Ringer, with him. Robert has heard that his mother is living in Mill Springs, and the two children travel over 300 miles, riding the rails in the hopes of reaching Robert's mother by Christmas. Robert and Abiah encounter both goodness and evil on their trek in this touching story of destitute children during the Depression.

Stanley, Jerry. *Children of the Dust Bowl: The True Story of the School at Weedpatch Camp.* Crown, 1992. 85p. (4-8) Non-fic.

This nonfiction book tells of the destitute Okies, poor dirt farmers from Oklahoma, Texas, Arkansas, and Missouri, who left their homes during the Depression and moved to California where they heard agricultural jobs were available. Most of these people found no work and deplorable living conditions until the federal government built several farm-labor camps to house them. The Okies faced vehement discrimination and much of the book is devoted to the building of Weedpatch School at the Arvin Camp. The black-and-white archival photographs are as valuable as the text and show a people courageous and determined in the face of adversity. John Steinbeck's *The Grapes of Wrath* was based on the Okie experience in California. Includes bibliographic notes and an index.

Taylor, Mildred. *The Friendship.* Ill. by Max Ginsburg. Dial, 1987. 53p. (4-6) Fic.

The Logan family, which the author introduced in *Song of the Trees* (Dial, 1975), participates in this story set in rural Mississippi in the 1930s. Cassie Logan and her three brothers are in town one day when they witness an encounter between an elderly black man named Tom Bee and a white storeowner named John Wallace. Having once saved his life, Mr. Wallace gave Mr. Bee the "right" to call him by his first name, but this is simply not acceptable behavior in the South. Goaded by a group of white men and boys, Mr. Wallace shoots Mr. Bee in the leg when Mr. Bee continues to call him "John" instead of "Mr. Wallace" in public. The children are naturally upset and try to comprehend how such a thing could happen. This book is based on stories told by the author's father of his childhood in Mississippi during the Depression.

Taylor, Mildred. *Mississippi Bridge.* Ill. by Max Ginsburg. Dial, 1990. 64p. (4-6) Fic.

The narrator of this story, a 10-year-old white boy named Jeremy Simms, is disturbed as he watches a bus driver in his Mississippi home town making all of the black travelers get off the bus in order to make room for white riders. Later, when the bus goes off the bridge over the swollen Rosa Lee Creek during a rainstorm, Jeremy sees how the townspeople, both black and white, work together to save the passengers. The Logan children, featured in *Roll of Thunder, Hear My Cry,* appear briefly in this story. Black-and-white line drawings illustrate what is taking place, and the facial expressions of the participants are especially noteworthy.

Taylor, Mildred. *The Road to Memphis.* Dial, 1990. 290p. (6-8) Fic.

Now a senior in high school, 17-year-old Cassie Logan is attending school in Jackson, Mississippi, and planning for college. An unforeseen series of events in the fall of 1941, however, including a lovers' quarrel and a black friend's outrage against his white persecutors, forever changes the course of her life and propels her into the reality of the adult world. The story of the Logan family, seen in *Roll of Thunder, Hear My Cry* and *Let the Circle Be Unbroken,* continues in this splendid book about family love and support, friendship, and black-white relations in the South in the early 1940s.

Taylor, Mildred. *Roll of Thunder, Hear My Cry.* Ill. by Jerry Pinkney. Dial, 1976. 276p. (4-8) Fic.

Based on the childhood of the author's father, this story of prejudice and segregation in rural Mississippi during the 1930s is seen through the eyes of children. Ten-year-old Cassie Logan and her brothers walk each day to the poorly equipped black school, are discriminated against in town, and struggle within their family circle to earn enough money to hold onto the land that their Grandpa bought after he was emancipated. This powerful story of surviving prejudice also emphasizes the power of a loving and supportive family. The story of the Logans continues in *Let the Circle Be Unbroken* (Dial, 1981).

*Uchida, Yoshiko. *A Jar of Dreams.* Atheneum, 1981. (4-6) Fic. (Part 2, Unit 8, Sect. 2)

Van Raven, Pieter. *A Time of Troubles.* Scribner's, 1990. 180p. (6-8) Fic.

Set in the 1930s, this story follows 14-year-old Roy Purdy as he accompanies his ex-convict father across the Dust Bowl in the hopes of finding work in California. Finding the pay for fruit picking insufficient to even subsist, father and son find themselves on opposing sides as workers prepare to unionize and strike against the sub-human labor conditions. This powerful novel of action and conflict focuses on the plight of migrant farm workers, and on the hardships, courage, and desperation that marked the years of the Great Depression.

Weidt, Maryann N. *Stateswoman to the World: A Story About Eleanor Roosevelt.* Ill. by Lydia M. Anderson. Carolrhoda, 1991. [64]p. (4-6) Biog.

Whitmore, Arvella. *The Bread Winner.* Houghton Mifflin, 1990. 138p. (4-6) Fic.

The Depression is at its height in 1932 and Sarah Puckett's parents have just lost their family farm. They move into a dreary shack in the nearby town and Sarah endures cruel teasing at school while her parents unsuccessfully search for employment. A bright, hard-working girl, Sarah devises a plan to sell her prize-winning bread, which earns a living for Sarah and her mother while Sarah's father rides the rails looking for work. The Pucketts lose their shanty in a natural disaster, but good people come to their rescue and a new business, Pucketts' Blue-Ribbon Bakery, is born.

Wosmek, Frances. *A Brown Bird Singing.* Ill. by Ted Lewin. Lothrop, 1986. 120p. (4-6) Fic.

Set in a Minnesota Swedish community in the 1920s, this story tells of nine-year-old Anego, a Chippewa Indian girl who was adopted as a young child by a white family. Happy and adjusted with her family and school, Anego is suddenly faced with the possibility that her Native American father may come to reclaim her. Although Anego has experienced discrimination over the years, she does not feel at all Indian and does not wish to leave Mama and Papa Veselka. Soft black-and-white illustrations complete this fine, short novel that examines the topics of adoption, prejudice, and multi-racial families.

*Yep, Laurence. *The Star Fisher.* Morrow, 1991. (6-8) Fic. (Part 2, Unit 8, Sect. 2)

UNIT
twelve

World War II and the Holocaust

OBJECTIVES

1. In cooperative-learning groups or individually, the students will select a real or fictional person or small group, such as a family, to follow throughout the course of World War II and its aftermath. Through writing in their History Journals, the students will show their understanding of the impact of the war. Students will compare the experiences of people in the United States with those in European and Asian nations.
2. Students will interview persons who lived during World War II, or use newspapers from the era to learn about such topics as the home front, invasions of Europe, the Holocaust, and individual roles during the war years.
3. Students will read nonfiction accounts of the Holocaust and respond in their History Journals to the Nazi edicts against the Jews.

LEARNING ACTIVITIES

1. How World War II Affected Our Lives

Begin by listing people who were affected by World War II. This list may include members of the students' families, and people from many different nations and ethnic groups. The book list will suggest many different people, such as Yankele and his parents who fled the Nazis in *Along the Tracks*; Patty Bergen in *Summer of My German Soldier*; a Japanese-American family as portrayed in *The Journey* and *Journey to Topaz*; Mii in *Hiroshima No Pika*; or the young people and adults in the short stories in *Echoes of War*.

In small groups or individually, the students will select real or fictional persons who lived during World War II. In their History Journals, the students will write about the effects of the war on these people by describing their lives before, during, and after the war, emphasizing the process, necessity, and effects of changes. All members of cooperative-learning groups should have read the same book so that they can contribute to an in-depth assessment of the effects of the war.

Compare the experiences of people in the United States with those of people who lived in European and Asian countries on a chart using basic human needs as the components of comparison. The purpose is to examine the effects of war on civilian populations within the arena of war and beyond.

2. Eyewitness Accounts

Based on their reading, students will prepare questions they would like answered by guest speakers who lived during World War II. Questions and topics may include the home front, the war in Asia and the Pacific, invasion of Europe, the Holocaust, and the person's role during the war years. It will aid the speakers to have a list of questions prior to their appearance in the classroom.

As an alternative to the interviews, copies of newspapers from the era may be used. The news stories, letters to the editor, advertisements, and announcements will aid the students in constructing an "eyewitness account" of the war years.

3. Never Again!

Begin study of the Holocaust by reading *nonfiction* with the students in order to emphasize the harsh reality of the Nazi persecution of Jews. Barbara Rogasky's *Smoke and Ashes: The Story of the Holocaust* provides historical background information plus excerpts from diaries, eyewitness accounts, and photographs from the concentration camps. The true stories of bravery and compassion in Milton Meltzer's *Rescue: The Story of How Gentiles Saved Jews in the Holocaust* will serve as a tribute to the enduring goodness of the human spirit.

Inge Auerbacher tells the story of her childhood spent in the Terezin concentration camp in *I Am a Star: Child of the Holocaust*. Through this account, the readers will see the effects of the growing Nazi persecution leading to the "final solution"—the extermination of the Jews. In *Hide and Seek*, Ida Vos tells her story of being hidden by people who helped her family survive. *Along the Tracks*, also based on the life of a real person, tells of how six-year-old Yankele's Jewish family fled from the Nazis. Yankele gets separated from his mother and spends the next six years as one the "abandoned ones," the homeless children who lived on the streets of Russia.

After reading some of these horrendous but poignant true stories, the students should be ready to read fictional accounts similar to the real stories told in *Rescue: The Story of How Gentiles Saved Jews in the Holocaust*. For good fictional works, see *The Devil's Arithmetic; Number the Stars; Bridge to Freedom;* and *Waiting for Anya*.

Under the title, "Never Again!," have students write in their History Journals about the Holocaust and how they could help assure that this abominable event is never repeated. Leave the form of the response open so that students may write poetry, essays, or use drawings to convey their reactions. Ask students to share their responses with members of the class.

BOOK LIST

Note: Starred (*) books are reviewed in a previous section or unit of this book.

Aaron, Chester. *Alex, Who Won His War.* Walker, 1991. 156p. (6-8) Fic.

Fourteen-year-old Alex Kellar, living in Pequod, Connecticut, longs to contribute to the war effort. His parents work at the nearby submarine base and his beloved older brother, Oliver, is fighting in Europe. After Alex finds the body of a dead German on the beach, he is captured, along with two elderly ladies who live nearby, by two Nazi saboteurs. Caught between his revulsion at having to assist the enemy and his need to protect the women, Alex searches for a solution to this predicament. This is a fast-paced and exciting story about one boy's adventure on the home front during the Second World War.

Aaseng, Nathan. *Navajo Code Talkers.* Walker, 1992. 114p. (4-8) Non-fic.

This excellent account of the role of the Navajo Marines who became the "code talkers" in World War II offers an overview of the Navajos' relationship with white Americans, an explanation of Navajo beliefs, a description of the structure and complexity of the Navajo language and the development of the code, and a summary of the war in the Pacific. First-hand accounts of the code talkers' experiences document the progression of the war throughout the Pacific theater. The code talkers believed their most significant contributions were in being able to contact their commanders with information about where units needed reinforcements, accurately directing artillery fire, and sending and receiving secret information. Although the Navajo do not have a word for "patriotism," the code talkers' bravery, intelligence, and courage is well-served in this book. Includes photographs.

Auerbacher, Inge. *I Am a Star: Child of the Holocaust.* Prentice-Hall, 1986. 87p. (4-8) Biog.

The author tells of her own experience from the ages of seven to ten, while imprisoned with her parents in the Terezin concentration camp in Czechoslovakia from 1942 to 1945. Her personal story is embedded in the historical setting of Hitler's rise to power, the rise of anti-Semitism in Germany, and the Nazis' "final solution"—the extermination of the Jews. Auerbacher was one of 100 children to survive out of the 15,000 children who were imprisoned in Terezin, and the grim facts of the Holocaust are intertwined with Auerbacher's personal story and with her poems stemming from her experience. Both the narrative and poetry are moving and somber.

Avi. *"Who Was That Masked Man, Anyway?"* Orchard, 1992. 170p. (4-8) Fic.

In a unique blending of scripts from 1940s radio adventure stories and dialogue among book characters, Avi spins a humorous story of sixth-grader Frankie Wattleson as he tries to bring the excitement of his beloved radio programs into his New York City life. His best friend, Mario Calvino, lives in the next building and reluctantly shares Frankie's imaginative antics. When Frankie's brother comes home after being wounded in the Pacific theater of the war, Frankie plans an elaborate escapade to cheer up his depressed brother and his favorite teacher, Miss Gomez, whose fiancé died in the war. Although his plans go awry, Frankie accomplishes his goal and brings laughter to those he really cares about. This book is a natural for readers' theater.

Barrie, Barbara. *Lone Star.* Delacorte, 1990. 183p. (4-8) Fic.

When this Jewish family from Chicago moves to Texas in 1944, Jane Miller, a fifth grader, tries to fit into this mostly Christian community. The formerly affluent family has to adjust to economic hardships and Southern culture. Jane is lonely and tries to understand her own faith and that of her new Christian friends. Jane's Orthodox Jewish grandfather makes her attempt at acceptance even more difficult. However, as the family and the local Jewish congregation learn about the Holocaust and the fate of their relatives in Europe, the family solidifies, and Jane grows to understand the strength and endurance of her family and its faith.

Bergman, Tamar. *Along the Tracks.* Trans. by Michael Swirsky. Houghton Mifflin, 1991. 245p. (6-8) Fic.

In the early years of the Second World War, a six-year-old Jewish boy named Yankele flees from the Nazi invasion of Poland with his family. The family settles in the Crimea for a while until the Germans press forward and once again force the family further east. During their journey, Yankele becomes separated from his mother and for the next six years is one of the "abandoned ones"—homeless children who ride the rails in Russia, steal food, and sleep in coal piles for warmth during the cold winters. Yankele is a real person and this poignant story is based on his childhood during World War II.

Bunting, Eve. *Terrible Things: An Allegory of the Holocaust.* Ill. by Stephen Gammell. Jewish Publication Society, 1989. [32]p. (4-6) Fic.

This allegorical tale opens with a peaceful forest environment where the animals get along with each other and share the surroundings. But one day the Terrible Things come and take away all of the creatures with feathers. Little Rabbit wonders what the birds have done to upset the Terrible Things, but everyone looks away and tells him to be quiet and not question. Again and again the Terrible Things come, without any reason or provocation, taking away the various animals. Little Rabbit manages to hide when they come for the white animals, and escapes to warn the rest of the forest animals about the horror. Children will clearly understand that sometimes one must stand up for one's beliefs, even if one stands alone.

Cormier, Robert. *Tunes for Bears to Dance To.* Delacorte, 1992. 101p. (4-6) Fic.

Post-World-War-II America is the setting for this story about an 11-year-old boy named Henry Cassavant who faces some difficult choices. The death of his older brother has left Henry's father in a severe depression, while his mother is working hard to keep the family together. Even Henry is contributing to the household by working for nasty Mr. Hairston at the local grocery store. Henry has befriended an elderly Jewish Holocaust survivor who has carved a beautiful village out of wood. For no apparent reason, Mr. Hairston asks Henry to smash the village and threatens to fire Henry, and even his mother, if Henry does not comply. This is a thought-provoking novel of moral choices.

Davis, Daniel S. *Behind Barbed Wire: The Imprisonment of Japanese Americans During World War II.* Dutton, 1982. 166p. (4-8) Non-fic.

When Franklin Roosevelt signed Executive Order 9066 early in 1942, the lives of 120,000 Japanese Americans were changed forever. This book tells their story. These Americans lost their homes and farms when they were transported to relocation camps in some of the most desolate places in the United States. Living conditions were primitive at best, some Japanese even had to live in remodeled horse stalls, and readers will understand the shock and sense of betrayal felt by the Japanese Americans. The author discusses everyday life in the camps, how lawyers were arguing for Japanese rights in the American courts, the impressive records of the all-Japanese U.S. fighting units, and adjusting to civilian life at the close of the war. Includes many archival photographs, a bibliography, and index.

Faber, Doris. *Harry Truman.* Abelard-Schuman, 1972. 96p. (4-6) Biog.

Fife, Dale. *North of Danger.* Dutton, 1978. 72p. (4-6) Fic.

When the British arrive in Spitsbergen, Norway, in 1940 to evacuate the inhabitants because of the approaching Nazis, 12-year-old Arne Kristiansen remains behind. Arne's father, a scientist on a mission far to the north, is wanted by the Gestapo for having fought in the resistance. Scared that his father will walk into a trap when he comes home, Arne travels over 200 miles on skis to warn him. Along the way, Arne encounters an old German who teaches him about trust, bigotry, and endurance. Based on a true story, this exciting tale about a courageous boy would be a good read-aloud selection.

*Freedman, Russell. *Franklin Delano Roosevelt.* Clarion, 1990. (6-8) Biog. (Part 2, Unit 11)

Greene, Bette. *The Summer of My German Soldier.* Dial, 1973. 230p. (6-8) Fic.

Set in the small town of Jenkinsville, Arkansas, during the war years, this is the story of 12-year-old Patty Bergen, a lonely Jewish girl who is constantly belittled by her parents. When a group of German prisoners-of-war are sent to her home town, Patty befriends a young German named Anton Reiker who impresses her with his intelligence, courtesy, and respectful treatment. When Anton escapes, Patty discovers his hiding place, but cannot bring herself to turn him in and is eventually prosecuted for treason. This powerful coming-of-age novel touches on prejudice, loyalty, religious differences, conscience, child abuse, and human dignity.

Griese, Arnold A. *The Wind Is Not a River.* Ill. by Glo Coalson. Crowell, 1978. 108p. (6-8) Fic.

The small Aleutian island of Attu during World War II is the setting for this novel about a young girl named Sasan and her younger brother, Sidak. Although the war is raging, this remote island does not feel its effects until Japanese forces invade the island in June 1942. All the islanders except Sasan and Sidak are captured by the Japanese and the siblings struggle to evade capture. When they encounter a wounded Japanese soldier, they must decide whether to follow the Old Ways as Grandmother taught them and help their enemy, or turn their backs. This is an exciting story of two children on their own who must make some difficult choices.

Hahn, Mary Downing. *Stepping on the Cracks.* Clarion, 1991. 218p. (6-8) Fic.
A small town in Maryland in 1944 is the setting for this story about two girls, 11-year-old Margaret Baker, and her friend, Elizabeth, who must come to grips with matters of conscience when they discover an army deserter named Stuart hiding in the woods. Stuart is the gentle brother of the town bully, Gordy Smith, whom the girls hate. When Stuart's pneumonia worsens, Margaret and Elizabeth team up with Gordy to help save Stuart, and in the process begin to understand the painful life Gordy has experienced with an abusive, alcoholic father. With her beloved brother fighting in Europe, Margaret wrestles with her feelings about Stuart's anti-war stance in this timeless story of moral ambiguity and maturation.

Hamanaka, Sheila. *The Journey: Japanese Americans, Racism, and Renewal.* Book Design by Steve Frederick. Orchard, 1990. 40p. (4-8) Non-fic.
This picture book's brutal subject matter makes it a choice for older readers. This is the story of the author's experiences as a child during World War II in a Japanese "relocation center." Children will learn about racism and discrimination against the Japanese following the attack on Pearl Harbor, what Japanese Americans endured, and how old wounds have come to be healed. The striking, realistic illustrations feature portions of a 25-foot mural that inspired the story.

Härtling, Peter. *Crutches.* Trans. from the German by Elizabeth D. Crawford. Lothrop, 1988. 164p. (6-8) Fic.
In the devastation of European cities at the close of World War II, many people were homeless and searching for loved ones. Among this number is 12-year-old Thomas, who was separated from his mother when they tried to board a train from Brunn to Vienna to find relatives. Thomas wanders around Vienna and finds only the doorway to his aunt's home remains standing. He follows a man on crutches, hoping to escape being picked up by the Russian soldiers. Crutches and Thomas team up as scavengers for food and housing, hoping to remain together as displaced persons. The portrayal of human caring amid the postwar chaos is based on the author's own experience. This is an outstanding and bittersweet story of friendship and the survival of humankind despite the deprivation of war.

Hest, Amy. *Love You, Soldier.* Four Winds, 1991. 47p. (4-6) Fic.
During the Second World War, seven-year-old Katie, her mother, and her mother's pregnant friend, Louise, live together in an apartment in New York City while their soldier-husbands are away. Katie helps Louise when

her baby is born, and learns to love the child. They all support each other when the dreaded news comes that Katie's father has been killed. This poignant story, which makes the hardships of World War II understandable to children, deals gently but realistically with loss through the development of love and hope. As their neighbor observes, "Love is risky, but it's worth it."

Hoobler, Dorothy, and Thomas Hoobler. *An Album of World War II.* Watts, 1977. 96p. (4-6) Non-fic.

Dividing World War II into two separate theaters—the war in Europe and the war in Asia—the authors trace the events that led to the outbreak of war; the significant land, naval, and air campaigns; the fall of Europe; life on the home front; the resistance movement; the liberation of Europe; and, finally, the dropping of the atomic bomb on Japan. The excellent use of archival photographs, which accompany the clearly written text, will help middle readers visualize and understand the horror and destruction of this global war. Includes maps and an index.

Hotze, Sollace. *Summer Endings.* Clarion, 1991. 165p. (4-8) Fic.

During 1945, the war in Europe ended in May, and Japan surrendered in August. For 12-year-old Christine Kosinski, a Polish immigrant living in Chicago, this momentous summer was the end of childhood as she said good-bye to her sister, watched the Cubs baseball games from the porch of their apartment, and danced at the Aragon Ballroom in celebration of the end of the war. Amid the everyday events of roller-skating to the cemetery, eating ice cream on hot summer days, and sharing secrets with her best friend, is the continuing worry about her father who was unable to leave Poland with his family in 1939. This romantic story is richly detailed with the sense of time and place—summer in the city at the close of the Second World War.

*Innocenti, Roberto. *Rose Blanche.* Creative Education, Inc., 1985. (4-6) Fic. (Part 1, Unit 10)

Isserman, Maurice. *World War II.* Facts on File, 1991. 184p. (6-8) Non-fic.

Kudlinski, Kathleen V. *Pearl Harbor is Burning! A Story of World War II.* Ill. by Ronald Himler. Viking, 1991. 54p. (4-6) Fic.

Ten-year-old Frank, a newcomer to Hawaii, meets Kenji, a Japanese-American boy, who shares his interest in baseball. The boys trade baseball cards and ethnic snacks while they sit in Frank's treehouse. From this perch they watch in fascination and horror as Pearl Harbor is bombed by the Japanese, and cheer when the U.S. Navy scores some hits. With Frank's parents away at work, Frank spends the night of December 7, 1941, with

Kenji's family and learns about their loyalty to the United States and their respect for their Japanese heritage. This lively story, part of the "Once Upon America Series," not only describes the events at Pearl Harbor, but also explores the meaning of patriotism and friendship.

Laird, Christa. *Shadow of the Wall.* Greenwillow, 1990. 144p. (6-8) Fic.

Although not quite 14 years old, Misha Edelman has seen more horror in his young life than most people see in a whole lifetime. The year is 1942 and Misha is living in Dr. Janusz Korczak's orphanage in the Warsaw Ghetto with his two younger sisters. Beatings, killings, hunger, fright, cruelty, and constant stress are daily occurrences in Misha's existence in this touching story of a young boy caught up in the Holocaust. Life for the Edelman children becomes even more tenuous when Mrs. Edelman dies and the Nazis tighten their control in the Ghetto. The author successfully blends real and fictional characters in this powerful novel about the Jewish struggle for survival during the Second World War.

Lowry, Lois. *Number the Stars.* Houghton Mifflin, 1989. 137p. (4-6) Fic.

This story is set during the Nazi occupation of Copenhagen, Denmark, in 1943. Ten-year-old Annemarie Johansen and her family are drawn into the plans of the Danish Resistance as they help their Jewish friends escape to neutral Sweden. This well-told, exciting story portrays the courage and human decency of average Danish citizens, including children, such as Annemarie and her Jewish friend, Ellen. This excellent read-aloud book is useful for examining responses to persecution and racism.

Macy, Sue. *A Whole New Ball Game: The Story of the All-American Girls Professional Baseball League.* Henry Holt, 1993. 140p. (4-8) Non-fic.

In an effort to raise home-front morale during World War II, Philip Wrigley, owner of the Chicago Cubs, formed the All-American Girls Softball League with four teams. Although it took a while for fans to become serious about baseball players who hit like Ted Williams but looked like Scarlett O'Hara, the eyes of the nation were soon upon these midwestern women's baseball teams. The book traces the early years of the AAGPBL, the femininity angle, life on the road, and the eventual demise of the League. The author makes excellent use of original source material and includes many quotes from the players themselves. The photographs are fascinating and the book includes a chronology, bibliography, and index. Another well-written book on this topic is Diana Star Helmer's *Belles of the Ballpark* (Millbrook Press, 1993).

Magorian, Michelle. *Good Night, Mr. Tom.* Harper & Row, 1981. 318p. (6-8) Fic.

In the fall of 1939, a nine-year-old, undersized boy named Willie Beech is evacuated from war-torn London and sent to live in the English countryside with a gruff old man named Mr. Tom. An abused child, Willie learns that life can be different and for the first time in his life is surrounded by people who care. Mr. Tom grows to love the boy and helps Willie learn to think for himself. The realism of this touching story, including the difficult subject of child abuse, is well-depicted and will show young readers how World War II affected the lives of children in England.

Maruki, Toshi. *Hiroshima No Pika.* Lothrop, 1980. [48]p. (4-6) Non-fic.

The horror of the atomic bombs dropped on the city of Hiroshima is graphically told in this picture book. Seven-year-old Mii and her parents are at breakfast on the morning of August 6, 1945, when the Flash disrupted their lives forever. The author shows utters chaos—people fleeing, dead bodies, and pain and suffering everywhere. Hiroshima is rubble, devoid of vegetation or buildings. Mii never grew after the Flash and her father died the following autumn. The message in this book is necessary, but potent, and care should be taken with younger readers.

Marvin, Isabel R. *Bridge to Freedom.* Jewish Publication Society of America, 1991. 136p. (4-8) Fic.

The unlikely combination of a 15-year-old German army deserter named Kurt Muller and a Jewish schoolgirl named Rachel Gildemeister are the central characters in this fast-paced story that takes place in western Germany during the last months of the war. Kurt and Rachel discover each other while hiding in an abandoned wine cellar and decide to pool their resources in an effort to get Rachel across the border to her relatives in Belgium. To escape, they must cross the Remagen Bridge across the Rhine before they are captured by the approaching Allied troops. Both sides of the conflict are reflected in Rachel and Kurt's stories. Both boys and girls will enjoy this story.

Mazer, Harry. *The Last Mission.* Delacorte, 1979. 182p. (6-8) Fic.

In 1944, high-school freshman Jack Raab steals his older brother's birth certificate and enlists in the Air Corps. Being large and well-developed for his age, Jack is accepted and this book describes the horrors of war from the perspective of an adolescent caught up in something he was not prepared for. The glamour and romance of war is quickly dispelled for Jack when he becomes a waist gunner on a B-17 bomber—the loss of sleep, stress, poor food, and the whole uncertainty of life become all too real for Jack. The book makes for exciting reading, especially when Jack's plane is shot down over Czechoslovakia.

Meltzer, Milton. *Rescue: The Story of How Gentiles Saved Jews in the Holocaust.* Harper & Row, 1988. 168p. (6-8) Non-fic.

Morpurgo, Michael. *Waiting for Anya.* Viking, 1991. 172p. (4-8) Fic.

In this dramatic novel, which takes place in southern France during World War II, a 12-year-old shepherd named Jo Lalande discovers that Benjamin, the son-in-law of a local widow, is hiding Jewish children at her farm and smuggling them over the border into Spain. When German soldiers come and occupy the village, Benjamin's work becomes even more risky. Benjamin is waiting for his daughter, Anya, to show up at the farm after a long separation and the action builds to a climax as the Germans close in on the operation, which by now has enlisted the help of all of the townspeople. Both the French and Germans are shown as real people in this novel of good and evil.

Rogasky, Barbara. *Smoke and Ashes: The Story of the Holocaust.* Holiday, 1988. 187p. (6-8) Non-fic.

Beginning with the rise of anti-Semitism in Germany, the author traces Nazi ascendency under Hitler, the war against the Jews, how the Jews were deported and herded into ghettos across Europe, and how they were interned and exterminated in concentration camps. Resistance and survival techniques are disclosed, along with the efforts of Gentiles to save their neighbors and friends. This difficult story is told with objectivity and compassion, often citing eyewitness accounts of what took place. Some of the pictures included are painful to look at, but this story must be told. Includes a bibliography and index. Another fine overview of the Holocaust is Miriam Chaikin's *A Nightmare in History: The Holocaust, 1933-1945* (Clarion, 1987).

Savin, Marcia. *The Moon Bridge.* Scholastic, 1992. 231p. (6-8) Fic.

Ten-year-old Ruthie Fox is in the fifth grade in 1941 when the Japanese bomb Pearl Harbor. Despite peer pressure, Ruthie becomes friends with Mitzi Fujimoto, a classmate of Japanese heritage, and the two girls share some special times. Ruthie watches as increased restrictions are placed on Japanese Americans and she is shocked when Mitzi and her family are rounded up and sent away. The second half of this story consists of letters written by Ruthie to Mitzi, although she never mails them since she does not know where the Fujimotos have been sent. At the close of the war, Ruthie and Mitzi meet to see if their friendship has stood the test of time and war.

Sender, Ruth Minsky. *To Life.* Macmillan, 1988. 229p. (6-8) Non-Fic.

The members of the Minska family are the focus of this compelling, fictionalized memoir of the problems faced by Jewish survivors of the

Holocaust. As the story opens in 1945, 19-year-old Riva Minska has just been liberated from a labor camp after surviving a stay in Auschwitz. Originally from Poland, she wanders throughout Europe, searching for relatives. Riva marries another survivor and the two end up in a displaced persons' camp in Germany, where they hope to emigrate to the United States. Flashbacks tell of the Nazi horror, and this poignant book, full of joys and bitter disappointments, is a fine tribute to the human spirit. *To Life* is a sequel to *The Cage* (Macmillan, 1986) and is based on the experiences of the author's family.

Sullivan, George. *The Day Pearl Harbor Was Bombed: A Photo History of World War II.* Scholastic, 1991. 96p. (4-8) Non-fic.

Taylor, Theodore. *The Cay.* Doubleday, 1969. 137p. (4-8) Fic.

In 1942, 11-year-old Phillip Enright is living with his parents on the Caribbean island of Curaçao, but when German submarines attack the local harbor, Mrs. Enright flees with Phillip. When their ship is torpedoed, Phillip is knocked on the head and wakes up to find himself on a raft with an old black man named Timothy and a cat. After drifting for a week, they land on a deserted island. As Phillip goes blind as a result of his injury, he must overcome his prejudicial feelings towards Timothy, on whom he depends more and more. This well-written, action-packed story would be a good read-aloud choice. Perhaps students will be interested in reading the sequel, *Timothy of the Cay* (Harcourt Brace Jovanovich, 1993).

Thesman, Jean. *Molly Donnelly.* Houghton Mifflin, 1993. 186p. (4-8) Fic.

Margaret Mary Donnelly is 12 years old and living in Seattle when war breaks out in 1941. Early the next year, Molly's friend and next-door-neighbor Emily Tamanaka disappears along with her Japanese family, and life changes for the family as Molly's father and Uncle Charlie begin work at the Boeing factory. This novel takes Molly through the four years of the war as she changes from a child into a young woman, experiencing deprivation, first love, sorrow at the death of a loved one, and troubles within a dysfunctional family. This story provides a realistic portrayal of the urban home front during World War II.

*Uchida, Yoshiko. *The Invisible Thread.* Julian Messner, 1991. (4-8) Biog. (Part 2, Unit 8, Sect. 2)

Uchida, Yoshiko. *Journey to Topaz: A Story of the Japanese-American Evacuation.* Ill. by Donald Carrik. Scribner's, 1971. (6-8) Fic.

Soon after the Japanese attack on Pearl Harbor, 11-year-old Yuki Sakane's father is interned in a prison camp in Montana. Eventually, the entire Sakane family is relocated from their Berkeley, California, home—first to the Tanforan Race Track Assembly Center, and later to Topaz, Utah. In

Topaz the family encounters dust, wretched living conditions, tuberculosis, and a shooting fatality. Eventually, Mr. Sakane is reunited with his family in Topaz, and, at the close of the book, the Sakane family is once again relocated, this time to Salt Lake City. Uchida narrates a painful and personal story seen through the eyes of a strong and loving family. The story of the Sakane family continues after the end of World War II in *Journey Home* (Atheneum, 1978).

Vos, Ida. *Hide and Seek.* Translated by Terese Edelstein and Inez Smidt. Houghton Mifflin, 1981. 132p. (4-6) Fic.

Based on the author's experiences as a child in Holland during World War II, this is the story of eight-year-old Rachel Hartog and the hardships her Jewish family experienced under Hitler's regime. As more and more restrictions are placed on Jews, Rachel's family eventually goes into hiding. Rachel and her younger sister, Esther, are separated from their parents and for years the girls cannot go outside. The short chapters deal with children's concerns and are written in a style that will be understandable to young readers. Although Rachel's immediate family was spared during the Holocaust, the Hartogs lost over 100 members of their extended family.

Westall, Robert. *Echoes of War.* Farrar, 1991. 89p. (6-8) Fic.

This collection of five stories deals with the effects of war, even decades after peace, on both young people and adults. The author successfully captures the physical, emotional, and psychological uncertainty of wartime. In "Gifts from the Sea," a young boy searching for treasures by the seashore discovers the body of a woman, and in "The Making of Me," a small boy is frightened of his shell-shocked grandfather until he is left alone with him and Grandpa shares some stories out of his past. Westall's powerful sketches connect the terrors of war with everyday life in a book that should lead to some interesting discussions.

White, Florence M. *First Woman in Congress: Jeannette Rankin.* Julian Messner, 1980. 95p. (4-6) Biog.

Whitman, Sylvia. *V Is for Victory: The American Home Front During World War II.* Lerner, 1993. 80p. (4-6) Non-fic.

Yolen, Jane. *The Devil's Arithmetic.* Viking Kestrel, 1988. 170p. (4-8) Fic.

As the story opens, Hannah, a 13-year-old Jewish girl living in New Rochelle, New York, complains that all the Jewish holidays are about remembering. As she reluctantly participates in the Passover Seder, she is transported back in time to the 1940s to a small village in Poland. Hannah becomes Chaya who has just recovered from a serious illness and is horrified when Nazis herd her uncle's wedding party into trucks to be "resettled."

The details of life in Auschwitz are all the more horrifying as Hannah/ Chaya recalls what she learned about the Holocaust, but is helpless to change events. The author's use of the time-travel vehicle and historical events is well done with an appropriate conclusion.

❋ ❋ ❋ ❋ ❋ ❋ ❋ ❋ ❋
UNIT
thirteen
❋ ❋ ❋ ❋ ❋ ❋ ❋ ❋ ❋

The Middle Decades of the Twentieth Century

OBJECTIVES

1. Students will continue the time line/flow chart begun in Units 9 and 10 in order to show the growth of the United States as a world power since 1945.
2. To include recent immigration in this unit, see Unit 8, Activities 4–8, and the book list, Unit 8, Section 2.
3. In order to examine the shift to the computer age, students will construct and conduct a survey of computer use among adults.
4. Students will construct a memorial wall bulletin board showing the names, dates, and accomplishments of the people involved in the pursuit of civil and human rights throughout American history.
5. Using newspapers, magazines, and photographs students will select articles and illustrations that show positive environmental actions.
6. The students will review their History Journals, time lines, maps, and book lists in order to select events and persons to compare using semantic differentials, such as: *democracy/totalitarianism; integration/persecution; loyalty/treason.*
7. Students will select from the Bill of Rights, the rights that are most important to them personally, and state examples of how these rights are implemented in their lives and in the lives of others.

8. After reviewing their History Journals, time lines, maps, and charts constructed throughout the school year, students will select 10 significant events in the history of the United States.

LEARNING ACTIVITIES

1. The United States as a World Power

Using textbooks and other references, the students will identify events since 1945 that involve the United States as a significant world power. These events, such as the Korean War and Cuban Missile Crisis, will be placed on the time line. As the students identify these events, they will find that the United States and the USSR were the major nations involved in many of the situations.

If the time line is continued to the present time, students will also note that even after the dissolution of the USSR, world events still involve the United States and nations torn between communism and democratic forms of government.

2. Surveying the New Industrial Revolution

With the aid of the teacher, the students will construct a survey of computer use among people, aged 20 and older. If each student surveyed four adults, the class would have a sample of approximately 100 people. The example in Chart 15 may be used for collecting data.

Tabulate the results by age and compare by graphing. What age groups have used computers the most? Which the least? Why are there differences among the various age groups? Which jobs make no use of computers? How are computers used in homes? In schools?

3. The Memorial Wall of Human Rights

Select a large bulletin board or wall space that can be dedicated to the construction of an American History Memorial Wall of Human Rights. Students will fill out a 5" x 7" card stating the person's name, the dates of that person's life, and a brief description of how and when this person worked for human rights. Include people from the twentieth century and from earlier periods so as to include the writers of the Bill of Rights, the abolitionists, the early advocates of women's rights, and others. The cards will be placed on the Memorial Wall in chronological order. Encourage the students to list members of their own families and themselves, as appropriate.

4. How Can We Be Environmentally Wise?

Individually, in small groups, or as a class project, have students identify and collect newspaper and magazine articles, illustrations, and their own photographs that show positive environmental actions. Try to emphasize positive environmental actions pursued in the schools and the local community. These collections could be displayed as scrapbooks or a bulletin board.

As a class, select those activities that could realistically be pursued by individuals or by the class. Plan to implement some of these positive environmental actions. Record the project with photographs and display the photos in the city hall and the public library.

Survey of Computer Use

Please check the appropriate boxes below.

Your present age:
❏ 20-29   ❏ 30-39   ❏ 40-49   ❏ 50-59
❏ 60-69   ❏ 70-79   ❏ 80 and older

1. Have you ever used a computer as part of your employment?
   ❏ yes   ❏ no
   If yes, at what age did you first use a computer in your work?_____

2. Are you currently using a computer in your work?
   ❏ yes   ❏ no
   If yes, what is your job?_____

2. As a student, did you have access to a computer in:
   ❏ elementary school
   ❏ middle school
   ❏ high school
   ❏ college
   ❏ job training

3. Did you have a computer of your own or at home when you were in:
   ❏ elementary school
   ❏ middle school
   ❏ high school
   ❏ college
   ❏ job training

4. Outside of your own work, where do you see computers being used? Please list at least three specific places such as your bank and local retail stores.

5. Do you currently have a computer at home?
   ❏ yes   ❏ no
   How is the computer used in your home?_____

CHART 15 Survey of Computer Use

5. The Gray Areas in History

As a class, the students will select events and persons from their History Journals, time lines, maps, and book lists. These persons and events will then be placed on the semantic differentials in order to compare and contrast. For example, on the continuum from democracy to totalitarianism, where would students place people, such as Thomas Jefferson, Abraham Lincoln, Franklin Roosevelt, Adolf Hitler, Joseph Stalin, Martin Luther King, Jr., and other leaders?

democracy————————————————————————totalitarianism

On a continuum of *integration/persecution*, where would students place slavery, the Holocaust, women's suffrage, "Jim Crow" laws, Brown vs. Topeka? Try applying the differential of *loyalty/treason* to the American Revolution from the viewpoints of Patriots *and* Loyalists. *Conservation/preservation* will bring out the differences in wise land and resource use. *Women's work/ men's work* as applied to various time periods will elicit a growing understanding of change over time.

The students will discover that in some areas of concern, there are strong differences from one time period to another reflecting the changes in laws, social concerns, and living conditions.

6. The Bill of Rights

After the students have had some experience dealing with the semantics differentials, have the students read Avi's *Nothing But the Truth: A Documentary Novel* as the foundation for discussing the differential *censorship/freedom of speech*. This thought-provoking book is well suited to readers' theater and will generate discussion of how individual rights are defined, restricted, supported, and understood.

Follow the discussion of *Nothing But the Truth* by having the students write in their History Journals about their most valuable rights, selected from the Bill of Rights. For each right, the students will state examples of how this right is implemented in their lives, *and* in the lives of others. In order to comprehend the application of the Bill of Rights to all, students must be able to extend their own most precious rights to others.

7. Ten Significant Events in the History of the United States

As a way of reviewing the history of the United States and differentiating between significant and merely interesting events, students will make a list of the most important happenings in the history of the United States. Start by brainstorming a long list of events. Then determine how these events tie together. For example, the Battle of Gettysburg was a significant happening but was part of a larger event—the Civil War. In the process of grouping events, the students will be identifying, summarizing, and reviewing the major events in our history, and they may indeed identify more than 10 truly significant events.

BOOK LIST

Note: Starred (*) books are reviewed in a previous section or unit of this book.

*Altman, Susan. *Extraordinary Black Americans: From Colonial to Contemporary Times.* Childrens Press, 1989. (4-8) Biog. (Part 2, Unit 3)

*Archer, Jules. *Breaking Barriers: The Feminist Revolution from Susan B. Anthony to Margaret Sanger to Betty Friedan.* Viking, 1991. (6-8) Biog. (Part 2, Unit 9)

Ashabranner, Brent. *Always to Remember: The Story of the Vietnam Veterans Memorial.* Photos. by Jennifer Ashabranner. Dodd, Mead, 1988. 101p. (6-8) Non-fic.

Ashabranner, Brent. *Dark Harvest: Migrant Farmworkers in America.* Photos. by Paul Conklin. Dodd, Mead, 1985. 150p. (6-8) Non-fic.

With sensitivity and insightful commentary, the author describes the work and lives of America's migrant workers, 70% of whom are Hispanic, 15% black, and 10% white. Many individual migrants are quoted throughout this volume which emphasizes the importance of the work done by the migrant farm laborers and the injustices of their lives. Despite the adversities of poor pay, health and safety hazards, child labor violations, and deplorable living conditions, the author uncovers the strength of family life and loyalties among the migrants.

Ashton, Stephen. *The Cold War.* Batsford Ltd., 1990. 64p. (6-8) Non-fic.

Atkin, S. Beth. *Voices from the Fields: Children of Migrant Farmworkers Tell Their Stories.* Little, Brown, 1993. 96p. (4-8) Non-fic.

Through nine very candid and personal interviews, readers will learn what life is like for the children of migrant farmworkers. The children, who range in age from nine to teenagers, tell of hot, tiring days picking in the strawberry or lettuce fields, discrimination experienced in school and communities, what it is like to be in a gang, small, often-crowded homes, their aspirations for education and a better life, and, most poignantly, the love and support of their families. The photographs that accompany the text tell their own story of these youngsters who are striving to achieve something in the land of plenty. This is an outstanding book.

Avi. *Nothing But the Truth: A Documentary Novel.* Orchard, 1991. 177p. (6-8) Fic.

This unique book *must* be read in its entirety in order to comprehend the importance of respect, freedom, and responsibility within the context of truth. A high school freshman named Philip Malloy hums along with the tape of the national anthem when it is played each morning during homeroom. When Philip is eventually suspended for his disrespect, the actions by Philip's parents, principal, teacher, school board members, and the media are reported in documentary transcripts of conversations, letters, school memos, diary entries, and newspaper articles. Through this unusual presentation, readers discover the "truth" of the situation. This book would be an excellent source of discussion of human rights, freedom of speech, and individual responsibility, and some of the scripted conversations, set in context, could become readers' theater.

Davis, Ossie. *Just Like Martin.* Simon & Schuster, 1992. 215p. (4-8) Fic.

Fourteen-year-old Isaac Stone is very focused—he wants to become a preacher like Martin Luther King, Jr., and he takes his responsibilities as Junior Assistant Pastor at Holy Oak Baptist Church very seriously. It is the summer of 1963 in Alabama, and Stone is very disappointed when his father will not let him participate in the March on Washington. Mr. Stone came home from the Korean War a changed man and his wife's death has made him even stranger. Remaining nonviolent is a challenge to young Stone, especially when a bomb goes off in the church, killing two children. As racial tensions mount in the small community, Stone and his father eventually settle tensions at home. This is a well-done portrait of life in a small southern town during the civil rights era.

Faber, Doris, and Harold Faber. *Nature and the Environment.* Scribner's, 1991. 296p. (6-8) Biog.

International in scope, this extensive work contains the diverse and interesting stories of 26 naturalists, conservationists, and environmentalists whose work has made a lasting impact on preserving the natural beauty of the world in which we live. In each of the well-written biographies, the authors explore the childhood interests and love of nature that fashioned the lives and careers of such people as Rachel Carson, Carl Linnaeus, Theodore Roosevelt, and George Washington Carver. The authors have included many photographs, archival illustrations, a bibliography, and an index.

George, Jean Craighead. *The Talking Earth*. Harper & Row, 1983. 151p. (4-8) Fic.

Set in the present day, this story concerns a young adolescent Seminole named Billie Wind, who does not believe her people's teachings about a great serpent in the Everglades, about animals talking to people, or about little people who live underground. Her punishment for not believing is to spend several days alone in the Everglades, where she recalls the teachings of the Seminoles, gathers food, makes a raft, listens to the birds and animals for what they have to tell her, and eventually finds her way home. In the process, Billie Wind learns that the animals do indeed have much to say.This book would be an excellent resource for examining current environmental problems.

George, Jean Craighead. *Water Sky*. Harper & Row, 1987. 212p. (6-8) Fic.

Lincoln, an adolescent white boy, goes to Alaska to seek his uncle and to visit the Eskimo family of Vincent Ologak. He finds Vincent camped on the ice awaiting the appearance of a whale to help the village. Lincoln learns much about the blend of Eskimo and white cultures, while discovering his own physical and inner strength. This coming-of-age story is rich in detail about the Eskimo way of life and reverence for life. Compare this view of Eskimo culture, seen through the experiences of a white boy, with the view presented in Jean Craighead George's *Julie of the Wolves* (Harper & Row, 1972), where an Eskimo girl examines her own culture.

Guy, Rosa. *The Ups and Downs of Carl Davis III*. Delacorte, 1989. 113p. (4-8) Fic.

In this touching series of letters from a precocious 12-year-old boy to his parents, Carl Davis III describes his bewilderment when he is sent from New York City to a small town in South Carolina to live with his grandmother. His parents feel Carl will be safe from drugs down there, and Carl writes of his dismay in school where he finds his teachers ignorant of black history. Carl steadfastly maintains his sense of self and pride, despite the prejudice directed towards him and his grandmother, as he gradually comes to like his grandparent and small-town life. These letters could be the basis for a rich student discussion.

Harrison, Barbara, and Daniel Terris. *A Twilight Struggle: The Life of John Fitzgerald Kennedy*. Lothrop, 1992. 159p. (4-8) Biog.

Haskins, James. *I Am Somebody! A Biography of Jesse Jackson*. Enslow Pub., 1992. 112p. (6-8) Biog.

Born in 1941 in Greenville, South Carolina, the Rev. Jesse Jackson grew up to become an international leader. A hard worker in school, Jackson graduated from the Agricultural and Technical College in Greensboro, where he became a leader in student government, as well as quarterback of the football team. In 1964, Jackson enrolled in the Chicago Theological Seminary, having already become involved in the Civil Rights Movement. Haskins is honest about Jackson's life, including the difficulties he encountered with the SCLC and his troubles during the 1988 presidential campaign. The book concludes with Jackson's current agenda and includes a bibliography and index. For younger readers, a good choice is Patricia McKissack's *Jesse Jackson: A Biography* (Scholastic, 1989).

Haskins, James. *Thurgood Marshall: A Life for Justice.* Henry Holt, 1992. 163p. (4-8) Non-Fic.

Thurgood Marshall, born in 1908, accomplished more changes in civil rights than any other person in the twentieth century. As a lawyer, then judge, he worked tirelessly to implement the principles of the Constitution for everyone. His work on behalf of African Americans took him into dangerous situations where white people, accustomed to the traditions of the Jim Crow laws, wanted no changes. As a lawyer for the NAACP, he tested the "separate but equal" concept as applied to public schools, and in 1954 he won the landmark case that declared segregation unconstitutional—*Brown vs. Topeka Board of Education.* As a justice of the Supreme Court, Marshall's mission was to continue to support the Constitution for all Americans. This well-written biography of a remarkable man includes a bibliography.

Haskins, Jim. *The Day Martin Luther King, Jr. Was Shot: A Photo History of the Civil Rights Movement.* Scholastic, 1992. 96p. (4-6) Non-fic.

Haskins, Jim. *One More River to Cross: The Stories of Twelve Black Americans.* Scholastic, 1992. 215p. (4-8) Biog.

The African Americans included in this biography are Crispus Attucks, Madam C.J. Walker, Matthew Henson, Marian Anderson, Ralph Bunche, Charles R. Drew, Romare Bearden, Fannie Lou Hamer, Eddie Robinson, Shirley Chisholm, Malcom X, and Ronald McNair. They all had to overcome racial barriers and most had to overcome the additional obstacle of poverty. The significant contributions these Americans made to society include a doctor who broke ground in isolating and storing blood plasma, one of the first two men to reach the North Pole, a world-class singer, the first black American to win the Nobel Peace Prize, the first black woman elected to the U.S. House of Representatives, and several civil rights activists. The brief biographies are full of information and the author includes photographs, a bibliography, and an index.

Herlihy, Dirlie. *Ludie's Song.* Dial, 1988. 212p. (4-8) Fic.

Twelve-year-old Martha Armstrong is visiting her aunt and uncle for the summer in a small Georgia town in the early 1950s. Martha is fascinated by a horribly-disfigured, autistic black girl named Ludie, and, eventually, Martha becomes friends with Ludie and her family. As the story progresses, Martha struggles with the unfairness of designating a group of people inferior based on the color of their skin and her actions inadvertently set off a series of events that forever change her life. This well-crafted story portrays bigotry and hate through a child's eyes.

Hirschfelder, Arlene B., and Beverly R. Singer, selectors. *Rising Voices: Writings of Young Native Americans.* Scribner's, 1992. 115p. (4-8) Non-fic.

This collection of essays and poems by Native American youth addresses identity, home, family, community, Native American history, education, ritual, and the realities of being a Native person in the United States today. Readers will learn about what it means to be an Indian, the role of grandparents, tribal closeness, prayer, the relationship between people and land, and how Native Americans must fight stereotyping and discrimination. The editors introduce each chapter with a brief background statement and include information about each young author. This excellent anthology should be used with any unit on Native American culture.

Hoobler, Dorothy, and Thomas Hoobler. *Vietnam, Why We Fought: An Illustrated History.* Knopf, 1990. 196p. (4-8) Non-fic.

Igus, Toyomi. *Great Women in the Struggle: An Introduction for Young Readers.* Just Us Books, 1991. 107p. (4-8) Biog.

This book, volume two of the "Book of Black Heroes" series, includes page-long biographies of over 85 black women who have made significant contributions to both their race and gender. The book is organized along topical lines and includes chapters on freedom fighters, educators, writers, fine artists, performing artists, athletes, lawyers, politicians, scientists, and healers. Each entry includes a photograph or illustration, birthday and birthplace, and information on adversities each woman had to overcome, along with significant achievements. This is a good introduction to the study of black women in America. Includes a chronology, bibliography, and index.

Isserman, Maurice. *The Korean War.* Facts on File, 1992. 117p. (4-8) Non-fic.

Lasky, Kathryn. *Pageant.* Four Winds, 1986. 221p. (6-8) Fic.

Set in Indianapolis during the early 1960s, this story focuses on Sarah Benjamin, a Jewish teenager who attends an all-girls Christian high school.

The author's humor and superior characterizations present Midwest America at the beginning of the "New Frontier" decade. This fast-paced, coming-of-age novel discusses adolescent anxieties, the pressures of the 1960s, and the love of the nuclear family, as well as raising the issues of stereotyping, discrimination, and censorship.

Levine, Ellen. *Freedom's Children: Young Civil Rights Activists Tell Their Own Stories.* Putnam, 1993. 167p. (6-8) Non-fic.

This book is a collection of the stories of 30 African-American children and teenagers who experienced segregation and the civil rights era first-hand during the 1950s and 1960s. The author interviewed the young participants, whose tales tell of "colored only" bus seats, drinking fountains, and restaurants; bombings; being taught to avoid eye contact with white people; the Montgomery bus boycott; integrating the schools; freedom rides; the Children's Crusade and subsequent incarcerations; and escalating violence. The narratives, told in the first person, are a living testimony to the courage and fortitude of an oppressed people who stood up for their rights under the Constitution. Includes photographs, chronology, "Who's Who" of participants, bibliography, and index.

Malmgren, Dallin. *The Ninth Issue.* Delacorte, 1989. 181p. (6-8) Fic.

New to a big high school in San Antonio, Texas, senior Blue Hocker is devastated when he is too late to try out for football. Needing an extracurricular activity, Blue joins the peculiar mix of students on the staff of the school's newspaper, the *Town Crier*. The paper's advisor, Mr. Choate, is innovative and gives the staff free rein. When the students begin to question administrative actions, such as preferential treatment for school athletes and what appears to be drug testing for the faculty, the principal tries, unsuccessfully, to control the newspaper's stories and decides not to renew Mr. Choate's contract. This action creates a great controversy in this skillful exploration of constitutional and interpersonal issues.

Marrin, Albert. *America and Vietnam: The Elephant and the Tiger.* Viking, 1992. 277p. (6-8) Non-fic.

The first several chapters of this book tell the history of Vietnam, including the ascendancy of Ho Chi Minh, the difficulties following the end of World War II, and the splitting of Vietnam into north and south. Marrin explains the "domino theory" which led the United States into its longest and most unsuccessful war, spanning the terms of several presidents. Marrin examines the conduct of the war under Lyndon Johnson and Richard Nixon, including the general unpreparedness of the young soldiers for the terrorist type of warfare being carried out in Vietnam, and how soldiers used drugs as a coping mechanism. War crimes committed by American forces are related along with the anti-war movement on the home front. The honest text makes excellent use of eyewitness accounts and historical photographs. Includes a bibliography and index.

McKissack, Patricia. *Martin Luther King: A Man to Remember.* Children's Press, 1984. 128p. (4-8) Biog.

McKissack, Patricia, and Fredrick McKissack. *The Civil Rights Movement in America from 1865 to the Present.* Children's Press, 1987. 320p. (6-8) Non-fic.

This excellent and comprehensive history divides the struggle for civil rights into three chronological periods: 1865 to 1900, 1901 to 1954, and 1955 to the present. Although focusing on the rights of African Americans, the authors also discuss other groups who have suffered discrimination, including Native Americans, Asians, Hispanics, women, the disabled, immigrants, and children. The text is well-written and will be understood by young readers. The authors make great use of original sources, including newspaper articles, legal documents, political speeches, and personal accounts. The many illustrations and photographs are fascinating and closely tied to the text. Includes a bibliography and index. Highly recommended.

McKissack, Patricia, and Fredrick McKissack. *Taking a Stand Against Racism and Racial Discrimination.* Franklin Watts, 1990. 157p. (6-8) Non-fic.

The McKissacks successfully present the topic of racism—its beginnings, how racism and discrimination have developed in the United States, different forms of racism, and its recent resurgence. The authors trace racial issues in American government from 1776 to the present day, followed by chapters on leaders, such as W.E.B. Du Bois, Booker T. Washington, Rosa Parks, Martin Luther King, Jr., and lesser known people, such as Portland Birchfield and George Sakaguchi. The final chapter urges readers who feel they have been discriminated against to take action, but to always examine the situation carefully before taking a stand. Includes a list of civil rights organizations, a bibliography, and index.

*Mohr, Nicholasa. *Felita.* Dial, 1979. (4-6) Fic. (Part 2, Unit 8, Sect. 2)

Moore, Charles. *Powerful Days: The Civil Rights Photography of Charles Moore.* Text by Michael Durham. Stewart, Tabori & Chang, 1991. 207p. (4-8) Non-fic.

Children of all ages will find the photographs of Charles Moore riveting. Moore, through his work in *Life* magazine, chronicled the trauma of the civil rights era between 1958 and 1965. Perhaps for the first time, students will begin to see what these brave men and women underwent in their fight for their constitutional rights—demonstrators being pummeled by fire hoses, dogs unleashed against protestors, the march on Selma, Alabama, desegregating the schools with the use of force, and a host of other spellbinding events. Durham's text puts occurrences in historical perspective, often using Charles Moore's own words, in this tribute to an emotional and hard-fought struggle.

Moore, Yvette. *Freedom Songs.* Orchard, 1991. 168p. (6-8) Fic.

In 1963, 14-year-old Sheryl, an African-American girl, and her family drive from their home in Brooklyn, New York, to visit their family in rural North Carolina for the Easter holiday. Sheryl has always loved the South, but she loses her innocence when she is humiliated after using a "whites only" drinking fountain in the local dime store. The family is divided when Uncle Pete, home from college, announces that he is going to become a freedom rider that summer. Back in Brooklyn, Sheryl and her friends take an active role in the Civil Rights Movement, and the family becomes unified when Uncle Pete is mortally wounded. This well-written story evokes the mood surrounding the fight for civil rights in the United States in the early 1960s.

Myers, Walter Dean. *Malcolm X: By Any Means Necessary: A Biography.* Scholastic, 1993. 210p. (6-8) Biog.

Nelson, Theresa. *And One for All.* Orchard, 1989. 182p. (6-8) Fic.

In 1966, the life of an average family living in White Plains, New York, is forever changed by the Vietnam War when the oldest son, Wing, enlists in the Marines on his eighteenth birthday. Occurrences are seen from the perspective of his younger sister, 12-year-old Geraldine, and events on the home front are well-portrayed, including Wing's restlessness and school problems, his friendship with a boy who later becomes an anti-war demonstrator, and the family's interpersonal relations. This well-written story uses complex characters and realistic dialogue to present the era of the Vietnam conflict in an understandable light.

Parks, Rosa, with Jim Haskins. *Rosa Parks: My Story.* Dial, 1992. 192p. (6-8) Biog.

Rosa McCauley Parks' autobiography begins with her childhood years growing up in her grandparents' rural home in Alabama. Parks' mother and grandmother were strong women who instilled in her fortitude and a sense of self-worth. Parks recounts with candor her school years, her marriage with Raymond Parks, and the origins of her activism in Montgomery, Alabama. In December 1955, Parks led what became a year-long fight against the city's and state's segregation laws; her memories of the struggle are clear and impressive. The book includes the recollections of key people in the Civil Rights Movement, such as Martin Luther King, Jr. and E.D. Nixon. Numerous historical photographs enrich the text.

Paterson, Katherine. *Park's Quest.* Lodestar, 1988. 148p. (6-8) Fic.

Eleven-year-old Parkington Waddell Broughton V and his widowed mother live in Washington, D.C. Park wonders about his father who died in Vietnam, but his mother is reluctant to shed any light. Although they have had almost no contact with Mr. Broughton's family, Park convinces his mother to let him visit his paternal grandfather. While at the farm of his stroke-ridden grandfather, Park meets the uncle he did not know he had. His uncle is married to a Vietnamese woman whose daughter lives with them. Through contacts with the girl, who is also 11, Park learns that they have the same father and that his mother divorced his father after she learned of the daughter. This painful story of love and loss is poignantly told.

Powledge, Fred. *We Shall Overcome: Heroes of the Civil Rights Movement.* Scribner's, 1993. (6-8) Non-fic.

Provensen, Alice, and Martin Provensen. *Shaker Lane.* Viking Kestrel, 1987. [32]p. (4-6) Fic.

A deceptively simple story line portrays the changes that take place when farm land is sold off in small parcels at a very low price. The people who buy the land that the old ladies can no longer care for build poorly constructed little houses. The residents are depicted as rural poor white families and the children are teased as the "poorhouse Shaker" kids. When a dam built near Shaker Lane floods the area, the families move away and no one questions the state's right of eminent domain. The book raises many questions about whose rights and needs are served by state projects, and the story needs thorough and careful discussion and associated research.

*Rappaport, Doreen, ed. *American Women: Their Lives in Their Words: A Documentary History.* Crowell, 1990. (6-8) Non-fic. (Part 2, Unit 3)

Rodriguez, Consuelo. *César Chávez.* Chelsea House, 1991. 111p. (4-8) Biog.

Part of the "Hispanics of Achievement" series, this is a biography of a Mexican-American labor leader César Chávez, who was best known for his work on behalf of the migrant farm workers of America. After a drawn-out strike, Chávez and his union, the National Farm Workers Association, won a contract for California migrant grape pickers in 1970. Through means of a national boycott and a hunger strike, all the while emphasizing nonviolence, Chávez was successful. Chávez's childhood as a migrant farm worker is detailed along with his more recent accomplishments prior to his death in 1993. Includes many photographs, a chronology, bibliography, and index.

Siegel, Beatrice. *The Year They Walked: Rosa Parks and the Montgomery Bus Boycott.* Four Winds Press, 1992. 103p. (6-8) Non-fic.

Talbert, Marc. *The Purple Heart.* HarperCollins, 1992. 135p. (4-6) Fic.

Luke Canvin cannot believe that the morose and sickly looking man who has just returned from Vietnam in 1967 is his confident, brawny, construction-worker father. Getting no explanation from his mother, Luke does not know what to think or how to act. Luke takes his father's Purple Heart medal and fabricates stories to tell his friends, but is anguished when he loses the medal. Luke and his father eventually confront their fears and open the door to communication. The characters are complex and well-developed and readers will comprehend the uncertainty and discord of the homecoming and ultimate reconciliation.

Taylor, Mildred. *The Gold Cadillac.* Dial, 1987. 43p. (4-6) Fic.

This story, drawn from the author's childhood in Toledo, Ohio, centers on Lois and Wilma and the new gold Cadillac their father has just purchased. The year is 1950 and the family decides to visit relatives in Mississippi, despite the fact that it could be "dangerous" for this African-American family. Once they drive into Tennessee, the girls start to see signs that read "White Only, Colored Not Allowed," and their father has to explain about the ignorance that brings about prejudice and segregation. When Papa is jailed in Mississippi because the authorities think he has stolen the car, the life of this family is forever altered. Taylor skillfully presents the topic of bigotry in a manner that children will easily understand in this story that also highlights family love and support.

Turner, Glennette Tilley. *Take a Walk in Their Shoes.* Dutton, 1989. 175p. (4-6) Biog.

Fourteen African-American men and women, mainly from the twentieth century, are portrayed in succinct, informative selections. Each biographical sketch is followed by the script for a skit drawn from that person's life. Turner includes people in medicine, entertainment, academe, and the abolition and civil rights movements. Both the biographies and the skits candidly and objectively present the hardships, prejudice, and injustices that these people fought to overcome. The author gives permission to use the skits for non-profit performances.

Walter, Mildred Pitts. *Girl on the Outside.* Lothrop, 1982. (6-8) Fic.

This fictionalized account of the desegregation process is based on the integration of Central High School in Little Rock, Arkansas, in 1957. The story centers on two girls—senior Sophia Stuart, an affluent and popular white student, and sophomore Eva Collins, one of the black girls who has agreed to attend the white high school. The action in the book takes place in the space of a week, shifting between the two households, as tensions in the town build. Readers will see both sides of the issue and share in the fears and uncertainties experienced by both blacks and whites in this emotion-ally charged situation.

Wilkinson, Barbara. *Not Separate, Not Equal.* Harper & Row, 1987. 152p. (6-8) Fic.

The year is 1965 and 17-year-old Malene Freeman is one of six black students who have been selected to integrate the all-white Pineridge High School in southwest Georgia. The story opens with a crazed white person letting his dogs attack Malene as she is walking to school—just the latest incident in a year full of tension and anxiety for these six students. Their feelings are clearly brought out during their group discussions—the manner in which they coped with the many "discourtesies" they experienced throughout the year. A dramatic incident at the close of the story forever alters the courses of their lives.

*Yep, Laurence. *The Lost Garden.* Julian Messner, 1991. (6-8) Biog. (Part 2, Unit 8, Sect. 2)

SELECT
BIBLIOGRAPHY

✿ ✿ ✿ ✿ ✿ ✿ ✿ ✿

Adamson, Lynda C. *A Reference Guide to Historical Fiction for Children and Young Adults*. Westport, CT: Greenwood Press, 1987.

Allen, Adela Artola. "The School Media Center and the Promotion of Literature for Hispanic Children." *Library Trends* 41 (Winter 1993): 437-61.

Billing, Edith. "Children's Literature as a Springboard to Content Areas." *Reading Teacher* 30 (May 1977): 855-59.

Brodie, Carolyn, ed. *Exploring the Plains States through Literature*. Phoenix: Oryx Press, 1994.

California State Department of Education. Language Arts and Language Unit. *Recommended Readings in Literature, Kindergarten Through Grade Eight*. Sacramento: California State Department of Education, 1986.

Champion, Sandra. "The Adolescent Quest for Meaning Through Multicultural Readings: A Case Study." *Library Trends* 41 (Winter 1993): 462-92.

Children's Catalog. 16th ed. New York: H.W. Wilson, 1991.

Cianciolo, Patricia Jean, ed. *Picture Books for Children*. Chicago: American Library Association, 1973.

Collins, Carol Jones. "A Tool for Change: Young Adult Literature in the Lives of Young Adult African-Americans." *Library Trends* 41 (Winter 1993): 378-92.

Connet, Dorothy. "When Using Literature in Your History-Social Science Program, Don't Forget to Include History-Social Science!" *Social Studies Review* 28 (Winter 1989): 41-51.

Doll, Carol A., ed. *Exploring the Pacific States through Literature*. Phoenix: Oryx Press, 1994.

Donavin, Denise Perry. *Best of the Best for Children: Books, Magazines, Videos, Audio, Software, Toys, Travel*. New York: Random House, 1992.

Eakin, Mary K., comp. *Good Books for Children: A Selection of Outstanding Children's Books Published 1950-65*. 3rd ed. Chicago: University of Chicago Press, 1966.

Freeman, Evelyn B., and Linda Levstik. "Recreating the Past: Historical Fiction in the Social Studies Curriculum." *The Elementary School Journal* 88 (March 1988): 329-37.

Freeman, Judy. *Books Kids Will Sit Still For: The Complete Read-Aloud Guide*. 2nd ed. New York: R.R. Bowker, 1990.

Frey, P. Diane, ed. *Exploring the Northeast States through Literature*. Phoenix: Oryx Press, 1994.

Gillespie, John T. *Best Books for Junior High Readers*. New Providence, NJ: R.R. Bowker, 1991.

—. *The Elementary School Paperback Collection*. Chicago: American Library Association, 1985.

—. *The Junior High School Paperback Collection*. Chicago: American Library Association, 1985.

Gillespie, John T., and Corinne J. Naden, eds. *Best Books for Children: Preschool Through Grade 6*. 3rd ed. New York: R.R. Bowker, 1990.

Haviland, Virginia. *The Best of Children's Books, 1965-1978, Including 1979 Addenda*. New York: University Press Books, 1981.

Hickman, Janet, and Bernice E. Cullinan. *Children's Literature in the Classroom: Weaving Charlotte's Web*. Needham Heights, MA: Christopher-Gordon Publishers, Inc., 1989.

Hirschfelder, Arlene B. *American Indian Stereotypes in the World of Children: A Reader and Bibliography*. Metuchen, NJ: Scarecrow Press, 1982.

—. "Native American Literature for Children and Young Adults." *Library Trends* 41 (Winter 1993): 414-36.

Howard, Elizabeth F. *America as Story: Historical Fiction for Secondary Schools*. Chicago: American Library Association, 1988.

Huck, Charlotte S., Susan Helper, and Janet Hickman. *Children's Literature in the Elementary School*. 4th ed. New York: Holt, Rinehart & Winston, 1987.

James, Michael, and James Zarrillo. "Teaching History with Children's Literature: A Concept-Based, Interdisciplinary Approach." *The Social Studies* 80 (July/Aug. 1989): 153-58.

Jenkins, Esther C., and Mary C. Austin. *Literature for Children About Asians and Asian Americans: Analysis and Annotated Bibliography, With Additional Readings for Adults.* New York: Greenwood Press, 1987.

Jett-Simpson, Mary. *Adventuring with Books: A Booklist for Pre-K-Grade 6.* 9th ed. Urbana, IL: National Council of Teachers of English, 1989.

Junior High School Library Catalog. 6th ed. New York: H.W. Wilson, 1990.

Keach, Everett T., Jr. "Social Studies Instruction Through Children's Literature." *Elementary School Journal* 75 (Nov. 1974): 98-102.

Khorana, Meena G. "Break Your Silence: A Call to Asian Indian Children's Writers." *Library Trends* 41 (Winter 1993): 393-413.

Kruse, Ginny Moore, and Kathleen T. Horning. *Multicultural Literature for Children and Young Adults: A Selected Listing of Books, 1980-1990, By and About People of Color.* 3rd ed. Madison, WI: Cooperative Children's Book Center, University of Wisconsin-Madison, 1991.

Kuipers, Barbara J. *American Indian Reference Books for Children and Young Adults.* Englewood, CO: Libraries Unlimited, 1991.

Latrobe, Kathy, ed. *Exploring the Great Lakes States through Literature.* Phoenix: Oryx Press, 1994.

Laughlin, Mildred Knight, and Letty S. Watt. *Developing Learning Skills through Children's Literature: An Idea Book for K-5 Classrooms and Libraries.* Phoenix: Oryx Press, 1986.

Laughlin, Mildred Knight, and Patricia Payne Kardaleff. *Literature-Based Social Studies: Children's Books and Activities to Enrich the K-5 Curriculum.* Phoenix: Oryx Press, 1991.

Lee, Lauren K. *The Elementary School Library Collection: A Guide to Books and Other Media, Phases 1-2-3.* 18th ed. Williamsport, PA: Brodart Company, 1992.

Lima, Carolyn W. *A to Zoo: Subject Access to Children's Picture Books.* 3rd ed. New York: R.R. Bowker, 1989.

Lindgren, Morri V., editor. *The Multicolored Mirror: Cultural Substance in Literature for Children and Young Adults.* Fort Atkinson, WI: Highsmith Press, 1991.

Lipson, Eden Ross. *The New York Times Parent's Guide to the Best Books for Children.* New York: Times Books, 1988.

MacCann, Donnarae, and Olga Richard. "Picture Books and Native Americans: An Interview with Naomi Caldwell-Wood." *Wilson Library Bulletin* 67 (Feb. 1993): 30-34; 112

McGowan, Tom, and Meredith McGowan. *Telling America's Story: Teaching American History Through Children's Literature.* New Berlin, WI: Jenson Publications, 1989.

Monson, Dianne L., ed. *Adventuring with Books: A Booklist for Pre-K-Grade 6.* New ed. Urbana, IL: National Council of Teachers of English, 1985.

Nabokov, Peter, ed. *Native American Testimony: An Anthology of Indian and White Relations: First Encounter to Dispossession.* New York: T.Y. Crowell, 1978.

"Notable 1992 Children's Trade Books in the Field of Social Studies." *Social Education* 57 (April/May 1993): 197-208.

"Notable 1991 Children's Trade Books in the Field of Social Studies." *Social Education* 56 (April/May 1992): 253-64.

"Notable 1990 Children's Trade Books in the Field of Social Studies." *Social Education* 55 (April/May 1991): 253-60.

"Notable 1989 Children's Trade Books in the Field of Social Studies." *Social Education* 54 (April/May 1990): 219-26.

"Notable 1988 Children's Trade Books in the Field of Social Studies." *Social Education* 53 (April/May 1989): 233-40.

"Notable 1987 Children's Trade Books in the Field of Social Studies." *Social Education* 52 (April/May 1988): 312-19.

"Notable 1986 Children's Trade Books in the Field of Social Studies." *Social Education* 51 (April/May 1987): 290-301.

"Notable 1985 Children's Trade Books in the Field of Social Studies." *Social Education* 50 (April/May 1986): 294-302.

"Notable 1984 Children's Trade Books in the Field of Social Studies." *Social Education* 49 (April 1985): 322-30.

"Notable Children's Trade Books in the Field of Social Studies." *Social Education* 48 (May 1984): 369-81.

"Notable Children's Trade Books in the Field of Social Studies." *Social Education* 47 (April 1983): 241-52.

"Notable Children's Trade Books in the Field of Social Studies." *Social Education* 46 (April 1982): 281-87.

"Notable Children's Trade Books in the Field of Social Studies." *Social Education* 45 (April 1981): 282-86.

O'Brien, Kathy. "Using Children's Literature in the History-Social Studies Curriculum." *Social Studies Review* 28 (Fall 1989): 53-63.

Rudman, Masha Kabakow, ed. *Children's Literature: Resource for the Classroom.* Needham Heights, MA: Christopher-Gordon Publishers, Inc., 1989.

Sanacore, Joseph. "Creating the Lifetime Reading Habit in Social Studies." *Journal of Reading* 33 (March 1990): 414-18.

Sharp, Pat Tipton, ed. *Exploring the Southwest States through Literature.* Phoenix: Oryx Press, 1994.

Slapin, Beverly, and Doris Seale. *Through Indian Eyes: The Native American Experience in Books for Children.* Philadelphia: New Society Publishers, 1992.

Smith, Karen Patricia. "The Multicultural Ethic and Connections to Literature for Children and Young Adults." *Library Trends* 41 (Winter 1993): 340-53.

Smith, Sharyl, ed. *Exploring the Mountain States through Literature.* Phoenix: Oryx Press, 1994.

Sutherland, Zena. *The Best in Children's Books: The University of Chicago Guide to Children's Literature, 1973-1978.* Chicago: University of Chicago Press, 1980.

—. *The Best in Children's Books: The University of Chicago Guide to Children's Literature, 1979-1984.* Chicago: University of Chicago Press, 1986.

—. *History in Children's Books: An Annotated Bibliography for Schools and Libraries.* Brooklawn, NJ: McKinley Publishing Co., 1967.

Sutherland, Zena, May Hill Arbuthnot, and Dianne L. Monson. *Children's Books.* 8th ed. Glenview, IL: Scott, Foresman, 1991.

Sutherland, Zena, Betsy Hearne, and Roger Sutton, eds. *The Best in Children's Books: The University of Chicago Guide to Children's Literature, 1985-1990.* Chicago: The University of Chicago Press, 1991.

Sutherland, Zena, and Myra Cohn Livingston, eds. *The Scott, Foresman Anthology of Children's Literature.* Glenview, IL: Scott, Foresman, 1984.

Taba, Hilda, Mary C. Durkin, Jack R. Fraenkel, and Anthony H. McNaughton. *A Teacher's Handbook to Elementary Social Studies: An Inductive Approach.* 2nd ed. Reading, MA: Addison-Wesley, 1971.

Tiedt, Pamela L., and Iris M. Tiedt. *Multicultural Teaching: A Handbook of Activities, Information and Resources.* 2nd ed. Boston: Allyn and Bacon, 1986.

Tjoumas, Renee. "Native American Literature for Young People: A Survey of Collection Development Methods in Public Libraries." *Library Trends* 41 (Winter 1993): 493-523.

Vandergrift, Kay E. "A Feminist Perspective on Multicultural Children's Literature in the Middle Years of the Twentieth Century." *Library Trends* 41 (Winter 1993): 354-77.

VanMeter, Vandelia. *American History for Children and Young Adults: An Annotated Bibliographic Index.* Englewood, CO: Libraries Unlimited, 1990.

Veltze, Linda, ed. *Exploring the Southeast States through Literature.* Phoenix: Oryx Press, 1994.

Watt, Letty S., and Terri Parker Street. *Developing Learning Skills Through Children's Literature: An Idea Book for K-5 Classrooms and Libraries, Volume 2.* Phoenix: Oryx Press, 1994.

Winkel, Lois. *Mother Goose Comes First: An Annotated Guide to the Best Books and Recordings for Your Preschool Child.* New York: Henry Holt, 1990.

INDEX

❀ ❀ ❀ ❀ ❀ ❀ ❀ ❀ ❀

by Linda Webster

IAKM 4863 8|9| 94 (h1)